The Best of Times on the Chesapeake Bay

An Account of a Rock Hall Waterman

Lived by
Captain
Lawrence
William Simns

Written by
Robert L.
Rich, Jr.

Schiffer Publishing Ltd

4880 Lower Valley Road • Atglen, PA 19310

Dedications

In celebration of his birth, Captain Larry has dedicated this book to his first great grandson, Landon David Nordhoff, who was born on August 7, 2009, in Chestertown, Maryland in great health.

In honor of his special life, the author has dedicated this book to John Malone Bannan, Jr. for significantly advancing our writing project days before his premature death on September 2, 2010.

Schiffer Books are available at special discounts for bulk purchases for sales promotions or premiums. Special editions, including personalized covers, corporate imprints, and excerpts can be created in large quantities for special needs. For more information contact the publisher:

Published by Schiffer Publishing, Ltd.
4880 Lower Valley Road
Atglen, PA 19310
Phone: (610) 593-1777; Fax: (610) 593-2002
E-mail: Info@schifferbooks.com

For the largest selection of fine reference books on this and related subjects,
please visit our website at **www.schifferbooks.com**
We are always looking for people to write books on new and related subjects.
If you have an idea for a book, please contact us at
proposals@schifferbooks.com

This book may be purchased from the publisher.
Please try your bookstore first.
You may write for a free catalog.

In Europe, Schiffer books are distributed by
Bushwood Books
6 Marksbury Ave.
Kew Gardens
Surrey TW9 4JF England
Phone: 44 (0) 20 8392 8585; Fax: 44 (0) 20 8392 9876
E-mail: info@bushwoodbooks.co.uk
Website: www.bushwoodbooks.co.uk

Designed by Mark David Bowyer
Type set in American Garamond BT / Zurich BT

ISBN: 978-0-7643-4277-6
Printed in the United States of America

Contents

Acknowledgments

Larry's Acknowledgements

To my children Dawn, Larry Jr., Robert, Jamie, Ricky, Susan, Scotty, and Eddie, I hope my account helps you understand how and why I have spent so much of my life focused on the watermen of Maryland. Even now, as an old timer, I'm still consumed with solving fishery and water quality issues that should have been solved decades ago.

To my mother Rebecca, thank you for raising Joanne, Richard, and me at home in Rock Hall. Thank you for teaching me about the importance of family and community. Mom, you prepared my heart so I could one day walk with God when I was mature enough.

To my father Clifton, now gone, thank you for playing an active role in my life when I was young. Dad, you prepared my mind to follow the water and to love nature. You taught me to work hard, work smart, never quit, and to look forward. Thankfully, you taught me to cultivate relationships in every generation and helped me see a window where I could become a Mason.

To the watermen of Maryland whom I serve, I hope this book honors your past and inspires you towards a better future. It has been my privilege to serve as president of the Maryland Watermen's Association for these past forty years. Please know you are an important part of my personal, professional, and spiritual growth, and I treasure my relationship with you.

And to my wife Carolyn, thank you for your constant support during this writing project which has necessarily spilled into the time that I had put aside for you and me.

Foreword

Some time ago, I asked Larry Simns, president of the Maryland Watermen's Association, how it was that he'd managed to stay in office for decades.

"It's simple," he said with a smile. "I don't let 'em vote."

His easygoing manner belies his biography. Every challenge a commercial fisherman can face, afloat, ashore, or within his heart, Larry Simns has faced. And there is no question in my mind that he is the wisest and most effective leader within the U.S. fishing industry. That's not an assertion I make offhandedly. I've been around Maine commercial fishermen since I was 9 years old, and over the last decade and a half at *National Fisherman* I've gotten to know fishermen and industry leaders from throughout the United States.

For example, Alaska's Dave Benton, Zeke Grader of California, George Barisich of Louisiana, Jimmy Ruhle of North Carolina, and David Cousens of Maine, among others, have proved to be tireless and effective advocates for fishermen. And if they stay active for fifty years, lead their troops through enough battles, and win enough wars, we may someday look upon one or another of them as "the Larry Simns of his era."

As the largest estuary in the United States, Chesapeake Bay is both a Garden of Eden and a sump serving six states. It is also a maelstrom of political currents. With 17.2 million people living in the Chesapeake watershed, there's vast use of its resources, commercial fishing being but one – underfunded – component of its stakeholder demographic.

Then there's recreational fishing. Most commercial fishermen I know have a live-and-let-live attitude when it comes to competition. A fisherman knows it's not just his fellow permit holders he's competing with; there are predator species, the march of seasons, the evolving behavior of his quarry and environmental changes to confront. Why obsess about guys with poles? As Linda Greenlaw once told me, "A good fisherman will get his trip."

Unfortunately, many recreational fishermen do not share this encompassing view. When abundance becomes an issue, as happened with Chesapeake rockfish, anglers are quick to single out commercial fishing as the reason for decline. The fact that sport fishermen often outnumber and out-harvest commercial watermen becomes irrelevant.

Larry, a fourth-generation waterman, began fishing in the 1950s and came into his own in the 1960s. Indeed, it's been half a century since he first realized that the days when a fisherman had only the fish, the price, and the weather to worry about were drawing to an end.

His awakening began when outsiders planned to develop a small, unspoiled island in his home county of Kent, but it was not long before a gnawing uneasiness within him about water quality came face to face with the collapse of oysters. If Larry had been inclined to view Chesapeake watermen as a monolithic brotherhood, the oyster crisis of the late 1960s, which pitted county against county according to the health of local reefs, soon taught him otherwise.

Yet he found within himself the ability not just to work with watermen from throughout the Chesapeake, but to derive satisfaction from doing so, and he emerged from the oyster crisis as the president of the nascent Maryland Watermen's Association, a position he still holds.

And make no mistake; his endurance is not attributable to autocratic impulse, but to an intuitive grasp that politics is the art of the possible. "Don't ever draw a line in the sand," he warned me more than a decade ago, as I began writing editorials at *National Fisherman*. "Because as soon as you do, they'll push you back over it."

It's like this: Everyone knows the watermen can't have the entire rockfish allocation; Larry is shrewd enough to know how much they can get. Without question, however, his zest for realpolitik is matched by his commitment to principle. For all of his advocacy on behalf of watermen, he has never focused simply on economic survival. From his earliest days, Larry has been full of reverence for the Chesapeake and certain of his place in its wondrous ecosystem. His focus has always been the community of watermen, on the families who for generations have lived beside the Chesapeake, their lives shaped by its tides.

And that is why, as long ago as the 1950s, a time of abundance when conventional wisdom held that "you can't pollute that ocean, that ocean's too big," Larry understood that water quality is the linchpin of marine life – and life ashore, as well.

—Jerry Fraser
Group Publisher of *National Fisherman & WORKBOAT*
Portland, Maine 2012

Preface

In the spring of 1978, I accepted a crewmember position on an old Virginia built workboat working for a Talbot County waterman. Working on shares, we combined our strengths to catch live eels for the European fresh market and small eels to be sold salted for local trot-liners. Unfortunately, our daily harvests in April were terrible and after covering my monthly fuel, meal, toll, and hotel expenses, I netted $17. I have never worked so hard for so little. I had never been so cold for so long, either. But, I also never saw so many beautiful sunrises or met so many hardworking, fun-loving people. Though it's been over thirty years since I worked on the Susquehanna Flats, I haven't experienced another job I enjoyed more than working as a crewmember on a Chesapeake Bay workboat.

That September, I left the beauty of the waters to finish my degree in agriculture from The University of Delaware. After enduring a negative cash flow for months, I resolved to find a job on dry land that could produce a paycheck every two weeks. I also promised myself not to find work that was so heavily dependent on the abundance of Mother Nature.

With mentoring support from my advisor, Dr. Ulrich Carl Toensmeyer, I managed to graduate in the summer of 1980 and find a sales position in Dallas, Texas working for American Cyanamid Company. With this abrupt move from my beloved Chesapeake Bay area to cotton country, I shattered my dreams of owning a small grain farm and serving as a crewmember in Maryland. Ironically, I purchased a Maryland commercial fishing license so I could harvest oysters on Eastern Bay, just in case my decision to work with plants was a mistake.

Working with plants and people was the right spot for me. In time, I lived in several prime agricultural areas of America including Texas, Mississippi, Tennessee, Iowa, Georgia, and – surprisingly – New Jersey. Through an aggressive travel schedule driven by my roles in sales and marketing, I ultimately traveled to every state in America. I was fascinated with every facet of production agriculture and still find pleasure and purpose in farming, gardening, and landscaping. In the long run, I remain sure that by harnessing the power of plants, the United States of America will be in the best position to lead the way in providing food and fiber for a planet with over 7 billion people.

No matter how hard I tried to expand my territory and leave Maryland behind, I never successfully could get the beautiful state out of my mind. It is one of only a few states in America that can legitimately boast of having significant mountains, oceans, marshes, and four true seasons. More importantly, Maryland was loaded with water, wheat, and waterfowl, and also contained my home town of Annapolis. Almost every fall, I would get homesick for Maryland particularly on windy, cool days during the corn harvest. So, with Emily now a "tar heel" and Rob finishing his thesis at The University of Vermont, I left my life in Lancaster as an executive, lacrosse coach, and neighbor to see what God had planned for me on the Eastern Shore of Maryland.

When I first met Captain Larry Simns for breakfast on October 30, 2008, I was disheartened when he said, "Bob, we could use your consulting assistance at the Maryland Watermen's Association but we don't have any money." That hurt bad enough, but I felt worse a few moments later when the runny eggs I had ordered slid off my plate and onto my pants. I had been patiently waiting since 1976 to meet the legendary waterman from Rock Hall and now I'm sitting across from him with egg yolk splattered all over myself. I feared that my first impression would also become my last.

I expected Larry to laugh at me but he didn't. Instead, he laughed with me and then convinced me that watermen are used to making a mess. His smile and his laugh caught my attention. Knowing I was not going to land a consulting contract with this industry leader, I decided to make the best of my breakfast and learn more about him anyway. We talked for a couple of hours about everything. As we walked towards our pickup trucks to go our separate ways, I turned to Larry and asked him if he would like me to write about his life. Knowing full well I was not a writer or a waterman, he smiled and said, "Let's write a chapter about my great grandfather and see how it goes."

Bob and Larry on *Little Dawn*. *Courtesy of Debra Himelwright Rich @ 2010.*

Introduction

I was born on September 18, 1937, in a small fishing and farming community called Rock Hall. By the time I was 6, I had already cast my dream of becoming the fourth-generation from my family to make a living by harvesting seafood on the Chesapeake Bay. At that time in Maryland's history, I witnessed an abundance of oysters, fish, and crabs that seemed infinite. The schools of shad, rockfish, and menhaden were incredible and so were the numbers and diversity of waterfowl that flew up and down the Mid-Atlantic Flyway. Kent County was simply loaded with wildlife, waterfowl, and waterways and I loved every acre of it.

As I was growing up in the fifties, real improvements in harvesting equipment evolved quickly which made commercial fishermen more successful because we could fish harder and longer with a greater margin of safety. The cotton threads we typically used in our gill nets were replaced with synthetic fibers which lasted longer and caught more fish. Diesel and gas engines were adapted for marine uses which allowed the watermen to go right to the fish and also allowed them to venture farther from home. Significantly, the introduction of hydraulic power for marine uses transformed the Maryland seafood industry into an efficient, reliable supplier of fresh, quality seafood for the east coast. Hydraulics, plus the conversion from wood to fiberglass boats, really changed the trajectory of watermen's success.

By the time the sixties rolled around, all aspects of the commercial fishing industry had jelled together. Clearly, the fish were wildly abundant all over the waters of Maryland. But just as important, the navigation and harvesting equipment had dramatically improved as well so it was easier to find and catch the fish. Without question, this decade became my best of times on the Chesapeake Bay. Even under sustained fishing pressure, each fishery remained healthy and reproduced sustainably in the wild. From my view, the waters of Maryland were clean and clear. My workboats were seaworthy, efficient and durable which enabled me to roam all over the Chesapeake. Because I was trained by the best captains in Kent County, I knew what I was doing and was a good waterman. From a professional perspective, it was a great time in my life. I made a good living and had lots of fun.

By the seventies, however, troubles started to become obvious to all users and stakeholders associated with the Chesapeake Bay watershed. The oyster fishery, which for centuries seemed to be indestructible, was ravaged by two diseases. The shad fishery, my favorite species to harvest, was also in big trouble. Even the water clarity was fading and soil particles were easy to see floating in the water column. All of these factors, and more, made the seventies an unsettling period for all commercial fishermen of Maryland. But our lives as fishermen changed dramatically when Hurricane Agnes crawled up the East Coast. This early season storm dumped millions of gallons of excess fresh water into the Chesapeake Bay in a short period of time. Worse, these flood waters carried tons of topsoil and chemicals from New York south to Virginia which filled the Susquehanna River and therefore the Chesapeake Bay with an excess of toxins of all kinds.

By the end of June in 1972, my best of times had changed as watermen all over Maryland scrambled to survive the aftermath of Agnes. Almost overnight, the direction of my life changed from being a self-made waterman into a leader consumed with saving the fisheries so we could sustain all fishermen. Completely untrained to lead men, let alone commercial fishermen, I became immersed in solving fishery problems and spent huge amounts of time in Annapolis, Maryland's State Capital. Of course, I still wanted to make money harvesting fish, oysters, and crabs to feed my family. Unfortunately, the watermen communities around Maryland had not groomed leaders to represent them in Annapolis. I assumed a leadership role within the Kent County Watermen's Association which rapidly became a big assignment when the oyster fishery collapsed. Ready or not, I became president of The Maryland Watermen's Association in 1973.

After all these years, I am still at the helm of the Maryland Watermen's Association. Though much has changed since I first started, I still spend most of my time working for clean water, stronger fisheries, and opportunities for working watermen. Thankfully, I continue to operate a profitable charter boat business on *Dawn II* with my sons, Larry Jr. and Scotty, and my grandson, Brent. I also have a number of grandchildren near Rock Hall to enjoy as time permits. When they are mature enough, I hope to teach them what I know about the Chesapeake Bay and her surviving watermen. I want them to know, at the very least, what the Chesapeake Bay was like in her prime.

When Bob first started to write about my life, I figured I would write about my best of times in places like Solomons, Annapolis, and Betterton. I didn't have any "pie in the sky" expectations about our book. I thought it would be interesting just to write them down so my grandchildren could read them as they matured. As I started to share these stories one by one, my mind flooded over with many memories of good times and great people. In no time, our simple writing project became a real labor of love for us both. Since I didn't keep a journal or take many pictures when I was young, Bob and I patiently cobbled together the basic order of events from 1937 to 1998 as best we could.

We spent hours talking on *Dawn II*, in our trucks or at the Larrimore Farm in Centreville. We also attended book signings, trade shows, conferences, and museums to try to piece my life together. Bob interviewed a number of family and industry leaders to help him capture the big-picture events. Bob studied a number of quality books and websites to help him get it all straight. Please be advised that some dates may not be correct (or in the correct order) and the spelling of places and people may not be perfect either. I hope these unintended errors cause no harm and do not distract my readers from finding value in our book.

When I reflect back on the number of people who have volunteered their time to help us write this book, I have been amazed and also humbled by this outpouring of guidance, encouragement and trust. Only God could have brought that many people together to help one fisherman and one farmer write a book like this. To give where credit is due, I do offer two messages of hope in the back of the book to help interested readers see how my growing faith has played a role in starting and finishing this book. The first message is written for anyone considering a life as a commercial fisherman anywhere in America. The second message is written for people seeking a stronger faith; this is an intimate summary of my testimony – warts and all.

Thank you for carving time out your life to read about the Chesapeake Bay and her working watermen as seen through my eyes. I do hope you learn something new or see an old problem in a different light. I hope the information I have shared will be of some future value as we work together to restore all of the waters of Maryland back to prime while there is still time.

Part One
Learning the Seasons
(1937 – 1951)

Chapter One
Captain Willie

My great grandfather's name was Willie Stevens and his first job after elementary school was to work as a junior crewmember on a fishing boat. He started his working life around 1875 and progressed as a waterman until he achieved the level of captain (non-military) in the early 1900s. Later, as an experienced captain, he purchased two progressively better sailing workboats to harvest fish on the Chesapeake Bay. In his prime and final fishing years of the 1920s and 1930s, Captain Willie was the owner and operator of a beautiful, black hulled pungy boat called *Lightning*.

In his time, all workboats were either powered from the wind using sails or human muscles using oars. Steam engines had not yet been adapted for use in commercial fishing vessels used on the Chesapeake. Steam was only used for ocean-going freighters and large passenger ships and ferries. On the waters of Maryland, the watermen used sailing canoes, skipjacks, bugeyes and pungy boats to harvest oysters, crabs, and fish. Of these workboats, the pungy boats had the most length and beam (width) and were widely used to haul freight like lumber, tomatoes, wheat, and peaches when not in use harvesting fish.

Captain Willie was a true fisherman and he refused to gear up *Lightning* to haul freight. In his mind, *Lightning* was too beautiful to haul logs or hay. He believed his beautiful boat should only be used to catch fish and he never changed his view on that point. In those days, hundreds of pungy boats worked the waters of Maryland and it must have been a magnificent sight. Today, however, all of them have been burned, sunk, or pulled up into the marsh to rot away. One way or another, all the original pungy boats built by man have now been returned to the earth.

Sadly, because the pungy boat captains have also passed away, there is no one left from those generations to tell their stories.

The specific role they served in the Maryland seafood industry is quickly fading away from our memories. In fact, there are very few old photographs around to help young people see how graceful these old boats used to be. Fortunately, a few forward thinking people created a replica of a pungy boat called *The Lady Maryland*. She, alone, keeps the past alive as she sails up and down the Chesapeake Bay. A magnificent workboat, she remains to honor this part of Maryland history.

To catch a lot of fish, Captain Willie didn't use high-end technologies or fancy marine equipment. He used simple tools he made himself out of wood, steel, and cotton. His most important resource on board *Lightning* were his crewmembers as they were responsible for doing all the work while fishing. Generally, he traveled with a crew of four or five seasoned fishermen to optimize his profits. In addition to a share of the profits, each fisherman was entitled to a sleeping bunk and enough food and water to stay out on the water for up to three weeks.

In addition to his people, Captain Willie owned a small fleet of rowboats to work alongside *Lightning* while fishing. In the early 1900s, watermen had many ways and systems to catch finfish. Watermen used pound nets, gill nets, fyke nets, haul seines, purse nets, and hook and line. As both a master fisherman and a master sailor, Captain Willie only used the purse seine net to harvest fish in the Chesapeake Bay. He believed that the purse seine net was the most efficient and effective way to harvest striped bass, American shad, perch, butterfish, croaker, sea trout, and spot.

As a young boy, he had learned how to use every kind of net or traps available but he liked the process and results of using the purse seine net. As his only system, he invested his entire life in becoming a specialist with a purse seine net. I believe his pure love for sailing inspired him to use the purse seine instead of a stationary tool like the pound net. An adept navigator, Captain Willie used primitive navigational and nautical instruments not much better than the equipment used by the Europeans to discover America. Even with crude equipment, Captain Willie knew how to navigate in the shallow waters of the Chesapeake Bay, which, even with modern equipment, is hard for sailors. With no electrical power on board, Captain Willie used the laws of nature and his knowledge to go fishing and come home.

On board, the captain and each crewmember had specific responsibilities to accomplish every day. The crewmembers were responsible for giving the captain 100 percent of their time, energy, and heart while on a fishing trip. Risking their lives frequently, these men worked like machines to get the work done in bitterly cold winds and sweltering heat to earn their share of the profits. These men worked without the benefits of medical insurance, workman's compensation, a retirement plan, or unemployment. In spite of the dangers involved, there was no long-term disability coverage either. These men were primarily on board *Lightning* to make money. These men also wanted to be an active, contributing part of the American workforce. In those lean times, anyone who could work did work.

Captain Willie shouldered a greater burden as he was responsible for finding, catching, and selling fish profitably. He was also responsible for the safety of his crewmembers, so he spent hours maintaining his equipment and gear. Since emergency medical care was not accessible to a sailing workboat, Captain Willie worked hard to prevent onboard accidents from occurring. For this reason, *Lightning* was impeccably maintained. The captain was also responsible for providing each crewmember with a place to sleep and enough food and water to keep the men strong. The captain was responsible for selling the harvest and then dividing up the gross profits into shares.

There was no official scoreboard or published ranking system that publicly announced which captains caught the most fish or made the most profit. But there was also no need for such a formal system. Everyone in Rock Hall knew which captains paid good money and which ones just got by. Communication by way of the fishermen grapevine insured that the crewmembers knew where the good, steady money could be made. Likewise, the captains knew which crewmembers were good men and which ones were lazy, hard to work with, or dangerous. Once a crewmember earned a spot on a good boat like *Lightning*, he would do almost anything to protect his spot on that boat. In the back of their minds, they knew they could be replaced in a heartbeat if they were fired, quit, or died.

A Chesapeake Bay pungy boat. *Courtesy of Ann Crane Harlan*.

Chapter Two

Fishing with a Purse Seine

In all four seasons, Captain Willie's two purposes in life were to catch a lot of fish and to get his crew back home safely. No fishing trip was considered a success until the boat was tied up at the mooring and all dockside chores were done. Over time, the best captains emerged as the leaders of the fleet based on their abilities to read the waters and sense where the fish were. Using a mixture of experience, real time observations, and a sixth sense, successful men like Captain Willie had a real feel for the waters of Maryland, almost like a pulse.

To deliver consistently good harvests, fishermen needed to know all they could about the life cycles of their target species and how they reacted to different environmental conditions. Similarly, the captains learned as much as they could about the life cycles of the baitfish the target species were consuming. By observing the waters and the fisheries for decades, Captain Willie knew a great deal about the predator prey relationship as this was the key to finding fish. Following his instincts and historical experiences with cycles and seasons, he would try to intercept migrating schools of fish based on the time of year and the temperature of the waters and air. As captain, his job was to get *Lightning* close to schools of fish moving up or down the Bay. To improve his odds of finding breaking fish, he would request a crewmember to serve as a lookout. These men would be looking for unsettled waters which often included a concentration of seagulls. Ideally, the lookout would find a school of "boiling" fish. This term describes the way waters bubble up and splash violently when big fish are chasing after smaller baitfish on the water's surface.

Once a school of fish had been identified, Captain Willie would quietly sail right into the area where the baitfish were being devoured by the larger fish. Once within range, he would dispatch two rowboats to encircle the school of fish with the purse seine net. Rowing in opposite directions, the men would drag their side of the net around the school until they met on the back side of the school of fish. The entire net would remain suspended close to the surface as they were held up by floating corks.

Following the first command, the full length of the net would be released and drop vertically in the water column. This would provide a physical, and nearly invisible, barrier that would keep the fish in a tight bunch. Once the net was in place, the second command would trigger the release of the "tom" which was a heavy cast iron weight. As the tom sank rapidly, it would force all sections of the net below the fish to cinch at the bottom. With the net "pursed," the fish were trapped inside a massive net.

Once the net was pursed, the rowboats would reconnect with the mother ship *Lightning*. Using heavy dip nets, the men would manually lift the live fish out of the net and dump them out on the bottom of the boat. Other crewmembers would sort out the catch based by species and size. Keepers would be moved to the fish hold where they would be cooled down with ice. Non-target species were discarded overboard without injury.

There was nothing fancy or amazing about using a purse seine net. It was simply hard, backbreaking work and required endurance and courage.

Captain Willie's entire life was centered on purse seine fishing with a pungy boat. He had other interests and could do many things, but his true driver and passion in life was commercial fishing. He aspired to be the best in every way. But not every year was a good one. In certain years, he said the fishing was "poor." He assumed the lean years were directly related to weather or environmental cycles that were out of his control. He considered the hard years as just part of working and living in the natural world. Though we never talked about it, I don't think he ever would have concluded that water quality or excess harvesting pressure was to blame.

Based on the stories I heard from him and about him, I'm certain that Captain Willie's best of times were in the years prior to 1939. Following World War I and the Great Depression, Americans eagerly consumed all fresh caught, wild fish they could get their hands on. Fresh fish sold at the markets were low cost, nutritious, and delicious and was a preferred meal when in season.

I'm sure he never wanted these good times to end; none of us ever do if we are honest with ourselves. Unfortunately, Captain Willie endured a tragic blow to his career when he was about 70 years old. Significantly, I am now in my 70s writing about his life.

Less than twenty nautical miles away, in Annapolis, lawmakers and regulators were concerned about the sustainability of a few finfish species. The issue had nothing to do with polluted waters. The issue was not related to watermen harvesting too many fish either.

The problem looming large in Annapolis was that marine engines were being adapted so they could be used to power commercial fishing vessels. Regulators and lawmakers in Annapolis feared that if sailing vessels using purse seine nets were converted to gasoline or diesel power that they would become too efficient and effective in harvesting seafood. At the time, rockfish and shad were the two species of greatest concern.

It was determined, somehow, that the evolutionary use of gasoline and diesel engines for marine uses was inevitable and unstoppable. It was assumed, wrongly, that every pungy boat captain would insert an engine into their pungy boat and discontinue the use of their sails. Back then, face-to-face dialogues between regulators and local watermen like Captain Willie was not feasible. Information traveled primarily through word of mouth and the US Postal Service. I don't think many pungy boat captains beyond Anne Arundel County had much of a voice on this (or any) issue.

Tragically, this debate occurred in Annapolis without much input from the waterman or the seafood handlers. Over time, regulatory officials in Annapolis determined the best way to handle this emerging issue was to ban the use of purse seine nets in Maryland. With a stroke of a pen, a law was written outlawing the use of purse seine nets. There was no grandfather clause to help the old salts like Captain Willie. There was no bailout or stimulus package for him either. Abruptly, the new law ended an era that had served Maryland for centuries. The only way of life that my great grandfather knew anything about was now banned.

In a well-intended effort to preserve the rockfish, the experts in Annapolis created several new problems for the industry. Most importantly to my family, men like Captain Willie were devastated and destroyed. Too old and set in his ways to change, he was unable and unwilling to gear up *Lightning* to haul lumber. He was placed on this earth to be a sailor and a fisherman and nothing else. The simple truth was that banning the purse seine nets emasculated the old men who couldn't change.

Not surprisingly, this new law favored other watermen significantly. Pound netters, haul seiners, and gill netters all flourished because they had less competition and much better, faster access to the big schools of rockfish and shad. Instead of reducing harvesting pressure on the rockfish, the purse seine net moratorium triggered an increase in far more aggressive fishing systems in Maryland. In Virginia, the use of purse seine nets remained legal and marine engines were also allowed.

Specifically for my great grandfather, I'm sure a piece of him died when his only tool was taken from him. In his twilight years, he was unable to wrap his mind around the idea of a noisy and dangerous gasoline engine down into the hull of his beautiful *Lightning*. After nearly fifty years of success using only God's wind, why would anyone in Annapolis think he would change his ways? I realize he wasn't quite as old as Captain John Smith who famously sailed up the Chesapeake Bay, but he was too old to start fishing in boats powered with gasoline. The moratorium marked the end of his best of times and as a leader of the Kent County fleet.

What a difference it would have made if regulatory officials in Annapolis had banned the use of marine engines in pungy boats instead of banning the purse seine nets. It was the combination of both technologies that was causing the fears in Annapolis. Had he been denied the use of engine power, he could have fished for a few more years and ended his career with dignity and his head high. Instead, his nets rotted along the shore line and his crewmembers all left his side after decades of service. I can only imagine the pain Captain Willie endured as he dragged his beloved *Lightning* into the marsh for the last time. It must have been so hard to let go of his precious workboat, only to watch the laws of nature break her down board by board in the shallow water.

Chapter Three
Trotlining for Hard Crabs

Clearly, the State of Maryland didn't want purse seine nets used on the northern part of the Chesapeake Bay. Maybe regulators and fishery managers labored exhaustively about the long-term fate of individual fishermen like Captain Willie before they issued the moratorium. This moratorium, and its aftermath, impacted my family long before I was old enough to know any better. Though he was wounded, he was not dead and he maintained an important role in our family and in Rock Hall.

Even without *Lightning* or his purse seine nets to challenge him, Captain Willie continued to get up every morning to fish, eel, and crab from his old rowboat. Captain Willie was not a quitter. He never quit loving The Chesapeake Bay, Kent County watermen, and all of the fisheries of Maryland. Thankfully, he never quit on his responsibilities as my great grandfather either. After I was born in 1937, he waited until I was old enough to go fishing and crabbing with him during the summers.

By the summer of 1943, when I was 6, my parents agreed I was ready to spend time with Captain Willie. So every day of the summer, I spent all day fishing, crabbing, and eeling with this old man. It didn't matter to me that he was no longer one of the elite sailing captains. All I could see, as a child, was this old man wanted to spend quality time with me on the shores and waters around Rock Hall. I loved spending my days with Captain Willie.

For my hardworking parents, this emerging partnership worked well for them, too. Mom had bad knees and I know I wore her down sometimes with my curious and active nature. Though she never said anything about it, I know Mom was glad I could keep an eye on her grandfather as she worried about him falling overboard or being lonely. Besides, Dad already could see I was hooked on the watermen's ways and he instinctively knew that I would soak up all of the lessons from Captain Willie if I spent enough time with him.

At age 6, Dad felt I was too young to crab alone on Swan Creek and he knew I would be too small to really help Uncle Luke, Uncle Josh, and Captain Fusty.

All summer long, we were always together somewhere in Rock Hall or out on the water. Captain Willie was a gaunt man with a slight build. Sometimes, he appeared almost hollow looking but was remarkably strong and wiry. He had a nose like a hawk beak and high cheek bones. He wore a roughly trimmed handlebar mustache and a straw hat in the summer time. He was bowlegged enough for a hog to walk through his legs and he wore heavy, non-insulated black hip boots that were always rolled down below his knees. He liked to wear a button down shirt and a vest. He always wore long pants. He never learned to drive a car and never wore a life jacket. I don't think he could swim, though we never discussed it.

Physically, I was small for my age but I was also strong and scrappy. I had the same hawk beak nose. I never wore a shirt or shoes and my skin was as brown as a berry. My feet were as tough as cow leather. We traveled everywhere together on foot so we were always together walking and talking, which we both enjoyed.

Our conversations roamed from topic to topic and there was no subject that was off limits. I loved his stories and I loved the way he told them to me. It didn't bother me that he repeated himself now and then. I found his stories to be full of wisdom and dry humor. I liked the way he talked to me instead of *at* me. He didn't treat me like I was just another little boy just tagging along. Instead, he spoke to me as a future man and waterman which enabled me to see the world he knew past Rock Hall.

I didn't realize at the time, but I see clearly now that his stories played an important role in helping me to grow up and to succeed. I do believe we are all affected by the environment we are exposed to, particularly when we are young. At special moments, he would pull me in close and tell me simple truths about people and their ways. One of his favorites sayings was, "Larry, you've got to watch some church people. Lots of folks go to church to hide what they really are. Some of them will skin you. You have to figure out the difference for yourself." My great grandfather, forever a God-fearing man, but not a church attending man, wanted me to be alert and streetwise to hypocrites and smooth talkers even in a small town like Rock Hall.

One time he told me about an old man who moved mysteriously up from southern Maryland to start a new life in Rock Hall. This newcomer, often referred to as a "come-here" on the Eastern Shore, managed to successfully re-create himself in our community as a stand-up man of God with a noble past. Well, one Sunday afternoon, Captain Willie was near his shed chopping wood when this freshly pious man came up to him and verbally criticized my great grandfather for working on Sundays. In those days, the blue laws were in effect and many Christian congregations believed doing any kind of work on The Sabbath was wrong.

The two men started arguing over the spirit and letter of The Bible concerning working on Sundays. The argument got heated, and this newcomer picked up a piece of firewood and smacked Captain Willie over the head. In broad daylight on The Sabbath, the two old men (both in their eighties) had a fist fight over what they each believed God considered acceptable behavior. It was a sad display of Christianity gone amuck. Worn down and hurt, the fight ended with both men walking away angry. This time, Captain Willie had the upper hand because he knew the real reason why this man had moved to the safety of Rock Hall. In hindsight, I learned never to underestimate the wisdom that follows a man who has sailed all over the Chesapeake Bay.

I tried my best to keep Mom from hearing these stories about her grandfather but sometimes I got carried away and she would hear me telling my friends. She would get upset with her grandfather for telling me such things and for making our family look so crude. Sometimes, she would pitch a fit and tell me I could never go crabbing again with that old man because he was such a bad influence on me. I think she was partly embarrassed, but also afraid that I would stop going to church with her. Every time she would go on a rant, Dad and I would just smile at each other because we knew she loved her grandfather and we knew she couldn't possibly keep up with me all summer long. I always knew that I would be crabbing with him the next day no matter what she said the night before. It was a comical piece of family drama that still makes me smile. As an old timer myself, I must agree that some men and women do hide their true selves inside the safety of a church.

Though Captain Willie did not progress far past elementary school, he was a smart man who was constantly learning new things. Sometimes, I would find him alone in his shed reading old books and journals just to find new and better ways to fish and sail. From memory, he could recite historical registries of the tall ships that sailed the Chesapeake. He taught me the names and locations of every sail on every type of tall ship and periodically quizzed me to see if I could get them all right. We spent our share of rainy and windy days hanging out in his shed but what I loved most was when we went out on the water.

Every morning, I would jump out of my bed at 4 a.m. and meet him in front of his house. From there, we would walk down together to the docks, prepare the boat, and row out into the harbor. From the second I stepped onboard his boat, he treated me as a young crewmember. He valued my agility and balance and regularly used my small hands to get the work done. Like a true mentor, he always had small tasks lined up for me to learn, practice, and master. At first, I did simple jobs like bailing out the boat. As I demonstrated understanding and competency in the small jobs, he would find harder jobs for me to tackle and then master. Patiently, he showed me the right way to bait the trotline with chunks of eel. He also showed me how to cull (sort) crabs based on size, gender, and hardness. He wanted me to know the differences between a jimmie (male), a sook (female), a peeler, and a whitey.

He showed me new things all the time and regularly explained why one process worked better than others. He allowed my curiosity to roam a bit and often let me try things on my own even when he knew it would not work out. He let me fail now and then too but never scolded me for making mistakes or failing to follow his process. If I failed at some task repeatedly, he would slow down and explain what went wrong and why another process would work better. He taught me how to tie important knots like the bowline and half-hitch. He also showed me the right way to tie up a boat factoring in the rising and falling tides. He made sure I knew about boat safety and etiquette principles when working around other watermen.

As I demonstrated proficiency, he would smile at me and say, "You are getting it Larry." His positive feedback was quite motivating and it inspired me to learn and do more. One day, the moment came when he had said I was ready to learn how to row his crabbing skiff. For men of his generation and before, rowing was considered a primary competency to be considered a good waterman. Patiently, he showed me how to develop a smooth and rhythmic rowing and pushing action so the rowboat would glide consistently on the surface of the water without jerking or surging. He taught me how to push face-forward and how to row face-backward but he insisted I perfect the face-forward technique. It was his steadfast belief that a waterman must always be able to see clearly in front of him.

He helped me perfect my push and coast method which enabled him to scoop the crabs off the trotline with one sweeping motion. Captain Willie didn't just want me to know how to row his boat. He wanted me to row well. He knew that the better rowers caught more crabs because the crabs wouldn't prematurely drop off the trotline before we could dip them. To this day, I am amazed how few people know how to row at all, let alone with any pace or endurance.

Sometime during our first summer together, he started calling me "Willie" now and then. It was his subtle way of saying that I was making progress towards my dream of becoming a waterman and that we made a good team out on the water. As a young boy hearing those affirming words from a seasoned captain, I soaked up every bit of his approval and grew in my confidence. In his own way, he was saying, "I believe in you Larry," and that meant I was on track to be the next waterman in the Simns or Stevens family.

Though I was the student and he was the teacher, I could see that he found great pleasure in teaching me. He loved to pass on all he knew to someone who was willing to accept the guidance and old enough to physically do the work. He knew he was in charge of my safety while we spent time together and he looked after me well. Likewise, I think having the responsibility of teaching a young person new things gave him energy and purpose as an old man living his final years alone in Rock Hall.

In our second summer together, Captain Willie spent less time teaching me about crabbing and handling small boats. Once he could see that I had mastered the skills, he didn't force me to learn the same lesson over and over again. Instead of focusing on teaching me, we spent most of the summer crabbing so he could make enough money for groceries and coal. Most of the time, I rowed the boat while he dipped hard crabs off the line.

Larry pushing Captain Willie. *Courtesy of Ann Crane Harlan.*

Concerning blue crabs, we routinely caught ten to twelve bushels of hard crabs just working from 4AM to 10AM out of a rowboat. Crabs were everywhere and were as thick as mosquitoes at dark. It was normal to see anywhere from six to twelve crabs hanging on a chunk of eel as it came up the trotline. Nowadays, a waterman considers it a good day when he catches 5 bushels of hard crabs on a trotline after ten hours of work. Fortunately, the dockside price of a bushel of crabs is now better but not that much better.

As partners, we found a wonderful pace and rhythm to our work and most of the time we talked as we worked. Usually, I would just listen to his stories and ask a question now and then. As he dipped crabs and filled his bushel baskets, Captain Willie would tell me about his best of times. He told me what it was like to sail *Lightning* and how she handled so well in heavy seas. He told me how the purse seine nets worked and how the moratorium took his livelihood away. He told me about his hard times too so I would not foolishly assume that the life of a waterman was easy. It was impossible to listen to his stories without wishing I could have been his crewmember back when he sailed *Lightning*.

I mostly enjoyed hearing him talk about the raw power of the Chesapeake Bay to produce seafood. When he spoke of the massive schools of rockfish and shad that used to stretch for miles, I was filled with awe. He told me about the massive piles of oyster shells that used to pile up next to the shucking plants. He explained how discarded oyster shells were so plentiful that they were routinely used for building roads as they were readily available and cheaper than stones.

By 1945, Captain Willie and I had enjoyed three summers together and our time as partners had run its course. He knew I was growing up fast and needed to gain new experiences with more progressive watermen in Rock Hall. He didn't want to hold me back from growing just so he would have company working his trotline. In a selfless act of love, he gave me a send-off gift to honor our special relationship. To celebrate our three summers together and to affirm that I was ready to take the next step towards becoming a waterman, Captain Willie restored and then gave me one of his old rowboats so that I would have my own workboat.

From the same marsh where *Lightning* had been left to rot away, Captain Willie and I dragged out the best of his old, discarded rowboats. First, we cleaned her up and started "to make her right" as he would often say. We replaced all the rotten floorboards and repainted her bottom. We then outfitted her with a pair of old oarlocks that we found in his junk pile. Once right, we dragged her to the water's edge and swamped her in the shallow water. By soaking her in the water for a few days, the old wood would swell up and leak less.

He then rummaged around his shed until he found a few old eel pots. We replaced the damaged funnels so they would catch eels effectively and then we attached some lines with corks. To get me started, Captain Willie gave me a few biddie crabs to use as bait in the eels traps. By the way, a biddie crab is a live female crab that has had all of her legs and her apron removed which somehow attracts eels.

With my own workboat fully equipped to catch eels, Captain Willie encouraged me to go out alone to set my own eel pots. The next day, he would watch patiently from the dock while I rowed around to check and harvest my eels. Once docked, he helped me salt and store the eels in a barrel so he could use them later for his trotline. As a final gesture of his affirmation in me, he gave me his word that he would always buy my eels no matter what.

By helping me get started with my own workboat, he effectively launched me into becoming a money-making waterman complete with a boat, pots, and my first customer. This was a gift from him to only me. It was his way of thanking me for spending my time with an old man while everyone else was too busy to notice or care. Quietly, he was saying *I love you, Larry* and I'm glad we have shared these three summers together trotlining for hard crabs.

Chapter Four

Aunt Claris

Captain Josh Thomas married my mother's sister, Claris. They lived in Rock Hall and I regularly spent the night at their home when I was young. I learned so much about life just by spending time with them. Clearly, they invested a great deal of time in their marriage and I viewed them as inseparable and in love. They listened to each other thoughtfully and selflessly and helped each other with the daily chores. They knew of each other's struggles and fears. They both worked hard from dawn to dusk and only rested when all the work was done.

Uncle Josh ran the charter fishing operation while Aunt Claris ran the home and communicated with the customers. Uncle Josh was an exceptional waterman and made good money. Uniquely, he was both a fisherman and a businessman and he knew how to hold onto his earnings. He regularly re-invested his profits back into his workboat, his family, or his future. He always maintained an emergency fund to help the family and others get through the hard times. His work ethic was incredible. On evenings when I stayed over, I regularly would hear his feet shuffling around in the kitchen at 4 in the morning. I also remember seeing him come home after dark filthy, sunburned, and dead tired. As a young boy watching Uncle Josh come and go, I learned early on there was nothing glamorous or romantic about making a living as a waterman.

On cold nights, Uncle Josh insisted that I sleep without covering my hands and feet so my toes and fingers could adjust to the cold weather. It's not that he wanted me to be cold and uncomfortable in his home. He did want to expose me to one of the harsh realities of becoming a commercial fisherman. He knew that if I truly wanted to become a waterman I would have to condition my extremities to bitter cold temperatures. So, he started me out slowly by conditioning my fingers and toes to the cool night air. I learned from Uncle Josh that a man should not pursue a life as waterman if he was unable or unwilling to turn off his senses and work through pain.

Turning off the senses. *Courtesy of Ann Crane Harlan.*

Though Uncle Josh helped me prepare to become a waterman, it was his wife, Claris, who taught me about kindness, warmth, and love. She was a gentle woman who never raised her voice or spoke an angry word. She held a deep, sustained interest in all of God's creatures and creations. She loved to observe and appreciate anything that was alive. She was aware of my growing passion for the water and watermen, but she used her time with me to talk about other things. She always took an interest in what I was thinking and feeling about nature and about people. She never forced her opinions on me or judged me for having a different point of view. Instead, she would ask me simple questions and leave them with me to ponder for a while. She gave me time to think through my own beliefs and waited patiently for me to form my best answer. She never rushed our discussions and never interrupted my train of thought. She was gifted with the ability to relate to others and she took an active interest in whatever I cared about. She was an unselfish, gentle person who was always there with a kind word. I'm also certain she was the most environmentally aware and sensitive member of my family.

One day, while we were eating lunch on the back porch, she saw a spider. Seeing the spider triggered her to ask me what I thought about the proposed DDT ban that was being debated in Annapolis. As a young boy, I didn't have a clue what an insecticide was used for, let alone whether it was good or bad. When she could see that I didn't understand her question, she took the time to share her own thoughts about the chemical which she expressed in a non-judgmental, mature way.

Using simple words that I could follow, I was able to hear the depth and the breadth of her thinking about DDT. She explained that DDT was considered a miracle chemical because it killed the mosquitoes that carried malaria, which was killing millions of people around the world. She explained how millions of lives were being saved by wide-spread spraying of DDT where mosquitoes were breeding. She clearly saw the good side of DDT and helped me see the life-saving potential of the compound.

But closer to home, she also worried the DDT might be getting on Uncle Josh's hands when he worked on the Chesapeake Bay. She feared the scientists might be correct in alleging that DDT was thinning out the eggs of bald eagles and other birds. In her own mind, she was sure that the use of DDT in Maryland had all but wiped out her favorite bird: the osprey.

Until that moment, I had never heard of an osprey and I told her I didn't know anything about this bird. She explained that when she was a child, ospreys were a regular part of the Kent County shoreline. From her memory, she was certain that almost every channel post marker served as an active nesting site for adult ospreys to raise their chicks. I was too young to understand how DDT was able to kill a mosquito, but Aunt Claris got me thinking about the Chesapeake Bay from an aesthetic perspective as well as a place to make a living.

   It was a blessing to have Aunt Claris in my life to teach me a few soft skills that I would not likely pick up from my other relatives. As a result of that one conversation about a little spider, Aunt Claris triggered a lifelong curiosity over DDT and other chemicals used near the waters of Maryland to control pests. Years later, the applications of DDT were permanently banned in Maryland. At first, I didn't notice any change in the numbers of mosquitoes swarming from the marshes of the Eastern Shore. I didn't see any rebound of the awesome bird called an osprey. According to the scientists, it was going to take years of weathering and the passing of more time to break down the persistent residues of DDT.

   Today, ospreys are now as common in Maryland as they once were when Aunt Claris was a child. Not surprisingly, the osprey has become my favorite bird. I admire how they eat only fresh-killed meat and how they fiercely defend their young. When I see an osprey searching the waters for its next meal, I am reminded that wild creatures are resilient and adaptable and are able to coexist with humans if given half a chance. When I consider how the osprey returned from near extinction, I find hope in the possibility that we really could restore the Chesapeake Bay and her fisheries to her prime.

A successful osprey. *Courtesy of Ann Crane Harlan.*

Chapter Five

Dad

Without a doubt, my mother ran our household and provided all the structure my siblings and I needed to have a good start in life. She was a tireless provider and her love for her children was never in doubt. Mom worked outside of the home as a telephone exchange operator and also volunteered as an enemy aircraft spotter during WWII. Mom was steady and sure in her approach to discipline. She made sure I learned her Christian principles and values early. Whenever the doors of the Methodist Church were open, she would drag me along so I could be filled with The Holy Spirit. Ironically, it would take a full forty years and some hard times before I would recognize that it was Mom's strong faith that prepared me for a full, good life.

It was actually my father who had the skills and experiences I needed to become a waterman. He was a complete man and I knew he could teach me everything I needed to become a man and a waterman. Like many sons, I tried to be like him in every way, even though I wasn't physically or emotionally mature enough to do so.

He was kind, patient, smart, and resourceful. He was also curious, interesting, and selfless. He knew everyone in town and was liked and respected by most of them. He had deep friendships of all ages. My strongest memory of my father was the way he served as the town barber for many of the Kent County men and their sons. In his barber shop, Dad mentored many young people who were searching for their spot in Rock Hall. Without a doubt, I was blessed with a hands-on, full-time father who loved me.

Early in his life, my father had been a waterman in Rock Hall until a serious back injury forced him off the water. Once he and Mom fell in love, he saw the need to settle down so he could raise his family. He found his niche in cutting hair which enabled him to stay close to his watermen, farmer, and military friends. In nearby Tolchester, an active air defense system (Nike) was operational and my father cut hair for many of the employees.

My dad cut hair indoors to make a living but his true love and passion was to be outdoors. He loved everything about the Chesapeake Bay, including her marshes, woods, shorelines, and tributaries. Growing up around Dad, I had no choice but to be swept up into his passion for the outdoors.

Dad was active in the Masonic Order. Though I was too young to understand this organization or its purpose, I could tell that his role in this organization and therefore our community was significant. Almost every night, my father would close the barber shop and share a meal with his family. As soon as dinner was over, he would go back to his shop and meet with young men seeking to join the Masons. Later, as an adult, I would learn that he was teaching them the history and required lessons necessary to join the organization. I didn't grasp the importance of his work with the Masons, but I did notice that he and most of his close friends wore a distinctive ring bearing the Masonic symbol.

The Simns family lived on Sharp Street not far from Main Street. Inside, our living space was cramped but there was enough room for us all. I didn't know or care that we were poor as it seemed every family in town was just like us. We didn't have much, but we also didn't need much. We had a nice, simple life in the small fishing and farming village of Rock Hall.

Dad shaped the culture and focus of my early years as a child. He lived his entire life according to a handful of guiding principles that he probably learned from his mother and father. He instilled these same rules into me and made sure that I understood, believed, and followed them. Even as a child, I found his rules to be fair and forward thinking. Dad lived a life filled with commonsense, respect, and kindness towards others. The two themes that ran though every word or deed of my father was to be fair and to do the right thing.

Clearly, one of his favorite sayings was, "No one should get something for nothing." Dad believed deeply that hard work, initiative, and accountability were central to a man's worth and he never waffled on this principle. He believed that every American should work if they were physically and mentally able to. Because of this principle, Dad never gave me spending money to buy ice cream or watch a movie. I can't recall even having a discussion about getting an allowance. He expected me to finish all of my chores simply for the privilege of receiving his food, clothing, shelter, and love.

He never budged on this rule, but he did help me find jobs so I would have spending money. His efforts were directed towards finding me fresh sources of money so I could earn it myself. He bird-dogged the jobs, matched me up with the person who needed the job done, and let me work out the terms of the task. In his own way, Dad taught me to be frugal, intentional, and forward thinking about money matters. He wanted me to respect the value of money, even one penny, so I wouldn't be wasteful with money or fail to prepare for hard times.

One story, in particular, best illustrates how Dad taught me about money. When I was about 7 years old, a friend invited me to go swimming with his family at the Rock Hall Community Beach. To beat the Maryland heat and humidity, I asked Dad if I could go swimming. He said, "Sure, Larry, of course you can go." Without another word, he walked out of his barber shop and walked across the street to the hardware store. When he returned, he was holding a high-quality, expensive round dip net with a hardened, rounded front edge.

At first, I didn't see how my plans to go swimming had anything to do with this crab net. As he walked through the door, he said, "Larry, take this dip net with you and while you are there swimming, catch a half dozen soft crabs for our dinner." Without another word, I had his approval to go swimming with my friend as long as I caught dinner first. Since I had never gone soft shell crabbing before, nor had anyone taught me the tips to catch them efficiently, I spent all afternoon teaching myself how to catch six soft crabs. Less than a hundred feet away, I could see my friends having a blast swimming in the Chesapeake Bay. I got home just in time for Mom to cook up the soft crabs in a frying pan loaded with butter, salt, and pepper which when served on soft white bread were delicious.

Later that summer, I got a second invitation from my friend to go swimming. Again, I asked my father if I could go and he responded by saying "Sure, Larry, you can go swimming, but first you must pay for that dip net I bought you the last time you went swimming." Back then, soft crabs were $2.25 per dozen so I spent the rest of my summer paying for a dip net that I never asked for.

Soft shelling at Rock Hall Community Beach. *Courtesy of Ann Crane Harlan*.

I am certain that Dad was firm and rigid about money matters because of what he experienced during The Great Depression. Dad knew all about hard times and wanted to make sure his children could fend for themselves in good and bad times. I lived near Dad in Rock Hall for over sixty years and never did he change or soften his philosophy about making and saving money. In the way he learned from history, my father was a forward thinker with a bent towards being practical.

Dad taught me to believe in myself. He encouraged me to try new things and allowed me to fail, to a point, if there was a lesson associated with the mistake. All through his life, he practiced what he preached and took on some meaty challenges of his own. He took flying lessons so he could fly a small airplane around Kent, Cecil, and Queen Anne's County. He also built his own workboat from scratch on the lawn next to his house. It was always a pleasure to come by the house and find him working alongside my son, his grandson, Larry Jr. He would involve Larry in the process by asking him to bring tools or do some of the lighter carpentry work. In this way, he used his boat-building project as a way to help Larry stretch and mature.

By spending time with my father building and fixing things, he taught me most of the skills I would need to be an effective waterman. Gifted with patience and a practical mind, he taught me how to build crab pots, rebuild motors, handle a gun, make decoys, cut firewood, mend nets, splice rope, hammer a nail, and many other skills he felt I would need to survive on my own. I didn't realize he was teaching me life skills; I just thought he was showing me something.

When I was a young boy, I didn't realize how blessed I was to have a father and mother who loved me. I didn't fully grasp that some of my friends were living in broken, or breaking, homes. As a child, I didn't know that my father and mother had sacrificed so much to insure that I could live a full life. Truthfully, it wasn't until I struggled as a father myself that I fully understood that I was blessed with great parents.

Chapter Six
My Father's Friends

As I grew up in Rock Hall, I spent a lot of time with a group of able men I still refer to as "my father's friends." Most of them were watermen, a few were farmers, and the rest were small businessmen from Kent County. They differed significantly in terms of their ages and hobbies. But these men had an invisible bond that seemed to bind them together into a tight-knit group. Clearly, these men were successful in their chosen professions. They also were men of good character and community minded. They all loved to hunt and most of them liked to fish. But all of these men loved to spend time with my father.

I can't recall all of their names, but a few of Dad's best friends were Emil Myers, Captain Alfred "Dead Eye" Nordoff, Harry Hepbron, Walter Scoons, Billy Deford, Bobby Scoons, and Joe Downey. Some of the men were strictly duck hunters while others also liked to raccoon hunt as well. I think a few of them were part of the Masonic Order and a few more were also Christians. Whether they attended church or not, all of these men were God fearing and trustworthy. Because these men spent so much time with my father, they each carved out a spot for me to fit into their lives.

My father's best friend was Joe Downey. Joe owned the gas station directly across the street from my fathers' barber shop on Sharp Street. When things were slow, Dad and Joe would talk in the middle of the road. These men were inseparable, particularly during the hunting season. Because of their complimentary businesses and their welcoming natures, farmers and fishermen were always dropping in to see Joe and Dad, buy a soft drink, and catch up on the latest Rock Hall news. It was common for men to drop by Dad's place for a haircut while Joe filled their car with gas. This little spot on Sharp Street was a meeting place for many men from our community.

Joe was twenty years younger than my father and twenty years older than me but our age difference was not significant at all. Because Dad and Joe were best friends, I was, by proxy, always welcome in their company. Joe treated me like a son and regularly took me under his wing and helped when he could. He freely offered his wise counsel to me with no strings attached and never once did he come across as preachy or parental. He also helped me find odd jobs so that I would have spending money. Many times, he paid me for washing his customer's cars after they received their gasoline. He always thanked me for my hard, loyal work and paid me on the spot. He was our town's most successful entrepreneur, and by being near him, I learned how to treat customers fairly but also firmly. I admired his confidence, his intelligence, and his spunk. Joe, without a doubt, was my first mentor.

From Joe, I learned some important lessons on how he viewed and balanced his priorities. Joe believed that if a man didn't develop a life outside of work he was not living a full life. Like all of his friends, Joe worked very hard. But when he was done working, he knew how to play hard as well. Like my father, Joe was a firm believer in learning new things and taking prudent risks now and then. He too took flying lessons at the Rock Hall airport just for fun.

Joe was good at everything he attempted. He was a superb hunter and fisherman and seemed to know every detail about the life cycles of every species he was pursuing. Joe's greatest gift was in his ability to select, train, handle, and care for hunting dogs. In particular, Joe was a master hound-dog handler and trainer because he was so even, steady, and kind with his hunting dogs. He demonstrated a level of patience that was priceless for me to witness as a young boy. Joe had a sixth sense about dogs and I believe he could envision a finished, trained working dog in his mind's eye, even when the dog was just a pup. Joe could see an undeveloped strength in a dog.

One time, Joe bought and paid for two hunting dogs named Rattler and Fly. Joe paid a whopping $250 for this pair of healers (raccoon hunting dogs) in the early phase of his life when dollars were scarce. To illustrate the high costs of these dogs, be aware that Joe paid $1,000 for his gas station. When word spread around Kent County that Joe had paid $250 for two dogs, he was mocked for paying such a hefty price tag. But among his true friends, Joe said with his big toothy grin, "I know that was a lot of money. But when I saw those two dogs together, I just had to have them and hunt with them."

By spending time with Joe and Dad, I learned how to handle, discipline, and love hunting dogs. They both loved their dogs unconditionally and in return, they each received great pleasure while hunting with them. Dad was a master trainer of bird dogs including setters and pointers and Joe was a master trainer with hound dogs used for raccoon hunts.

These men taught me how to love dogs unconditionally. They believed it was better to have a dog and lose it than to never own one for fear of losing it. They also showed me I could understand the character of a man based on the way he handled his own dogs. Over time, I did observe and learn that some grown men are not patient or mature enough to ever own or handle a dog. Even now, nothing upsets me more than to see a great dog handled by a weak man.

Chapter Seven
My First Love

I loved to hunt the species my father loved to hunt. In the forties, deer populations were scarce. The dove hunting around home was good, but mostly appealed to land owners and their close friends. Dad loved to hunt quail, squirrels, and rabbits all fall and winter. But without a doubt, Dad's true love was duck hunting and naturally, duck hunting became my first love also.

I always knew when a duck hunt was "in the works" because a cluster of my father's friends would gather at the barber shop. To increase my chances of going along, I would shift my attitude around the house. I made sure my room was neat and my chores were done. I was also careful around Mom; I did not want to irritate Mom over something dumb which might prevent me from going the next morning. To be sure Dad didn't forget me, I placed my hip boots and hunting gear next to the front door.

Don't forget me!
Courtesy of Ann Crane Harlan.

Like my father, I loved every aspect of hunting for ducks. I loved listening to the hunters ramble about their great shots and their missed shots. I liked the camaraderie and the constant "cutting up" (a watermen slang expression for joking around). I liked seeing all the wildlife on the Chesapeake Bay. I liked seeing the waves, white caps, and the power of the winds. I liked seeing the sun rise and sun set. I liked watching weather fronts roll in. But most of all, I loved watching the ducks fly, toll (land), and swim.

In the mornings, we would hunt in our booby blind (stationary duck blind) 100 yards into the Chesapeake Bay due west of Eastern Neck Island. Here, we would hunt for diving ducks like canvasbacks, redheads, blackheads, golden eyes, and buffleheads. These fast-flying ducks were powerful, straight flying birds that flew up and down the Mid-Atlantic Flyway searching for the best place to eat.

In the evenings, we would hunt in a marsh blind for mallards, black ducks, widgeons, gadwalls, and teal. Hunting for puddle ducks was always a thrill because they were so intelligent, wary, and agile in flight. I liked hunting in the marshes because we could take our retrievers along to help locate and bring back our ducks. When I was a young boy, the three breeds we used to duck hunt with were the Labrador, Golden and Chesapeake Bay Retrievers. I admired all the breeds but my favorite breed has always been the Golden Retriever.

Once I secured an invitation to go hunting with Dad, I would go right to bed so I could get up early and be alert all morning. I was 6 years old the first time I went hunting for diving ducks, so I didn't carry a gun. I was so small I couldn't even see over the sides of the blind to watch the ducks fly over the decoys. So, I learned to peak through the cracks in the plywood while keeping absolutely quiet when the ducks were working (flying) near the booby blind. Though I wore layer after layer of clothes to stay warm, I was always cold, but I never said a word to anyone about how cold I was. I never whined or complained about anything while hunting because I wanted to be invited on the next hunt.

Since I was too young to shoot, the men all gave me little jobs to do while they hunted and talked. At first, I was in charge of picking up all the spent shotgun shells and bailing the rowboat. Several years later, I was entrusted with setting out decoys, picking up dead ducks, and chasing down cripples. From my father, I learned to never let a cripple die in the wild.

One skill I developed on my own was the ability to mark and identify every kind of duck both in flight and on the water. I was so curious and attentive to detail I quickly learned to tell the difference between male and female of each species even in low-light conditions. In time, I got so good at my duck identification skills, the hunters started to count on me to spot and identify the wild ducks.

Even after the hunt was over, I had many jobs to do on land. I was required to pick and clean dozens of wild ducks and hand deliver them to our family members, neighbors, or folks from Rock Hall who needed the meat to get by. My father made it clear that no wild duck should ever be wasted. He insisted that we ate, or gave away, everything that was shot. I put a lot of miles on my bike in the wintertime delivering freshly killed wild ducks.

Both before and after the duck season, there was always plenty of work to do. We had to build, or in some cases rebuild, the wooden framing of the duck blinds. We then had to "brush" the blinds which involved fastening marsh grasses and cedar branches to the blinds to help conceal the hunters from the ducks.

The job I enjoyed most was making and painting wooden decoys. The first step I learned was how to carve out the body from a block of white pine or cedar with a hatchet. Later, I was entrusted with a sharp knife to carve out the heads, which required more hand strength and control. When I was mature enough, Dad taught me how to weight the decoys so they looked real when floating on the water. Finally, he taught me how to paint the decoys to make them look alive. I'll never forget the moment my father let me paint the yellow eye on my first handmade decoy.

Painting the eye.
Courtesy of Ann Crane Harlan.

Looking back over the years, I am certain that my best of times started as I sat next to my father in a booby blind on the Chesapeake Bay. Even now, I still cherish those great hunts and wonderful days on the water. Just to be invited to sit amongst these high-quality, kind men and be a part of their good times was my gift. To be chosen to listen in as they talked about their fears, dreams, successes, and failures was truly an honor and a safe place to learn about life. Just to be there, I gleaned some of their wisdom which gave me hope.

Chapter Eight

Hunter Safety

My father taught me so many different skills that my friends considered me good at many things, but I was not gifted at anything. Dad instinctively knew that for me to become a successful waterman, I needed a broad range of skills, including mechanical, navigational, environmental, and social. As a young boy, he was preparing me to be a solid generalist. There was one skill set, however, in which my father insisted that I become an expert. Dad required me to learn everything I could about the proper care, handling, and use of all kinds of firearms. He expected me to be better than all others relative to gun handling and hunter safety. On this point, he would not bend his rules.

When I was young, there were no hunter safety courses. It was considered a father's responsibility to teach his son about hunting and hunter safety. Naturally, my father accepted his role as my firearms mentor and took the assignment very seriously. For years, he allowed me to walk in the woods or sit next to him in a duck blind, but did not allow me to carry or touch the guns. I was in training, so to speak, and I was required to sit and watch my father and other experienced hunters for years before he would let me take even an unloaded gun on a hunt.

One day, while we were squirrel hunting behind the house, my father asked me if I wanted to shoot at an old can with his Winchester Model 12 (sixteen gauge). I said, "Yes, I'm ready." I aimed and then pulled the trigger and the recoil from the gun almost knocked me to the ground. But with that one shot, I also became hooked on the use and care of firearms. Dad saw the spark in my eye, and from that day forward, he proceeded to teach me everything there was to learn about firearms, hunting, and wildlife.

His first teachings focused on how a gun was built and how it worked. Working together for hours, we would tear down each of his guns and put them back together in the right order. Through this foundational training, I learned how each type of gun worked, fit together, and what specific purpose each part served. Like a soldier, I became proficient at breaking the guns down and putting them back together. After I got really good at it, I was regularly asked by my father's customers to clean their guns while they got their hair cut. Because I had nimble, strong hands, I had the ability to properly position the delicate little springs common on the more popular shotguns.

Once I understood the mechanical parts of the guns, he proceeded to teach me every aspect of gun safety. He made sure that I could find the safety latch on every kind of gun. He also made sure I could safely unload the shells or bullets from both the chamber and the magazine. After I confirmed that "I got it," he would randomly test me to see if I demonstrated enough discipline in my safety processes. When I least expected it, he would hand me his pump shotgun to see if I would first check to see the breach was open and the gun was unloaded. If I didn't check the breach right then and there, even if I just saw him do it himself, he would "rake me over the coals." Even now as an old timer, I still check every gun around me to make sure the breach is open, the safety is on, and there are no shells left in the magazine.

When Dad felt I was ready, he allowed me to buy my first gun, which was a Model 12 Winchester with a 30" barrel. I paid $97 for it with the money I earned crabbing, washing cars, making donuts, and feeding pigs. As if I had never handled a Model 12 before, he proceeded to make sure I knew every aspect of this gun. Over and over again, he would repeat his time-tested philosophy about gun maintenance. He would say "Larry, if you take care of your gun properly, even in bad weather, it will take care of you." What he knew then and I now know as well, was this principle would later apply to my workboats, my pickups, my houses, and my marriages.

A Winchester Model 12. *Courtesy of Ann Crane Harlan.*

Surprisingly, he spent little time teaching me how to become a good shot. He did not concern himself with my desire to be an accurate and fast shooter. Instinctively, he knew it wasn't necessary to teach me to shoot well. He could see that I aspired to be a great hunter and he knew I would have to learn from others and develop my own style. All Dad cared about, really, was that I was safe with a gun and knew the proper hunting manners and traditions.

When I was young, Rock Hall was considered rural, and most families ate wild game and fish for most of their meals. All of my friends hunted, fished, and trapped with their fathers, uncles, or guardians. In fact, I can't recall one boy in my elementary class who didn't love to hunt and fish. Besides, America was deeply engaged in World War II, so our community was supportive of discussions about firearms, ammunition, and the proper use of guns to provide food. Kent County, like many Maryland counties, was fiercely patriotic in those years, so I grew up firmly believing in the right to bear arms.

How fortunate I was to have a father who was able to teach me the right way to handle, care, and use firearms. What a blessing to learn these important life lessons from a man who loved me. I hope my readers interested in learning about firearms can learn from a safety-minded person like my Dad. I believe the world would be a safer place if everyone who had a gun knew how to care for and handle it.

Chapter Nine

A Penny's Worth of Wind

We were hunting in the booby blind off Eastern Neck Island late in the duck season. The weatherman (now called a meteorologist) had forecast the winds to blow hard all morning and that a wintry mix of sleet, snow, and rain was probable. For duck hunters, this weather report was great news because fast-moving, dynamic weather events usually caused the ducks to move around. It was towards the end of the season, so my father allowed me to skip school so I could come along. On this particular hunt, we would also have a guest hunter not familiar with the traditions of Eastern Shore duck hunting.

While we loaded our decoys and gear into the skiff in the dark, I noticed there was absolutely no wind or waves at all. The Chesapeake Bay was "slick ca'm as a dish" which is an old eastern shore expression meaning the water was flat calm. With no waves to slow us down, we quickly unloaded our gear and set out the decoys so we would be ready to shoot at sunrise. Unfortunately, the strong winds never picked up and not a single duck flew anywhere near our duck blind after two hours of waiting. Without winds to push ducks around, ducks will often sit on the water all day.

Since I was now about 12 years old, I knew full well that either the weatherman was wrong or his timing was off. I could see this duck hunt was going to be unsuccessful and we would be going home soon enough. The men started to grumble a bit which is the normal way hunters express their frustration. At this point, we were all standing up in the blind and looking all around for a sign of a duck or a change in the weather.

The guest was particularly frustrated because he had taken a full day off from his job to come hunt ducks. Slowly, his low grumble evolved into a whine which irritated my father big time. Rule number one, as a guest, is to always keep your thoughts about the quality of the hunt to yourself. But our guest was not aware of our traditions and our ways. In a moment of despair, he reached into his pocket and pulled out a penny. Without hesitation, he threw the penny into the Chesapeake Bay and jokingly yelled out, "God, send us a penny's worth of wind to push in some ducks".

After hearing what I thought was a funny comment, I expected the other hunters to laugh along with our penny thrower. Instead, none of them would look at him or talk to him. Apparently, our guest had offended the other hunters in some way, but I wasn't sure how. At first, I figured they were irritated with him for whining like a child. Then, I logically assumed they were disappointed with him for wastefully throwing government property into the water. These men all grew up in The Depression so "a penny saved was a penny earned" to them.

As it turned out, the other hunters weren't even thinking about the loss of the penny. What they resented was how this guest hunter tried to bargain with God, even in jest, so he could selfishly kill a duck. Within the watermen circles around Rock Hall, it was understood that God's favor was never to be bought off, mocked, or defamed. Every God-fearing man in that duck blind knew that prayers and requests made to God were to be presented with reverence and a humble heart. Among watermen, requests for God were reserved exclusively for travel mercies or to receive enough wind to get back to port safely. Clearly, this guest hunter did not know, or think through, what he was doing when he mocked God.

The hunt had been a complete bust and now there was a new concern that God was offended while the men were out in deep water. Disgusted, my father said, "Let's get out of here." The other hunters agreed that it was time to go, so we all starting picking up our gear. Unfortunately, this hunt was not called off soon enough. Seemingly out of nowhere, the wicked winter storm predicted by the weatherman descended upon us while we gathered our gear. As predicted, we were pelted with sleet and rain as the winds blasted right into the front of our duck blind.

Naturally, the waves kicked up too, and soon were pounding hard against the side of our blind and our skiff. One by one, I watched a few of the decoys get dragged towards shore. Our real problem was unfolding without our knowledge. Somehow, our skiff had broken free and had already drifted out of reach. Surrounded by icy waters with no way home, it was a bad moment for each of us. Fortunately, I had not been the one to tie the knot that failed; that would have been too much for me to bear around all of these experienced men.

The storm blew hard for almost three hours. The storm moved exactly as forecast; it just arrived a couple of hours later than expected. Fortunately, an alert neighbor noticed my father and I had not returned from our morning hunting trip. Following his own intuition, he eased out in the rough waters in his own boat to check on us. He brought us back safely to Rock Hall and also helped us locate our lost skiff.

I never went hunting again with our not-so-funny guest. I still consider that one of the worst duck hunts of my life, but it was truly one of the most instructive too. As a young man hoping to build a career working on the Chesapeake Bay, I learned how quickly and fiercely a winter storm can descend. I learned something about being a guest in an unfamiliar place. Mostly, I gained a better understanding of what watermen mean when they say they are God-fearing men.

Chapter Ten

Running with the Big Dogs

When I was a young boy, our community went to great lengths to keep the populations of raccoons in check. In Maryland, raccoons were more than just a nuisance. They were viewed as a dangerous pest capable of causing real harm to humans and financial hardship for poultry farmers. Small children and domestic pets were considered most at risk to raccoon attack. Routinely, most farmers kept a rifle or shotgun in their trucks to use when a raccoon was observed lurking around the corn planters, chicken houses, or areas where children played.

Raccoons were aggressively trapped by professional trappers hired by farmers and landowners to keep the population in check. These trappers did not receive an hourly wage or a salary for their efforts. Trappers earned their income by trapping and skinning the raccoon for their hides. Once fully cured, these trappers would sell them to fur dealers who would sell these hides (often called pelts) to high-end makers of clothes who created glamorous coats for the wealthy. The lower quality pelts would be sold to hat and jacket makers who made warm, durable outer wear. In the forties, it was considered socially acceptable and even prudent to wear animal fur as clothing. And much of the raccoon meat was eaten as well.

At the time, the number of raccoons far exceeded the number of skilled trappers, and frequently, the population of raccoons would get out of control. When the populations spiked and became overly abundant, landowners would invite raccoon hunters with "coon hounds" to also help thin out the excess raccoons. (Today, there are populations of wild hogs in Texas that have become equally problematic and require the same efforts).

The general public supported the practice of raccoon hunting because they knew it reduced the risk of their family being exposed to rabies or distemper. We all knew people in our community who had been bitten by a raccoon and were forced to endure a very painful series of shots to be protected. Many of us knew of pets that had to be put down because they'd gotten into a fight with a raccoon (that was potentially rabid). Only a few residents in Kent County were naïve enough to allow a wild raccoon to come near or in their home to be fed like a pet. I was taught that a raccoon was a wild animal capable of causing violent attacks when hungry, sick, or backed into a corner.

A wise raccoon. *Courtesy of Ann Crane Harlan*.

I understand, to a point, why some people today find the old traditions of raccoon hunting to be distasteful. But where I come from, raccoon hunting was both encouraged and necessary to keep the highly adaptable raccoon in check. With no natural predators to keep their numbers down, raccoons adapted perfectly to living in barns and homes. In fact, raccoons actually thrive on man's wasteful nature and have no trouble finding food sources by raiding trash cans, bags of seed corn, and chicken houses.

Because raccoon hunting with my father and his friends was so impactful on my growing up in Rock Hall, I have chosen to share a few stories about my time hunting in the woods and marshes around Kent County. But first, I need to explain a little bit about the process of hunting raccoons with hounds. Raccoons, in nature, are nocturnal, which means they move around after dark in search of food. Generally, if a raccoon was seen in broad daylight, it was assumed to be sick and was to be avoided or killed.

Another important characteristic to know about raccoons is that they are omnivores, which means they eat meat, fish, and plants. Gifted with exceptional night vision and hearing, raccoons could find any source of food. Their sense of smell, however, was their strongest characteristic and raccoons would roam for miles to find fish, moles, snails, and even human garbage. Raccoons love to eat fresh eggs best of all, which made them a real problem for farmers who were raising chickens to feed their families.

Without a doubt, the raccoon was created in nature to be adaptable, cunning, and strong. Respected as fierce fighters on land and deadly in the water, raccoons were built to survive and even thrive around humans. But nature gave them a weakness too. When raccoons walk, climb, crawl, or swim, they leave a strong scent that hounds (bassets, healers, bloodhounds) can smell and follow. Wherever their feet and fur touch the earth, they leave an odorous trail that can be tracked even in the dark. Only in water can a raccoon partially mask his strong scent.

As hunters, we worked with the dogs that were naturally capable of detecting the smell of a raccoon. Working in large packs, we would release up to a dozen hounds into the woods or in the marsh. Barking and bellowing in the dark, the dogs would go back and forth through an area with their noses on the ground searching for a hot trail (scent). The hunters could tell when a hound found a hot trail because the sound and intensity of their bark would change. Once a hot trail was discovered, the other hunting dogs would join in on the chase and the trail of the raccoon would be followed until the scent was lost or until the raccoon was chased up into a tree.

The hunter's role in the hunt was to listen to the barks, keep an eye on the younger dogs, and shoot the raccoon out of the tree with a rifle once it was treed. The meat and the hides of the raccoon were either sold or given away. As a young boy, I considered raccoon hunting with dogs similar to using a falcon to hunt rabbits or a minnow to catch a fish. From day one, I loved to go raccoon hunting with my father. I wonder now how many mornings I fell asleep in elementary school after spending all night in the woods hunting raccoons.

Of all my memories of raccoon hunting, one hunt still stands out as the most comical. Though it happened when I was an adult, it reminds me of the good times we all enjoyed while hunting together on Eastern Neck Island. On this particular night, we were hunting along a narrow stretch of gravel road that had marshy water on both sides. We let the dogs out on the road next to the bridge and drove down the strip of land for about a mile.

If there was a raccoon in the area, we were pretty sure it would have to pass by this narrow section of land. In the dark, we all talked quietly among ourselves as the dogs barked and bellowed in the woods and marshes behind us. It was fun just to be standing there together in the dark near Senator Percy M. Hepbron's front yard. It really didn't matter at all whether we got a raccoon that night or not; the fellowship alone was good enough for us.

In no time at all, one of the older hounds smelled a fresh raccoon trail and the chase was on. I could hear the intensity of the dog barks get louder and more confident which meant the chase was coming right towards us. As the barking got really intense, I peered into the darkness thinking I might see a raccoon scurry by, but it was too dark where I was standing. So, we all kept listening and waiting for something to happen. Just then, I heard the strangest sound coming from within the pack of hound dogs. Amongst the heavy barks and bellows of the healers and the bloodhounds was a shrill, squeaky sound that we all knew was not a hound.

This *"yip, yip, yip"* sound continued and as hunters, we all fell out laughing over this new and strange sound. We started to speculate on what kind of animal might be making that *"yip, yip, yip"* sound. After a few moments, we agreed that it had to be a wild fox that somehow got mixed in with our pack of dogs. We laughed so hard at the thought that our pack of dogs now contained a fox. When hunting in the wilderness after dark, strange things do happen more often than not.

Now the barks and bellows were very loud and we were certain the raccoon and the dogs would soon pass by. Standing in a row like a bunch of crows sitting on a fence, we peered into the darkness to witness the chase unfold. Through the darkness, we could see the faint outline of a fast-moving raccoon as he passed about ten yards from us. Less than a minute later, the older dogs came rushing by, barking and bellowing. After a few more seconds, our younger dogs came by barking enthusiastically, but with less confidence. And, way in the back, Senator Hepbron's rat terrier came running down the trail running his little legs off trying to keep up with the pack.

It was a hysterical sight and we laughed to tears as we watched this little dog trying to keep up. Now we all knew what was creating that strange *yip, yip, yip* and we laughed again. But our laughter didn't last much longer because the pack treed the raccoon immediately after they passed us. Quickly, we realized that in the heat of the moment, one of the younger dogs might mistake the rat terrier for a raccoon and tear it to pieces. Or worse, we feared the raccoon might fall out of the tree and attack the rat terrier. We rushed to the tree and pulled the scrappy rat terrier off the hunt. Though her flesh was willing, we could not allow the little dog to run with the coon hounds.

Running with the big dogs. *Courtesy of Ann Crane Harlan*.

Chapter Eleven
Walking with Ame

While Joe Downey was clearly my first mentor, Mr. Emil Myers was my first hero. Emil ran Myers Store which provided groceries and supplies for many families in Kent County. During the duck-hunting season, Emil also sold food and supplies to the owners of the elite gunning clubs on Eastern Neck Island. He was a permanent resident of Rock Hall and a lifelong friend of Miss Helen Durding who owned and operated Durding's Store.

Nobody in town called him Emil, as his nickname was simply Ame. As a child, I considered him to be a gentle man who would do anything for anybody. He was a true jack-of-all-trades, as he could do everything well. He was well liked and was considered a stand up, significant man in Rock Hall. He was a close friend of my father's and therefore was a permanent part of the Simns family. Just to help out, he even cut my father's hair, since barbers can't cut their own hair (well).

Somehow, Ame was always there in the moment to help others. When we went raccoon hunting together, he would always keep an eye on me. Dad never asked him to help me, but he just knew he would be helping my Dad by helping me. In places where the water was too deep or the briars were too rough on my skin, Ame would lift me up on his broad shoulders and carry me until the walking was easier. He never made a fuss over helping me out nor did he seek affirmation from the other hunters for his effort. In this way, Ame enabled me to keep up when I was about 6 years old. By this simple act, Ame made me feel welcome and safe among the older men.

One night, Ame and I were alone walking around a big open field on the edge of the marsh. The moon was radiantly bright and I could see my breath in the cold night air. But, I didn't have enough light to see a full-grown bull on the far side of the field. Without our knowledge, the farmer had isolated his bull from the herd by locking him in this back field. Our peaceful moonlit walk was shattered when an alert hunter spotted the bull running in a full charge. Yelling at the top of his lungs, he said "Ame, run for the fence, a bull is charging you right now."

Needless to say, our conversation came to an abrupt end and Ame instinctively pushed me in the direction he wanted me to run. I ran as fast I could, but my little legs were no match for the size of the field and the distance still to be traveled. Ame ran behind me and stayed between me and the bull. As I got right up against the fence, Ame grabbed me by my belt and the back of my neck and threw me over the fence. He then climbed the fence forcing the bull to stop his charge. Still shaken up pretty badly, all I could say to this wonderful man was a muffled, "Thanks, Ame."

A full charge. *Courtesy of Ann Crane Harlan.*

Several years later, Ame and I were again walking around a rough patch of marsh on Eastern Neck Island when I learned something new from this unique man. On this particular evening, the tide along the Chester River was high which made the walking on the marsh hard for me. As always, Ame was walking beside me as we searched together for an easier path. I can't remember what we were talking about at the time, but we were into our normal dialogue between one man and one future man. Ame had this rare ability to talk with me about adult things but in a language and a tone that my young mind could follow. He never talked down to me, he always talked with me which made our time together so special.

As we walked in the darkness, we walked right into a foul-smelling part of the marsh. Abruptly, Ame stopped dead in his tracks and wouldn't move an inch closer. He was panicky and harshly grabbed my arm and dragged me away from the stinky spot on the marsh. I didn't understand what spooked him, but something inside Ame was telling him to get away from the terrible smell. He had trouble breathing and was anxious. For a moment, I feared that he was having a heart attack.

I sat quietly on the marsh grass while Ame calmed down. He apologized for being so abrupt and rough with me and told me he wanted to explain something real important to me. It frightened him how harshly he jerked me from the marsh and he wanted to explain what happened. He told me I was old enough to hear the truth about what caused him to run away so abruptly. Alone, under the stars, he proceeded to tell me a story about his service in World War II that changed the way I see water and water quality issues even today. With Ame now gone, I can share his story without causing him discomfort. I believe it is important for some younger readers to hear and grasp this story.

Though I didn't even know it at the time, this kind, gentle grocer had been a soldier stationed in the Philippines during World War II. One day, his unit was required to find and bring back fresh drinking water for the entire company so they could stay hydrated and healthy. This was a routine assignment for the soldiers, as Ame had found safe drinking water dozens of times before. As ordered, their unit returned with plenty of water, as the Philippines are a water-rich part of the planet.

Unfortunately, within a few hours of drinking from this water supply, every man who drank that water became deathly sick with severe diarrhea, cramps, and vomiting. The men were acutely sick.

Upon closer inspection, the unit leader discovered the new water supply didn't smell right. The remaining water supply was quarantined until the root cause of the sickness and the smell could be determined. No one had any clue what was wrong with the water because it looked fine to the naked eye. Plus, it had been located following the standard operating procedures for securing fresh water.

The remaining members of Ame's unit who had not sipped the "fresh water" were dispatched to double check the source of the drinking water. The unit found the exact point where the water was originally drawn and everything looked and smelled fine. Not satisfied, the unit proceeded to walk along the water system towards the headwaters. After a few minutes of hiking, the men came to a point where the water had spread out into a pond.

There, floating in shallow water, were over a dozen bloated bodies of enemy soldiers that had been killed in battle. Their bodies had been decomposing for several days in the hot sun and their flesh was rotting inside their uniforms. For Ame, the visual sight and smell of all that death was too much. He and the other men were sickened by this grotesque sight. Without a doubt, Ame was now certain what caused his comrades to get sick back at camp. They had removed what appeared to be clean water downstream from a supply that had been contaminated at the headwaters.

As I listened to his story, I didn't understand how a foul smell could trigger such an impulsive response within a man. I would learn later in my life that a man's sense of smell is not particularly strong, but is capable of evoking powerful memories. Clearly, the marsh we stumbled across that night while raccoon hunting was a vivid reminder of a nightmarish moment in the Philippines. As Ame finished his story, he had tears in his eyes and I was speechless. He signaled for me to get up, and we resumed our walk and reconnected with the other hunters. He never said another word about the smell on the marsh, and I never shared his story with anyone else – until now.

I don't remember if we got a raccoon that night or not. After receiving a personal lesson about the importance of clean headwaters, my mind was consumed with this experience. It was my first time to realize that war was not as glamorous, glorious, or romantic as it was portrayed in the picture shows. It shocked and even saddened me to learn that men could end up face down, bloated and forgotten by their own brothers in a puddle of water. Ame showed me that there was real pain and anguish when a family member was lost or killed in war. It became the moment when I understood the difference between killed in action, missing in action, and prisoner of war.

That night, I also learned that when the headwaters are fouled, then the whole water system is fouled too. Further, I learned that there is no such thing as safe drinking water if the headwaters are tainted with a toxin of any kind. After learning these lessons, I would never again take for granted that fresh drinking water was a basic right of being an American. Fresh water is a natural resource, just like a rockfish or a raccoon, requiring stewardship and conservation to be of sustainable value over time.

In the sharing of this one story, Ame taught me one other life lesson that remains valuable to me today. Prior to hearing this story, I had always assumed that my father's friend, Ame, was simply a good, mild-mannered grocer who happened to love raccoon hunting with my family. I had no idea that he was also a loyal, strong, dedicated soldier of The United States of America who fought half way around the globe so my family could worship, hunt, and fish freely in Rock Hall. I learned that until I walked a mile in someone else's shoes, I was not in a position to judge any man or his past. In one night, my impression of this man was deepened forever and Ame became my first true hero.

American Flag with 48 stars.
Courtesy of Ann Crane Harlan.

In the years to follow, I would spend countless hours in the mucky marsh trapping muskrats, hunting ducks, and chasing raccoons with dogs. Just by walking the marshes over and over again, I learned that each marsh has its own unique odor and even the same marsh can smell differently at different times of the year. Every now and then, I would come across a nasty smelling patch of mucky marsh that we now know is simply methane. However, just like Ame, I get spooked when I smell that odor and I get away from the spot as quickly as possible. For reasons I can't fully explain, that smell reminds me of death and I want no part of it before my time.

Chapter Twelve
Captain Lon's Pound Net

An important role model in my life was Captain Alonza "Lon" Hubbard. From the first day I was old enough to go fishing with him, Captain Lon took me under his wing and taught me many things about Rock Hall, watermen, and living a good, full life. For reasons beyond my understanding, Lon served as my unofficial Godfather when I was young and even kept an eye on me in my adult years when I was pushing hard and taking chances.

Captain Lon was a superb waterman and an even better pound net fisherman. A pound net is a permanent netting device used by watermen to catch fish migrating up and down the Chesapeake and its major rivers.

A pound net has three main sections that each perform a different function in the process. The hedge is positioned perpendicular to the shoreline and serves as an initial barrier for migrating fish. As the fish encounter the hedge, they panic and instinctively swim towards the deeper water which forces them to swim away from the shoreline.

As they swim along the hedging, the fish enter into an open area called the heart which holds the target and non-target species safely in the enclosed area. Still sensing danger, they continue to search for deeper water which forces them to push along the heart until they find and swim through a funnel. Once they pass through the funnel, they enter into the third section of the netting system called the pound which is a large containment area.

Here the fish will remain trapped alive until a waterman fishes them out with a dip net. The target species would be culled by species and size while the non-target species would be returned unharmed to the water. With the pound net system, no bait was required to attract the fish. Pound nets catch fish by interrupting and then intercepting their natural migration patterns. They are effective and still are widely used by fishermen today.

A pound net. *Courtesy of Ann Crane Harlan.*

By the time I was 10 years old in 1947, Captain Lon took my friend Hubbard Kendall and I along to fish the pound nets every day we were not in school. Hubbard was Captain Lon's sister's son so there was a family connection binding them together. Onboard, Hubbard and I were utility "helpers" for Captain Lon and we did whatever he told us to do. Usually, I was responsible for throwing back the little ones and the "trash fish" like toadfish. By the way, trash fish is no longer an acceptable description of these creatures. In our pound net, we caught striped bass, bluefish, perch, croaker, spot, sea trout, angelfish, and butterfish. Interestingly, Captain Lon caught the same species of fish that my Captain Willie had caught a generation before in his purse seine nets.

Looking back on our time together, I realize Captain Lon didn't really need my help on his workboat. He already had two able sons named Wilkens and Cope. Plus, he had two experienced crewmembers onboard named Jody Graves and Paddles Orr. Captain Lon not only carved out a spot for me on his boat, he also carved out a spot for me in his heart. What a blessing to have another mentor in my life to show me the ropes and get me started on the right path.

He was surely impressive with the way he handled his boat and his ability to catch fish. But what impressed me most was the way Captain Lon treated people. On board *The Gen Mac*, he hand-picked his crewmembers to make sure everyone got along, got the work done, and honored each other as fellow men. He experienced zero turnover on his boat which meant he never had to deal with green horns (inexperienced watermen) tearing up his equipment or wasting time. Every young waterman from Kent County wanted to land a spot on his boat but there was rarely an opening to compete for. In this way, Lon always had choices on shore which insured that he got excellent service and cooperation from his four crewmembers.

Another attribute that made Lon special was that his leadership style appeared to be color blind. In the forties, the black community lived apart from the white community. Segregation was a divisive and hurtful part of Maryland's culture and it severely tested the practical application of our nation's stated value of "one nation, under God." However, on board *The Gen Mac*, Lon expected the same level of service from all his crewmembers, whether they were his own sons or hired crewmembers. Lon required every man on board to pull their own weight, work without complaining, and to look out for one another. He didn't divvy up the dirty jobs based on skin color and he didn't pay shares differently, either.

Jody Graves was a black crewmember on board and he was very kind to me. In fact, he treated me like I was his own son. While working on the pound net, many times he would lift up my part of the net when the weight of the fish was too great for me to handle alone. On the way out to the fishing grounds, Jody and I would sit on the engine box and eat our lunches together. Often, he would share some of his meal with me as his lunch was always better. Sadly, it never dawned on me that I was not legally allowed to sit down with Jody Graves in a restaurant in Rock Hall. As a young boy, I was not mature enough to see the wrongness of discrimination. I did not fully understand the unfairness of discrimination until I witnessed it during the draft process for Viet Nam.

Captain Lon was not just a great waterman. He was truly a civic leader and served as a real catalyst for growth in Rock Hall. At just the right time, Lon built the Hubbard Pier Seafood Company from scratch. Through this vertically integrated business, he could make money at several different points. Because of his success, many other family businesses also were quite successful. Whenever I hear the expression that a high tide raises all boats, I am reminded how Captain Lon's vision helped us all be successful and significant in Rock Hall. Visionary men like Lon were good for Rock Hall and good for America.

One day while we were together, Lon told me about his military service deferral he encountered during World War I. As he was being inducted to become a soldier overseas, the reviewer noticed that Alonza Copeland Hubbard had the skills and experience to harvest seafood on the Chesapeake Bay. As a result, Lon was not enlisted as a soldier. Instead, he was required to go back to Rock Hall and harvest seafood to feed our servicemen and a growing America. In those days, farmers and fishermen were respected for their role in producing food that was used to keep our soldiers fit.

Chapter Thirteen

Family Ties

Because I was born into a family of watermen from both my mother's and father's sides of the family, I had direct access to three of the best watermen in Kent County. Uncle Luke, of the Thomas family, helped me perfect my skills with small workboats like rowboats, bateaus, garveys, and gilling skiffs. He was a master at handling small boats and he made sure I could operate and care for them properly. He also helped me learn how to operate and care for small engines. Best of all, Uncle Luke taught me how to read the bottoms of the Chesapeake Bay and her tributaries (rivers) which enabled me to catch the most fish and to save money on lost gear.

Uncle Josh was married to my Aunt Claris. Uncle Josh emerged as the most influential person in my life in terms of preparing me to become a progressive, hard-driving waterman. Early on, he inspired me to get active in The Kent County Watermen's Association because he knew that declining water quality was going to make it harder and harder to make a living on the water. He also taught me a great deal about leadership, making steady money and then saving that money so I could leverage my success in the lean years. Without question, Uncle Josh was the one waterman I attempted to pattern my life after.

Uncle Luke had a brother named Fusty who also was a waterman. Though he wasn't technically an uncle, he was clearly an important part of our family and of my life. Fusty operated a beautiful forty-two-foot workboat named *Lucky* and he regularly took his son Trapper (his real name was Glenwood Thomas) and me fishing whenever we could go. It was Fusty who taught me how to operate the four controls necessary to power and steer a workboat. Using only two hands, Fusty patiently taught me the right order in which to use the transmission, clutch and throttle while steering with the tiller (or steering wheel in the cabin).

It was no easy task for Fusty to teach Trapper and me how to operate this older system, but he stuck with it until he was comfortable that we could operate his workboat safely. He also taught us how to steer properly against the tides, currents, and waves so we could keep the gill nets from getting wrapped up in the wheel (propeller). Though it's been years now, I can still hear him say, "Larry, cut her away," while Trapper and he pulled in the nets.

Concerning his work ethic, Fusty was impossible for me to outwork. Over and over again, he would tell me his philosophy about working hard. He would say, "Larry, a house is a place to sleep and eat. If I'm not on my boat than I am in the shed. If I'm in the house, I will be either sleeping or eating. The only time a man should sit down is when he eats. If you have time to sit, then you have time to sleep. If you are not eating or sleeping you should be working". For sure, Trapper and I spent none of our time just hanging around Captain Fusty.

Captain Fusty was skilled at catching crabs, oysters, and fish. What made him so effective was that he could read the waters, read the bottom, and seemed to understand every detail about the life cycles of each fishery. But his greatest passion, by far, was top netting for shad in the upper part of the Chesapeake Bay. Fusty had refined every process needed to catch tons of shad and he was regularly one of the top fishermen in the fleet. I credit Captain Fusty for inspiring me to become a successful, profitable shad fisherman. In fact, it was Captain Fusty who first pointed out to me why fishing with top nets was often called "pretty fishing".

Of all of my uncles, Captain Fusty had the deepest appreciation for the historical aspects of commercial fishing. He held a deep respect for the generations of fishermen who came before him, and he admired how successful they were in spite of how very crude, primitive, and dangerous the equipment used to be. He convinced me that the old ways were not irrelevant.

Though Fusty was the first to adopt any new technology that would help him fish better or with a greater margin of safety, he continued to honor the old ways where it was practical. To keep a slice of Maryland's history alive for as long as he could, he preserved one of the old shanties. During the spring, he would tow it up close to the fishing grounds, and several crews used this shanty to eat their meals and relax. It wasn't necessary since he had a full cabin on *Lucky*, but he wanted to keep that part of the good old days alive for a little while longer. When Fusty was young, all the fishermen lived and ate meals in shanties when they weren't working with the top nets.

Mending nets at the shanties. *Courtesy of Ann Crane Harlan.*

Chapter Fourteen
Pretty Fishing

The sheer number of shad migrating up the Chesapeake Bay was astounding back in the forties. Back then, the old timers would tell stories of how the schools of shad were so thick they would darken the waters. As a young boy, I saw this abundance too and it was an awesome sight.

The shad fishery was only open for commercial harvesting during the annual "shad runs" which would start in late March and run through early June. Shad fishing was a spring thing, which meant the bitter cold winds of winter were behind us and the sultry days of summer had not yet come. So, while we worked with nets on the water and mended them each day on land, I watched the spring bloom in Kent and Cecil counties on a daily basis. I loved to watch the large trees gradually release their new leaves. I loved to watch the dogwoods start to flower. And I loved to watch the corn pop up in rows and the wheat start to green up. For whatever reason, I always felt closest to God in the spring during the shad run.

Even the process of selling our daily shad harvest to the fish buyers was special to me. Selling shad was not rough like shoveling oysters off the bottom of the boat or stacking dozens of bushel baskets full of crabs on a truck. In those days, shad was sold in wooden boxes in increments of 100 pounds. Slowly, we would place each shad down in a bed of crushed ice, belly side up, so they would lie side by side. We would ice them down again before creating another layer. When the box was all done, it reminded me of the way sardines were neatly packed into their little cans – only much larger. On an average day, we might have two tons of beautiful shad to pack on ice which meant we loaded forty wooden crates by hand.

The term "pretty fishing" doesn't really relate to the beauty of the fish, their abundance, or even the way we packed them into a wooden crate. The term "pretty fishing" described a number of the processes we used to set the nets each evening. First, every box of net was painstakingly organized so that every cork (buoy) and every ring (weight) would be released off the stern of the boat without a snag, hitch, or delay. In unison, two crewmembers would release the nets with precision, which was a beautiful process to witness.

But setting nets in the upper Chesapeake Bay was tricky and required complete cooperation from every captain working the same area. Since each boat was setting nearly three miles of drift nets, great care was taken to insure the nets stayed apart. To me, the most beautiful part of shad fishing was watching each boat set their nets against a setting sun in a straight line across the Chesapeake Bay.

Setting nets at sunset. *Courtesy of Ann Crane Harlan*.

By the time I was fourteen, in 1951, I knew the shad fishery was my favorite. I knew I could make more money catching crabs, oysters, and rockfish, but I loved to fish for shad with top nets. I fear that today's young people may never fully understand just how many shad once migrated up the Chesapeake Bay and into the Susquehanna River. There was a time, not so long ago, when the shad fishery in Rock Hall was more important to our community than the rockfish. If my readers remember nothing else from this book, please remember that the American Shad is still a beautiful fish and the fishery could be restored if America decides this species is important enough.

Part Two
Finding My Spot in Rock Hall
(1952 – 1958)

Chapter Fifteen
Teeming with Ducks

Every day after school in the fall and winter, I was always out in the woods, marshes, or fields hunting. Rain or shine, hot or cold, I would be hunting if a species of wild game was in season. I had no trouble finding places to hunt, either. In the early fifties, *No Trespassing* signs were rarely used because they were not necessary. Most landowners and farmers allowed me to hunt on their properties as long as I asked permission, cared for their land and their farm animals, and was considerate of the natural resources. As an expression of my appreciation, I would often give them a portion of the limit I shot on their property after I picked or skinned it. When hunting alone, I usually shot squirrels, rabbits, and quail.

By 1952, I was a fully committed, dedicated water-fowler. I loved every aspect of duck hunting and spent hours either planning to hunt, hunting, or cleaning up after a hunt. It was more than a hobby for me. All of my close friends were hunters too, and that is all we talked and thought about. Hunting served as a great place for me to build friendships and spend time in nature.

Though I hunted all wild game, nothing captured my heart and soul like hunting for wild ducks. Rock Hall was perfectly situated on the Mid-Atlantic Flyway. We were far enough south that overwintering ducks could survive the biting cold temperatures. Plus, the ducks had an abundance of natural duck food that could keep them fat all winter. Winter mortality due to winter starvation was low, which meant that ducks migrating north in March were plump and healthy for the breeding season.

Because of the sheer number of ducks that overwintered in our area, I developed a keen interest in learning everything I could about every kind of duck that flew to Kent County. I studied every detail I could find about diving, sea, and puddle ducks and never got tired of reading and learning about them. I hunted every kind of duck allowed by Maryland law and never turned down an opportunity to go duck hunting. I didn't care how cold it got, or how sick I was, I never missed a day duck hunting if I could help it.

It is hard to describe just how many ducks used to fly up and down the shoreline of Kent County. No photograph can fully capture the abundance and no book can adequately describe it, either. The sheer volume and diversity of wild ducks that used to overwinter in Kent County was simply indescribable. The mallards and black ducks were once so thick that entire headwaters of creeks would be filled with them. And diving ducks were once so plentiful they looked like a floating raft painted red, white, and black. The only word that comes close to describing the sheer number of ducks that migrated here was "teeming."

Often, my father and I would drive down to Eastern Neck Island to watch the ducks fly and swim. We didn't take our guns and we didn't talk much, either. We would just sit quietly in the truck and watch the birds move in their natural setting. It didn't matter whether we were watching diving ducks rafting up on the lee side of the shore or watching a pair of widgeon landing in a clump of marsh grass; we both loved to watch the ducks. Even today, watching ducks fly with my father remains one of my strongest and best memories of my Dad and me spending time together. I can still hear him say, "Larry, there are so many ducks swarming and swirling right now they almost block out the sun".

Blocking out the sun. *Courtesy of Ann Crane Harlan*.

Chapter Sixteen
Guiding Others

While still attending Rock Hall High School, I landed a job at a top gunning club in Maryland. At first, I was considered too young to lead hunters on paid duck hunts. So I was used as a utility employee who did a little bit of everything as needed. I was paid well and was even able to go hunting with the owners now and then. It was a great job for me.

Soon after I was hired, the manager and owners recognized that I had three skills that made me a likely candidate to become a hunting guide. First, I was an accurate shooter, so I could shoot behind weaker hunters and finish the ducks they had winged (crippled). Second, I was a hard worker and was willing to do every task at the club to help the customers have a good experience. Third, I was not visibly affected by the biting cold or hard work. In truth, I was cold like everyone else, but I refused to admit it to anyone at the club. I just endured. Third, I absolutely loved to duck hunt and my enthusiasm inspired the guests to love duck hunting also.

The owners asked me to guide some of their hunts which I readily agreed to. I was paid $75 per week and occasionally received small tips for "day guests;" the members didn't tip because they paid dues that covered my wages. This club catered to avid hunters who came back year after year to partake in a great duck hunt. The club also catered to the super wealthy sportsmen who visited at the club for a hunt of a lifetime. Some hunters wanted to shoot diving ducks while others wanted to shoot in the marshes and use their dogs. Frequently, we hunted both kinds of ducks on the same day. Whatever they wanted, it was my job to help them shoot the limit, enjoy the hunt, and get back to the lodge safely.

Ironically, because I was so young compared to everyone else in the duck blind, the guests would often discuss sensitive details of their lives as if I wasn't even there. Just by listening, I learned a lot about men's business strategies, personal struggles, and even their fears. I discovered that men of privilege were often dissatisfied with their lives beyond their achievements at work. I learned that some hunters came on the duck hunt to get away from their work and their families. I learned that men were willing to pay a small fortune just to have a good time. Some conversations were too sad to share in this book, but almost all of them helped me define what I wanted for my own life.

Most of the guests were agreeable men and women who simply wanted to spend a day in nature, have a good shoot, and bring home some fresh duck meat to share with their families. I enjoyed helping the hunters find success, so I didn't mind working for them. I willingly was there to get dirty, cold, and wet, so they could remain comfortable. Occasionally, I would have to guide an obnoxious loudmouth or a know-it-all, which made for long mornings in the duck blind. I generally just increased my tolerance and let their shooting results validate whether they were all talk or actually "as good as they claimed to be."

There were two kinds of hunters who truly eroded my enjoyment as a professional guide. I didn't like to work around hunters who lacked firearm-handling skills. As a paid guide, I was responsible for the safety of the hunters and the dogs, so it was always unsettling to have either a novice or a reckless gun handler along on the hunt.

Several times, I was so uncomfortable with the way certain hunters handled their guns that I had to take away their shooting privileges just to protect the others. This is not a pleasant task since the hunts were expensive. One morning, I was guiding for a large group when one of the hunters failed to secure his gun in the notch cut into the duck blind. Encumbered by his bulk hunting jacket, he bumped into his own gun which caused it to fall on the floor. Upon impact, the gun discharged on my side of the blind and blew a hole right through the plywood. Miraculously, the lead shot missed the club's dog and my legs.

The other kind of hunter I struggled with was the "big-shot" who came to the gunning club to fulfill a sick dream of being a "meat hunter." These rare, but problematic, sportsmen would muscle their way on Eastern Neck Island to kill as many ducks as their time and my patience would allow. They would shoot other people's birds and shoot over their limit. They were shooting more ducks than they could possibly eat. Several times, I had to abruptly end a duck hunt for all guests because one rogue sportsman wouldn't stop. Because I could lose my hunting license and my job (for breaking club rules), I stopped the meat hunters once I knew one was among us.

I always told the club owners which hunters were dangerous and which ones couldn't follow the rules. It was their role to make sure they didn't come back in future years. But I must say I met a number of blue-chip hunters who brought great traditions and respect to the club and to my life. As a young man trying to find my spot in the world, it was a blessing to be around good men who knew how to handle firearms, loved nature, and valued their fellow man. They were there for the hunt, not the kill, and they followed all of the club rules and followed my direction as their guide. In the blind, these men spoke about their families, careers, faith, and dreams. I gleaned many good ideas and perspectives by listening to these wise, older hunters.

Chapter Seventeen
Captain Cope

Guiding duck hunts and working for local watermen on weekends and during the summers kept me in spending money while I was living at home. I was not an exceptional student, but I did graduate from Rock Hall High School in 1956 while working many hours each week. I had no interest in going to college as I had already set my dream on becoming a full-time, successful waterman from Kent County.

To get started, I bought an old twenty-eight-foot workboat from Harry White called *Sea Mite* to run crab pots along the eastern side of the Chesapeake Bay. To save money, I worked alone from dawn to dusk and I fished my pots every day. As the price of hard crabs dropped off in the fall, I rigged up *Sea Mite* to harvest oysters using drop tongs. After Thanksgiving, I would remain on call to serve as a guide whenever the owners or the manager called me. On the days the club owners would rest the ducks, I would oyster alone.

As a newly married teenager with our first baby on the way, I struggled every day to find the balance between working hard and being a family man. I was biologically ready to be a father, but I was not emotionally, spiritually, and financially ready to be a good dad. With no money in the bank and no credit to my name, it seemed like I was always working just to make ends meet. We had no health insurance and nothing "in the cookie jar" to tide us over.

My wife, Nancy, and I lived in a small house we rented for $ 25 per month. It had no running water and no indoor toilet. It was a non-insulated home and the wind blew right through the walls and into our bones. Worst of all, I still had an "I am invincible" attitude common among male teenagers of my generation. I was pretty tough back then, but the reality was that I was one broken arm or one car wreck away from financial ruin. Not until I started living on my own did I fully realize what sacrifices Mom and Dad made while I was living at home.

While working alone that summer crabbing and then that winter oystering, I made an important self discovery about my future as a waterman. Though I enjoyed being alone and making all the decisions, I discovered I was limiting myself financially by operating on such thin margins and on such a small boat. If my dream was to harvest crabs and oysters in the Chester River for the rest of my life, *Sea Mite* would have been enough boat. But I wanted to be a progressive, top-end waterman like Uncle Josh and Captain Lon. I didn't want to just pay my bills and get by. I wanted to have a full life filled with experiences, success, and even failures, if need be.

Though my uncles and my father taught me all kinds of skills and strategies to harvest crabs and oysters, I lacked sufficient skills and experience to make a living fishing with gill nets. Captain Fusty got me started and lit a fire in my heart for shad fishing, but I knew it would take several more years to master both the art and science of fishing profitably with nets. At age 19, in 1956, it was clear to me that I needed to enlarge my territory by working with some of the best captains in Rock Hall.

My professional reputation around Kent County was strong but limited. I was considered a hard worker, agile on board, and tough enough to endure bitter cold temperatures. I was also known to be easy on equipment and a pretty quick learner. I was considered reliable, which meant I showed up every morning no matter what. I was also competitive in nature and motivated by money which are considered valuable traits in a crewmember. I was known, too, to have a hot temper and a tendency to overwork myself.

So, I put the word out among the fleet that I was looking for full-time work as a crewmember with an experienced gill netter. One day, while my father was cutting Wilkens Hubbard's hair, he mentioned I was on the lookout for an open spot on a fishing boat. Wilkens revealed that an experienced crewmember had just "up and quit" that same day leaving the Hubbard Pier Seafood Company workboat short one crewmember. Dad told Wilkens I wanted that spot and would be ready to fish right after Christmas. That same day, I received a call from Wilken's brother, Cope, asking if I wanted to be a junior crewmember on the *Lon Swann*.

I wanted and needed that job to reach my long-term dream of being a successful fisherman. I was disappointed the position offered was only a junior crewmember, which meant I would not receive a share of the boats profits. Instead, I would be paid a flat rate of $50 per week, plus room and board, and would be required to answer to both a tough captain and a harsh senior crewmember. I also worried about leaving my young bride in our drafty old house for long periods of time in the dead of winter. In the end, none of my concerns mattered at all. Either I wanted the job as presented or I didn't, and so I told Cope on the spot that I would work for him through the winter fisheries and the shad fishery. Right or wrong, I committed myself to six months of service on a workboat for a grand total of $1300.

After I accepted the job, Cope made sure I knew exactly what I had signed up for. He explained that I would make $50 per week for seven full days of work. He generously acknowledged that I would have my own bunk and would be able to eat as much as I wanted after the senior crewmember and he had finished. He told me clearly I would not partake in the boat's profits regardless of how successfully we fished or how hard I worked. He wanted me to be sure I knew I was going to be "low man" on board and most of the grungy jobs would be my responsibility. He told me I would not have time to guide at the gunning club in January. Finally, he advised me to find a reliable waterman to keep an eye on *Sea Mite* because we would likely be fishing down at Solomons for the month of January.

I remember the day I left my young bride and my baby girl, Dawn, just a few days after Christmas to start my new job. It's been over fifty years since that day, and it still makes me teary to think of the sacrifices Nancy and Dawn made so I could gain the experience to be waterman and a future leader. Imagine being a new Mom left all alone in a drafty old house with no running water. In many respects, signing on to work for Cope in Solomons was similar to a military deployment which places a huge hardship on the family that is left behind.

Wilkens drove me down to Solomons where Captain Cope had already readied the gear for opening day on January 1, 1957. Solomons was a beautiful, deep-water harbor town located at the mouth of the Patuxent River. It was a real fishing hub for the western shore of Maryland and workboats from all over Maryland annually returned to Solomons to fish and oyster. The water was salty enough and the prevailing winds were strong enough to keep the harbor and the fishing grounds ice free most of the time.

On board the *Lon Swann*, I was expected to be Cope's extra set of hands. Whatever and whenever he requested help, I stepped into that role and did it exactly as I was told. I was a utility man, a helper of sorts, and did everything the other men did at a fraction of their wage. I steered, pulled net, picked fish, scrubbed the boat, cooked meals, and fueled up the boat.

Cope was a take-charge Captain and his crewmembers understood that he was in charge. Cope was always in motion and ran himself, his workboat, and his crewmembers at full throttle whenever he could. On the water, he operated his workboat with a *blow-n-go* style and was considered "wild as killdeer" when roaming the Chesapeake Bay in search of fish. Because he ran hard all day long, he also tore up a lot of equipment and gear. Sometimes, I felt like I was just a piece of equipment.

Cope was a hands-on, in-the-moment captain and he knew how to do every task on his boat. Over his long career, Cope perfected every process on his workboat that would lead to a better harvest. Concerning the tasks required of me, he showed me exactly how he wanted things done and then he would watch me until he was sure I was following his way. Occasionally, he would allow me to try something my way, but usually I would end up doing it his way. Cope was a man of action and he taught me the basics and every tip I would need to become a proficient fisherman using nets.

Though he worked me to the bone, Cope gave me a great foundation in my first job as a junior crewmember. Beyond the skills he taught me, Cope exuded a passion for fishing on the Chesapeake Bay which was infectious and inspiring. By working alongside him, I too developed a thirst for fishing and I credit Cope for instilling in me a "can-do" attitude towards fishing and following the water. Between his attitude, his family resources, and his legendary work ethic, Captain Cope was a great first boss for me.

Though it often appeared that Cope was successful because he worked so hard and so long, I don't believe that was his key to success. Actually, Cope was a real student of the fisheries and learned everything he could about the life cycles of each target species and food source. Working the waters without an advanced degree in marine biology or statistics, Cope intuitively seemed to grasp the complexities and interdependencies of predator and their prey. To watch him read the waters was a special aspect of working with Cope on the *Lon Swann*.

Chapter Eighteen
Rite of Passage

Though I loved my first job working with Cope and was honored to have my spot on this boat, I hated being the low man on his workboat. From the moment I stepped on *Lon Swann*, the senior crewmember treated me like garbage and abused me verbally all day long. I was forced to do any grunt work that he could successfully offload onto me. I also had to answer to him and respond to his many commands. When I made mistakes onboard, he would yell at me and cruelly ridicule me in front of others when we were on shore. I hated working alongside this man and I winced every time he opened his mouth to shout at me.

Captain Cope could see that the chemistry between his two crewmembers was not good but he took no action to stop it. Cope had hired me to catch fish and do the work. It didn't matter to him that I was being tormented or that I was miserable around this waterman. Cope had warned me that I was going to be low man on the workboat, and he saw no need to fix a wrinkle in a process that was working well. After all, we were catching tons and tons of rockfish at a nice dockside price so there was no problem in his mind. The message he was sending to me was clear; suffer all winter and spring if I expected to receive $50 per week and a favorable recommendation from Cope in June.

By mid February, our time in Solomons was coming to an end and we prepared to travel back home to fish near Rock Hall. I was proud of myself for surviving the negative crewmember constantly abusing me. I had endured a living Hell, which filled me with a new confidence and pride. Somehow, I had developed a few coping skills I would need to ward off the few nasty people who seemed to show up in every job. My own level of maturity had progressed to the point where I was sure I could work for any captain on any workboat on the Chesapeake Bay.

Though I never did receive any affirming words from the senior crewmember, I did manage to gain the respect and trust of Captain Cope. In the long run, that was all I ever wanted and more than justified my decision to accept an assignment as a junior crewmember on the *Lon Swann*. After all, a favorable recommendation from a top captain is worth more to an emerging waterman than a wad of cash or pat on the back.

To be clear, Cope never said, "Great job Larry," or, "I am really glad that you worked for me this winter." That was not Cope's style and, for the most part, that was not the way watermen usually recognized their crew. Most of the time, crewmembers were rewarded for their good performance with large shares of the profits and that was the praise.

But on the morning we were scheduled to return to Rock Hall, Cope said to me, "Listen Larry, I am driving back to Rock Hall in the truck. I have some things to do before we go fishing tomorrow. So, I am expecting you to bring the *Lon Swann* up the Chesapeake Bay through this fog and be home by dark." With this one request, I knew Captain Cope trusted and believed in me or he would not have turned over his precious workboat to me.

I responded quickly with a "Yes sir" and then listened carefully as he shared with me the times, distances, and speeds he believed I should follow on my trip home. He then told me which landmarks to look out for if the fog ever lifted. He said, "Larry, you are in charge. I don't expect our senior crewmember to recover from his hangover anytime soon, so you'll have to get home on your own".

On the one hand, I was concerned about the fog that was now as thick as pea soup. Even for an experienced captain, fog can be very dangerous and it was a long trip back to Rock Hall. But on the other hand, I was excited to finally know that Captain Cope believed I was a good crewmember and could be trusted with navigating his workboat home in the fog. The fact that my tormenter was fast asleep in the bunk and wouldn't be in my face all day was just a gift.

Filled with a surge of confidence and my rough instructions from Cope, it never occurred to me to start my journey north in the fog with a prayer. I was an emerging, independent waterman trying to make my own mark in the world, so I never took the time to ask God for travel mercies through the fog. Instead, I untied the lines tethering *Lon Swann* to the dock and eased out of the harbor. Armed with nothing more than a watch, compass, tachometer, and a few bearings, I pushed up on the throttle until she leveled off. I then eased off on the power just a bit so I would have more time to react in the fog.

Mile by mile, I steered my way up the Chesapeake Bay looking as far out into the foggy mist as I could. The fog hid all the landmarks that Captain Cope had told me to look for. Since a large part of the trip would be traveled in the shipping channel, I stayed alert for the sounds or sightings of southbound freighters or tugs. Equally important, there were other workboats heading north towards Annapolis, Sparrows Point, Betterton, and Tilghman Island, so I also kept an eye off the stern to make sure another waterman didn't run up on me.

On a trip like this, no news is good news and I safely found my way past Cove Point, James Island, Bloody Point, and Thomas Point Lighthouse without ever seeing land. In fact, I never saw land or a landmark until I reached the sole span of the Chesapeake Bay Bridge. Even the pilings of The Bridge were hard to make out, but overhead I was able to hear and see traffic passing over the steel grates directly above me.

It was an extremely proud moment for me when I backed the *Lon Swann* into her slip at Rock Hall. No trip is a sure success until the workboat is safely docked and the engine is shut down. And there to greet me was Captain Cope who was visibly pleased I'd returned home before dark as he instructed. Quietly, Cope and I unloaded the gear that we weren't planning to use in the morning and I drove home to see my bride and my little girl. It was one of the most important days of my life.

Chapter Nineteen
Breakfast on the Sassafras

Even though I safely brought *Lon Swann* back to Rock Hall through the fog, I was still the low man onboard making $50 week. As promised, Cope would not increase my pay under any circumstances. Later that same winter, I was cooking eggs and bacon onboard while Cope was around the bend in the river setting nets for perch. I couldn't see them but I knew where they were setting nets. Cope had told me the perch were schooled up in the channel so he was setting his nets right in the channel which was legal but represented a real navigational hazard for other commercial vessels. I knew Cope was fishing right to the edge of the law.

While I cooked breakfast, a power vessel boat pulled up along-side the anchored *Lon Swann*. Once our boats were tethered together, a heavy-set man came onboard and planted his face about six inches from mine. Without any formal greeting or explanation of his purpose for boarding, he started to pepper me with hard, pointed questions about Cope and where he was fishing. He never gave me a chance to answer one question before he would fire off another. His questions were hard and direct and he wouldn't stop. I was unsure what or how to respond to this man with apparent authority.

While he pummeled me with questions, I went silent on him which irritated him. As he went on and on, I tried to figure out what he wanted from me and how I could give it to him without causing a problem between Cope and me. Clearly, this man was using his age, size, and authority to bully me into ratting on Captain Cope. At first, I was afraid of this man because he came on so strong. But since he persisted, he finally got under my skin and I resolved to tell him nothing. Technically, I was stonewalling.

My dilemma, as a 19-year-old waterman, was not easy to solve. On the one hand, I was certain Cope was fishing in or near a closed fishing area. I was also sure if I spilled my guts to this bully that Cope would get a fine and then he would fire me. On the other hand, my father taught me early in life to tell the truth and answer any questions directly when asked by men or women in authority.

Fortunately, the man with the hard questions never let up on me which meant I didn't really have a window to actually answer his questions. My stonewalling move really inflamed him which emboldened me even more. I just kept playing dumb and never caved in to any of his demands. To every question, I simply said, "I don't know, sir." Finally, he ran out of patience and in utter frustration said, "Well boy, you just don't know nothing about anything do you?" As respectfully as I could, I said, "No sir."

Furious, the man stepped off the *Lon Swann* while his crewman untied his vessel. I assumed he was going to chase down Cope, like a real man, and nail him for fishing in the channel. Instead, he went the other way which was cowardly. As I watched him disappear around another bend, I reflected on this short, but uncomfortable, exchange between a grown man and an emerging man. I concluded that I didn't like being called "boy" and I didn't like how he tried to use me to catch Cope. He didn't treat me fairly, probably because I was so young.

Chapter Twenty
The Farmers Market

The first half of 1957 had been almost perfect for Captain Cope. He had caught a record number of rockfish and perch in the winter fisheries, and was enjoying his best ever shad season that spring. With just a few days left in the shad season, Cope knew that his end of year revenue was going to be huge. And because he didn't have to pay me a full share, I knew I played a role in making him a lot of money. Cope was a content, happy waterman that spring and so was I.

Nancy and Dawn had survived the bitter cold winter in our little house and summertime was right around the corner. I had made good money working for Cope and more than enough to pay the rent, the grocery bills and the routine upkeep on *Sea Mite*. Even more important than the money, I had successfully carved out a spot as an experienced crewmember from Rock Hall. By successfully working with, and for, Cope, I was now an established, independent waterman who could crew for any captain in Maryland. Life, for the moment, was good to me.

One of my favorite parts about shad fishing was the camaraderie expressed among the watermen. Since many workboats were tied up at the same public landings, we all knew each other well and spent most of our days talking while we worked on our nets. We were always together eating and working. Back then, we even shared the same pay phone to call home. I can safely say that most of my best friends were formed along the Kent and Cecil county lines at the public landings at Betterton and off Turner's Creek.

Another part of the shad fishery I really enjoyed were the relationships the watermen had developed over the years with the local farmers. By late May, the weather was plenty warm, but not sultry and miserably hot like August. By mid May, the farmers had developed a pattern of coming around late in the morning to pick up a few fresh fish for lunch. They timed their visit so they could finish their morning chores and we would have time to get to shore with the fish. They never asked for more than one or two, and were always thankful to receive fresh shad roe to enjoy with their families.

In return, the farmers' wives would fill their pickup truck cabs with eggs, breads, milk, asparagus, and baked goods prepared right off the farms. These foods were fresh and were a welcome addition to the standard grub we would cook for ourselves. In terms of payment, there was no exchange of dollars. Instead, it was a mutual exchange of goods that we willingly shared with each other. It wasn't even a barter system, as we didn't concern ourselves with parity. We offered them a few fish now and then and in return we were given eggs, milk, or whatever they had. This farmers market was one of my favorite parts of the shad fishery.

This special relationship between the farmers and watermen lasted for decades until the shad fishery started to fail after Hurricane Agnes wiped out the bay grasses. Since then, this special bond between two important industries has grown apart somewhat. Ironically, at least in Kent County, commercial fishing and production agriculture are still viewed as important, vibrant industries necessary to keep America strong.

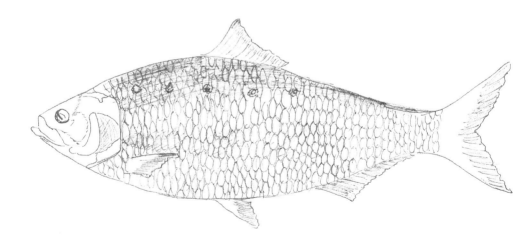

The American Shad. *Courtesy of Ann Crane Harlan*.

Chapter Twenty-One
Listing to Starboard

In the summer of 1957, I crabbed on *Sea Mite* and then tonged for oysters all fall. I worked as a duck hunting guide to make some extra money and to enjoy some fresh duck meat now and then. With the winter fishing season fast approaching, I strongly considered working with Captain Cope again because I knew he would pay me on shares and therefore I would do well. But, I didn't want to work on shares with his crewmember. As an experienced crewmember now, there was no reason to suffer when I could find other watermen to work with.

I was aware that *Sea Mite* was seaworthy but not long or wide enough to safely gill net in the icy cold waters of the Chesapeake Bay. I also didn't have the financial reserves to buy nets and take on the responsibilities of having a full crew. Even though Cope had taught me a lot, I still lacked enough experience to gill net effectively on my own.

So, I teamed up with two special watermen named Bobby Clark and Hubbard Kendall. We agreed to work in a three-way, equal partnership. We pooled our resources including our boats, nets, gear, and muscles to winter fish and then shad fish together. We used the standard share formula where the first third of the profits went to the boat owner to cover upkeep, fuel, and to buy new nets. The remaining profits would be shared equally between the three of us. I looked forward to working with two close friends that I knew would work hard, take risks, and still be fun to fish with. With this approach, I could play an active role in the day-to-day decision-making process and still not be overly exposed financially if the fishing was poor.

Right from the start, we did well catching rockfish during the winter fishing season. Fish were abundant and healthy, and as a result, our take home pay each day was excellent. Though the winter had been bitterly cold, the winds also never stopped blowing so the upper bay stayed open most of the winter. That winter, we never went down to Solomons, which saved us lots of money on fuel and meals. By late January, the ice had become problematic but the fishing was so good, we just worked around it. Every day, we burned a lot of fuel searching for open water so we could set our drift nets.

We knew the fish were there, and nothing powers a waterman to work hard or long hours like the opportunity to make a large haul of fish. But after spending a particularly cold night at the landing at Worton Creek, my partners and I jointly decided it was time to go home. The weather forecast was calling for a cold front to push strong winds up the Chesapeake Bay. We all felt it was the right time to get off the water and let this nasty winter storm pass on through.

Captain Cope was also working in Worton Creek and he agreed it was time to stop making money and get down to Rock Hall. For safety reasons, we stuck to our plan of traveling together alongside the *Lon Swann*. As the pair of workboats reached the open waters off Handy's Point, Captain Cope waved us over. As we pulled alongside, he informed us that he had changed his mind now that he was in open water and wanted to set a few nets over the Western Shore to see if he could make a quick strike on the rockfish. Bobby, Hubbard, and I were not interested in fishing our nets and we didn't like this change in plan. Because of his unique stature as the senior captain among both boats, we felt obligated to stay close to Cope while he tried his luck one more time.

Cope set a few nets where he believed the rockfish would be once the tide shifted. On board Hubbard's boat *Rose Elma*, we eased away from Cope and anchored in a wind-protected spot. Admittedly, I was irritated with Cope for changing his mind and asking us (me) to delay our return so he could catch some fish. I felt certain the weather forecast was accurate and felt we should have dead headed for Rock Hall at full speed. Selfishly, I wanted to be off the water and in my home when this storm passed over. But, I had agreed to let Cope fish a while and so I held my tongue and suffered in silence.

When the tide shifted, Cope started to pull in his nets. Seeing the crew working hard, we raised our anchor and started to ease close to where they were fishing. As soon as we pulled out of our protected cove, we were hammered with a steady blast of cold winds. In less than two hours, the winds had shifted from breezy to blustery and I knew we had all just made a big mistake by delaying our trip south. The fact that Cope caught zero rockfish in his nets made our poor judgment look that much dumber.

The Chesapeake Bay had gone from mild to wild. The air temperature had dropped sharply as well. With Cope's nets now on board, we started our trip home by steering southeast towards Rock Hall. We were warm and dry because we were huddled in the cabin with the heater running on full. But, I knew intuitively that we were not safe. With the wind blowing our bow spray onto the deck and the cabin, the spray water was immediately freezing on deck.

As we steered down the Chesapeake, the icing on deck got worse and worse. After less than an hour, much of the bow spray was frozen solid on deck. Unfortunately, based on our course and the direction of the wind, our starboard (right) side of both workboats were iced badly. By the time we reached Pooles Island in the center of the Chesapeake Bay, the *Rosa Elma* was loaded down with over six inches of ice which caused her to list (lean) badly to starboard. The weight of the ice pushed our boat down into the water and was becoming increasingly hard to steer. The decks were far too slippery and unstable to attempt to chip off the ice with an axe so it got thicker and thicker on the starboard side.

Though we were experienced watermen, we had made a critical mistake and were now in a place that was not safe at all. We were too far east to double back to Middle River or Back River. We were too far south to get to the Sassafras River. And with the coating of ice forcing us to list so hard to starboard, no one believed we could make it all the way to Rock Hall without rolling over. Ironically, the only place we could reach safely was back to Handy's Point. It was decision time!

From a distance, Captain Cope was alarmed to see *Rose Elma* leaning so far to starboard. Because she was a smaller and lighter boat, I'm sure it appeared from a distance like we were going to roll right over. But Cope's boat was listing badly, too. Pulling from his years of experience, Captain Cope determined the smart move for both boats was to return to the Chesapeake Landing inside Worton Creek to ride out the storm.

We limped and leaned across the Chesapeake Bay for over an hour before we finally eased into our slips at the landing. Of course, no other workboats were there because they had wisely decided to get out of there earlier in the day. After we ate dinner, I climbed into my bunk to get some sleep. But I never slept a wink, because I was furious over the predicament that I was now in. I was so mad at Cope I couldn't even talk to him. My greatest fear was that the *Rose Elma* would get iced in.

That night, the winds howled all night and the air dropped to single digits. If the heater on board our boat had failed, we would have frozen to death in our bunks. When I climbed out of the cabin to check out the ice, my worst nightmare had come true as both the *Rose Elma* and the *Lon Swann* were frozen solid in ice. Every part of the deck was covered with tons of blue ice. We were iced in hard and fast and I knew it would be weeks, perhaps even a month, before our workboat could be in open water again. Adding insult to injury, I was sure the rest of the fleet was operating in ice-free water on the Chesapeake not far from where we were stuck.

In a panic, we called our friends and asked them to come pick us up. As soon as we got to Rock Hall, Bobby, Hubbard, and I went on a massive search to see if we could beg, borrow, or steal an available workboat to keep on fishing. But all of the workboats were already spoken for or were locked up in ice somewhere else. We tried for over a week to find an available boat, but could not locate one. To his credit, the experienced Cope had already planned a backup plan for himself. Amazingly, he found a spot on the workboat *Oneida II,* operated by Captain Naudain Francis, and was fishing in Annapolis the next day.

This particular fishing trip put a real sour taste in my mouth for several reasons. First, I was furious with Cope for gambling with precious fishing time in a way that negatively impacted the less-experienced fishermen. Second, I realized I was not comfortable with consensus building when an important decision was being made concerning safety or fishing strategy. From this trip, I learned that I would rather go alone and be wrong than follow the herd and lose control of my destiny. Third, I was disappointed in myself for not following my own instincts, which had been sharpened by many great watermen.

It took me a while to cool down from losing weeks of prime rockfish income because of our mistakes. But, in time I did cool down. I couldn't stay mad at Cope long because I respected him more than I was mad at him. From this experience, however, I changed a number of my own strategies going forward. First, I would always have at least one back up plan in reserve. Second, I would not let my instincts be overridden by a herd mentality. Third, I would be more respectful to the laws of nature and the power of a winter storm.

Finally, I realized if I was truly planning to become a progressive, profitable waterman on the Chesapeake Bay like Uncle Josh, it was time for me to purchase a larger, wider workboat capable of getting me to the fishing grounds and back home again.

Chapter Twenty-Two
Captain Splint Downey

Onboard, crewmembers do most of the physical work. They are expected to work whenever the captain elects to leave the dock and, generally, are so well cross-trained they can perform most functions on the workboat, including serving as captain if need be. Usually, crewmembers work for a share of the profits after a boat share is paid to the captain to pay for the variable and fixed expense. When back in port, crewmembers either go home or go uptown. Most crewmembers leave the worries and heartaches about running the business to the captain.

The captain is responsible for insurance, mortgage, maintenance, licensing, regulations, logging, marketing, purchasing, inspections, and many more tasks. A seasoned captain performs all of these managerial functions while fishing with his crewmembers. Their minds are always in motion planning the next fishing trip, evaluating new gear, and maintaining their workboats. Some of them keep an office at home, but most of them keep their papers in the cabin or in their trucks. An important task for a captain is to maintain a quality crew, even when the fishery performance fluctuates wildly.

There are many watermen who have made nice livings serving as crewmembers only. They don't want the hassles that come with being the captain. So, on shore, the good crewmembers are always jockeying for position to become crewmembers with the best captains. In Maryland, best means the ability to catch the most fish, oysters, clams, and crabs. Until I was financially ready to serve as a captain on my own, I was a crewmember for several of the best captains and did real well financially.

Among the Kent County watermen, there was always an ongoing debate as to whether Captain Cope or Captain Splint was the best of the best. They both had nerves of steel and were fearless in their passion to catch rockfish, perch, and shad. They also had stamina, good problem-solving skills, and the ability to look forward. Importantly, Cope and Splint both had a sixth sense that helped them find fish, make money, and return safely each night.

In January of 1958, I started as a full-time, fully shared crewmember with Captain Maurice "Splint" Downey on his workboat *Mary C.* As I had hoped, Captain Cope did give me a favorable recommendation which opened up an opportunity to fish with one of the best watermen in Maryland. He was the master fisherman every captain aspired to be like and every young crewmember wanted to work for. His boat was regularly the top boat in terms of fish caught (and probably profits), so working for him was like money in the bank.

Though it was an honor to work for this legendary captain, serving as his crewmember was no cake walk. Splint's reputation around town revealed that he was tough and hard but also fair. His reputation also revealed that he was a man's man and his gifts of discipline, attention to detail, and work ethic were unmatched by any other watermen that I knew.

Splint was from the old school when it came to wages and a promise made. He expected his crewmembers to do exactly what they claimed they could do when they hired on. Over and over again, he would say, "Larry, you signed on for this job. You said you could do it, so do it. Work! And don't complain about it because there are plenty of people on shore who want your job." These words were not offered simply to humor or motivate his crewmembers. These words described exactly how he viewed his side of our working agreement and he meant them in both spirit and letter.

When I first started working for him, I felt as if I was just another piece of machinery for him to use as needed. He extended no feelings or interest whatsoever about the dreams, failures, fears, or needs of his crewmembers. It didn't matter to Splint whether a man was going through a divorce, was sick, tired, hungry, or injured. He never allowed a crewmember's personal life to slow down his success on the water.

In his mind, he believed he had hired a man to fish and nothing else. It's not that he didn't care or didn't have a heart. I know he cared about all of his crewmembers. He simply refused to allow feelings and personal issues to impede the forward progress on his workboat. With his firm beliefs, he guided a number of us to focus on the job, refrain from whining, and work together to make a good living. As an older waterman now, I see the brilliance in the simple approach he developed on the *Mary C.*

I'm sure my words about Splint's working style sound dramatic or perhaps even mythical, but Splint was the real deal. He was not impacted by cold, fatigue, or any amount of work. He outworked every one of his crewmembers every day. He never asked a crew member to do something that he wouldn't do or hadn't done himself. He never complained or whined about anything that happened to him. As a result, his crewmembers never whined or complained, either. We knew it would be a waste of time to ask Splint for sympathy or a bit of slack. Splint always pitched in with the manual labor if a crewmember needed or asked for help.

Captain Splint lived most of his life alone in a shanty on Eastern Neck Island. In the fall and early winter months, he was a senior hunting guide and manager of one of the elite gunning clubs. Between hunting seasons or days off at the club, Splint liked to hand-tong for oysters alone on the Chester River. In the summer and early fall, he ran a trotline alone, catching blue crabs for the basket trade.

During the fishing seasons from January through June, Captain Splint always hired two experienced crewmembers to help him get the work done and maximize his profits. Splint was a premiere gill netter and he used his low-sided, thirty-eight-foot workboat *Mary C* to get the job done. For six years, between 1958 and 1963, I worked for Captain Splint as a crewmember through the winter fishing seasons catching rockfish and perch and then the spring season top netting for shad.

Because Splint was so skilled and seasoned, I gained a lifetime worth of experience in a short period of time. By working with him, I made a lot of money, which enabled me to pay my home and boat mortgage and put some money aside for a bigger workboat. Importantly, Splint gave me the confidence and expertise to fish on my own.

One of my favorite early memories of working with Splint occurred in the winter of 1958 while fishing in Solomons. The weather had been bitterly cold for days and the *Mary C* was locked in ice right at the dock. Captain Splint, along with two other captains from Rock Hall, made the decision it was time to go home where we could ride out the cold snap. So, the three captains climbed into the front seat of Splint's Studebaker pickup truck. And in the back, the six younger watermen packed ourselves underneath a heavy tarp as Splint drove away from Solomons. It was ten degrees outside and the steel bed of the truck was miserably cold. The drive down Old Solomons Road was slick and it took us several hours just to get to Annapolis.

As we approached the Bay Bridge, Splint rolled down his window so he could pay the toll booth attendant. Back then, a fee was collected based on the number of passengers plus the vehicle. When the attendant asked Splint how many men were in the truck he said with a smile, "You know, it's so cold right now, I can't really remember. I know we have three up here but I can't remember if it was four or six back there under tarp."

Recognizing Splint's dry humor right away, she looked back to see if there really were passengers in the bed of the pickup truck. With a big smile, she shook her head as if both bewildered and amused, and said "Honey, if you really have men under that tarp in these freezing temperatures, I'll give you two for free." As our truck pulled away from the toll booth, all six of us lifted up the tarp and waved at her. She smiled and waved right back at us as Splint drove away. Although we were very cold, the six of us were laughing hysterically at our comical predicament.

Going home. *Courtesy of Ann Crane Harlan.*

Chapter Twenty-Three
Fog at Solomons

Though ice, wind, and high seas were the natural forces that regularly killed watermen, I have always considered fog to be a deadly force as well. Fog can be a real problem because it reduces or removes the watermen's ability to look forward and to see danger in a timely manner. It also distorts and masks sounds which impede our ability to fully use navigational aids like horns, whistles, and bells. Fog frequently slows down the early morning progress of watermen. But at its worst, the indirect effects of fog have killed even experienced watermen that have collided with other vessels, navigational devices, pilings, or even a floating chunk of ice.

Most of the time, fog is a temporary weather problem that passes with a little patience and perhaps a good breeze. But there are times when fog will creep in and hold for many hours and sometimes even days. Fog was a regular occurrence while we winter fished in Solomons. When fog was heavy and thick, most captains would just sit tight at the dock and wait until the sun burned off the fog.

Captain Splint approached fog a little bit more aggressively than most captains. Rather than wait around by the docks swapping "fish tales" with his fellow captains, Splint would always have us on ready on the *Mary C* so he could cruise out of the harbor the minute he saw the fog lifting. If the fog was light and misty, he would ease out of the harbor anyway. By slipping out first, he was assured of reaching the best fishing grounds first. Splint respected fog but he still ventured out before the others.

To help us navigate in the fog, we relied on a barometer, a compass, a timepiece, and a plunker line. We also had good navigational charts to show us water depths and the location of known submerged hazards. But even more reliable than the charts, we had Captain Splint's nearly perfect knowledge of the Chesapeake Bay waters and bottom. In terms of a sixth sense, few watermen had his feel for the waters and the fisheries. All things considered, I probably would place greater trust in Splint's gut feel than I would a navigational chart.

Sometimes, we would be out working the nets and a thick fog would roll in on top of us. This was 1958, quite a few years before radar, depth finders, GPS, and VHF-FM radar made navigation in fog so much better (as long as the power stays on). On the *Mary C*, we relied on each other to navigate safely through waters blanketed in fog. Working as a team, we used our collective senses including touch, sound, smell, sight, and taste to detect small differences in the water and in the atmosphere. To make sure everyone had a specific task in this situation, Splint assigned each of us (including himself) clear tasks and then expected us to do them right every time.

Splint assigned one crewmember the task of regularly checking the depth of the water as it passed underneath the workboat. In shallow water, we used a sounding pole which was simply a long stick we pushed into the water column until we felt the bottom. But in deeper water where we were winter fishing, we used a measuring device called a plunker line. A plunker line was simply a long rope that was marked in increments of one fathom (six feet) with a three-pound hollow cone lead weight on one end.

As the captain eased forward, the designated crewmember would throw the coiled plunker line ahead of the workboat so the weighted line would sink rapidly to the bottom. As the line passed alongside the boat, he would also keep tension on line so he could feel the vibration as the weight struck the bottom. Once down, the crewmember would clearly announce whether the bottom was sand, gravel, mud or oyster shell. Then he would pull up the line counting off the marks out loud in fathoms. Once the hollow cone reached the surface, the crewmember would double check to see if any mud was still in the cone. Immediately, he would recoil the line and repeat the process until the captain told him to stop measuring the depth.

There was nothing fancy about the plunker line system but it worked every time. I liked its simplicity and accuracy. I also liked that it required no batteries or nearby cell towers to work properly. Our plunker line never failed to measure the depth of the water keeping us safe from running aground. Captain Splint's knowledge of the Chesapeake Bay and its primary rivers was sufficient that we didn't regularly use the plunker line unless we were in fog or in waters that he was not familiar with. The old salts like Captain Splint knew the waters of Maryland by heart.

The second crewmember had an equally important task to perform when fog issues loomed. This crewmember was to serve as the primary lookout for any danger that was near. He would be stationed towards the bow of the boat and was charged with looking and listening into the murky fog for any sign of danger. His job was to spot hulls, buoys, and navigational markers before we made contact with them. His job was also to listen carefully for any sounds coming from any direction. It was one of those tasks that seemed easy as long as nothing was near us. With fog, you never really knew for sure if the journey was safe.

In low visibility situations caused by fog, it is essential to be able to hear warning devices from other vessels. But hearing sounds in the fog was hard for us because our boat generated noises too, including bow wake, exhaust, and moving parts of the engine. So, the lookout had to stay alert and focused at all times. He also had to be on ready to yell out a clear, concise command so the captain or other crewmember could execute the order immediately. This crewmember was the designated voice in the wilderness and would yell a simple command like "kick her away" or "stop." There was no time for discussion or debate.

All seasoned watermen have dealt with fog on the waters and the roadways of Maryland. I'm certain that every commercial fisherman has survived his share of close calls related directly or indirectly to fog. Fog can be particularly treacherous when working away from home port because the captains aren't as familiar with their surroundings. Fog has the ability to distort even a smart man's sense of direction and therefore his ability to navigate. Over my lifetime, I have come to appreciate how fog can needlessly destroy human life. As an old timer now, I believe that only a fool would not give fog its due respect.

Chapter Twenty-Four
Thump, Thump, Thump

A thick, wet blanket of fog had just overtaken *Mary C* while we were pulling nets in from deep water. We were fishing a few miles north of Solomons and were intentionally working in the shipping channel because that's where the fish were. Because of this fog, our visibility dropped to almost zero. We could no longer see other workboats or the navigational aids designed to guide us. Our real problem, however, was that we could no longer see north or south bound freighters making their way through the Chesapeake Bay.

Fog or no fog, Splint was expecting to catch a full load of fish that day. Since we were caught in the fog, we had no safe place to escape to without incurring more danger. Without missing a beat, Splint told us to keep pulling in our nets. Splint did assign me the additional task of serving as the lookout. So, we kept working and I kept listening and looking into the fog. I told Splint I could hear the faint "thump, thump, thump" coming from a freighter's wheel (propeller) but I could not tell if it was bound for Baltimore or Norfolk. Captain Splint heard me clearly and kept our direction steady as we pulled our nets over the side of the boat (called bow in).

I was hopeful the freighter's captain could see us on his radar and move around us. For a long time, I held a belief that freighter captains were more concerned about staying in the deep part of the channel than worrying about the location of a small fishing vessel. I also held a belief that most freighter captains would expect a fishing vessel to yield right of way to the much larger vessels coming through the channel. Though neither of these beliefs were helpful in keeping me calm and focused, I did think about these things as I pulled the nets and listened for dangers.

Without a visual sighting of the ship, Splint would not try to outrun or outwit the intentions of a captain piloting a freighter in the fog. Lacking a definitive location confirmed with my eyes or my ears, attempting to avert a collision would more than likely cause a collision. The better move for Splint was to identify the exact position of the freighter first and then take evasive action. As the thumping sound got closer and closer, I was looking for a black hull emerging out of the fog or for the sound of whooshing water (bow wake) which occurs as the bow slices through the water.

We worked in complete silence so we could hear the sounds around us clearly. The seconds passed like minutes as we peered into the fog. I still couldn't see anything but I sensed something wasn't right. Suddenly, I felt a faint upward movement of *Mary C*. At that moment, I saw the white bow wake against the black hulled freighter and instantly told Captain Splint to "kick her away." Fully prepared, Splint took the evasive action I commanded and we averted a direct collision.

As the freighter passed along side us in silence, I looked up to see two deckhands looking down at me. Not a word passed between the two vessels and just as quickly the "thump, thump, thump" sound faded into the fog. We kept fishing our nets as if nothing had happened and never said a word to one another. As I worked, I did wonder if the freighter's captain even knew we were there.

Chapter Twenty-Five

Three Fathoms

We were on a long run back to the harbor at Solomons when a fast moving fog rolled in on top of us. The fog was being pushed by a stiff breeze. In no time at all, our visibility dropped considerably and our ability to hear sounds was muted completely by the wind. Captain Splint was not comfortable with our new situation so he idled down the engine so he could cautiously guide us back to port using his own intuition and his dead reckoning skills.

Off in the distance, all three of us could hear a strange noise off our bow. We couldn't pinpoint the location of the sound, nor could we tell what was making the noise. Between the hum of our engine and the popping sounds of our exhaust system, we just heard odd sounds coming through the fog. Based on the course Splint had chosen, we thought it might be a patent tong rig working in deep water.

Captain Splint was in charge of navigating and steering the *Mary C*. My role was to look, listen and feel into the murky fog to see if I could determine what was causing the noise. The other crewmember was responsible for taking soundings of the bottom with the plunker line. As he shouted out the depths in fathoms, Splint instantly recognized we were off course because the bottom was hard and shallower than he had expected. Somehow, he had become disoriented in the fog and now he wasn't sure where we were relative to Solomons. The simple truth was that even our experienced, capable senior captain got turned around in fog.

My fellow crewmember kept testing the depth with the plunker line and his readings confirmed we were moving into shallow water. I can still hear him saying "10 fathoms, 8 fathoms, 6 fathoms, and finally, 3 fathoms." All along, he kept reporting a hard bottom. Just as he said "three fathoms," a skipjack powered by the stiff breeze glided right in front of us with both dredges over board. We didn't collide with her but their extended boom passed right in front of the *Mary C*. This could have been a very bad collision in icy cold water.

Chapter Twenty-Six
The Shangri La

Captain Bud Edwards was working in Solomons with his beautiful workboat *Shangri La*. Like most watermen who traveled to Calvert County each winter, Bud docked his boat with a special man named Mr. Obery who operated a marina called Obery Marine. Unlike other marina owners who catered primarily to elite pleasure boaters, Mr. Obery served and supported watermen.

In fact, he created a fee structure that worked well for us in good times and hard times. Rather than charge a flat weekly rate for the use of his slips (including water and electric), he charged each waterman a small percentage for each pound of fish or each bushel of oysters caught each day. He received payment directly from the waterman or from the fish buyer as agreed to by the men. It was all based on the honor system and sealed with a handshake.

His philosophy was that he only expected to make good money if his customers were also making good money. He knew if the fishing was good, we would have no trouble paying a generous slip fee. To his credit, he also knew when the fishing was poor, a fixed slip fee would cause a real hardship. I always felt Mr. Obery was truly a watermen's friend and most captains came back to him year after year without hesitation. I wish business could still be done with a firm handshake today, but I know those times have passed now.

Generally, captains prefer to get their gasoline or diesel tanks topped off in the evening so they can don't waste precious time filling up in the morning. No waterman likes to wait in line for fuel when it is prime time to fish. Most of the time, seas are more calm in the morning and tend to build up as the day progresses. One afternoon right before dusk, Captain Bud Edwards pulled into the marina to get some gasoline. The young dock attendant stepped on board *Shangri La* and started to pump gasoline into the fuel tank. In those days, the fuel pumps were slow and often the attendants would place a wooden wedge in the handle so he wouldn't have to hold the pump during the filling process. We all did it so we could get other tasks finished.

On the old wooden boats like *Shangri La*, access to the filling hole was not easy and it was very hard to monitor the fuel level. Most of the fuel nozzles did not have automatic cut-off valves either. In addition to all of these design weaknesses, the young man got distracted and momentarily forgot that the fuel was still pumping, which happens to us all. By accident, the tank overflowed and an unknown quantity of gasoline flowed directly into the bilge system of the workboat.

No one knows for sure how much excess gasoline was pumped into the bilge but it proved to be enough. Now aware of his mistake, the attendant shut off the gasoline supply at the pump. He then made a noble effort to get to the cabin to shut off the heater. But he was too late. When the fumes reached the heater in the cabin, there was an air-sucking whoosh sound and the cabin exploded. The force of the explosion lifted the cabin three feet off the deck. That same force blew the dock attendant off the *Shangri La* which saved him from burning to death.

A waterman working nearby plucked the young man out of the water. The *Shangri La* was now burning out of control in her slip. She was untied and pushed away from the dock so nearby workboats would not catch fire. I will never forget seeing the fire dance on the water all around the *Shangri La.* She burned right to the waterline and sank in the marina. From that day forward, I would never fully trust gasoline in marine settings again.

Chapter Twenty-Seven
Growing Pains

I was working a long set of crab pots alone on *Sea Mite* to support my family and to advance towards my goal of becoming a progressive waterman. I worked all the time. Crabs were plentiful and my focus was on volume since I had no control over the dockside price. Only on days when my seafood buyers declared "no market" would I stay in port. Things were going well for me and I was optimistic about my future.

My hopes for a great year came to an end thirty seconds after my son Larry Jr. was born on June 3, 1958 in Chestertown Maryland. Though our family doctor had warned us that our second child could develop a common blood disorder called "RH incompatibility," we had hoped that Larry would be spared this hardship. Unfortunately, his health failed immediately because his blood and immune systems were at war with one another. I didn't know if his blood was attacking his body or his body was attacking his blood. All we knew, for sure, was the doctor didn't see how Larry Jr. would survive.

It was hard to see him born strong and then lose weight, color, and vigor right in the hospital. I could hardly stand to see him lying in that tiny bed. Our doctor told us (again) that the only way to save Larry was to flush his tiny body with fresh blood until the harmful antibodies were diluted to a benign strength. Just the thought of my little boy having a needle stuck in his arms just about made me sick to my stomach.

Not even 21 years old, I was emotionally and spiritually unprepared to handle this health crisis. Unfortunately, everything I had been taught to become an effective waterman served no real value in saving Larry Jr. For the first time in my life, hard work and a never-quit attitude was not going to be enough to save Larry. I felt powerless, overwhelmed, alone, and afraid.

At the time, medical care on the Eastern Shore was not well developed, so high-risk patients like Larry were transferred to Annapolis, Wilmington, or Baltimore. For Larry to have a real shot at life, the doctor felt The University of Maryland Hospital in Baltimore was our best bet. Logistically, getting him to Baltimore from Rock Hall was not easy. By water or by air, the trip was less than twenty-five miles but there was no way we could transport him by workboat, and the state of the art helicopters we use today weren't available, either. Our only option to get to Baltimore was to cross The Bay Bridge at Annapolis or go North around the headwaters of the Chesapeake Bay and drive south.

As a young waterman, all of my money was in my boat. Not only did we not have insurance or a reserve of cash, we also didn't have a reliable car to get Larry to Baltimore. My car was "a junker." Unfortunately, I had not been cultivating my relationship with God in recent years either, so I didn't have a lot of faith in God or others to come to the rescue. Like many headstrong young men from my generation, I had convinced myself that I was the best person to solve my problems.

Fortunately, God came through for my little family even though I was not active with my own prayers or faith. In a tight-knit town like Rock Hall, word of Larry's illness spread like wildfire and everyone around me got the message that we needed help, prayers, and blood. Because of Mom's involvement with her church, everyone who was even remotely connected to the watermen community raised their hands and offered their assistance. Because of Dad's extensive network of friends cultivated at the barber shop, the Nike base, and the Masonic Order, help poured out from every part of Kent County.

Mom's friends provided the care for Dawn and Nancy and made a huge difference around the house. We received help with keeping our house neat and getting our laundry done. We received great meals everyday and always had quality folks to look after Dawn. Dad's friends pitched in operationally. In fact, dozens of hardworking farmers, watermen, lumberjacks, and soldiers made themselves available to help out.

The real challenge we faced was in finding enough compatible blood to flush Larry's little veins out. Dad made a special appeal for blood at the Nike base in Tolchester and with his deep ties to the Masons. In what I now recognize as a miracle, a long list of men and women agreed to go to Baltimore on their own time to donate their blood. Tommy Elburn, a rough-handed lumberjack and close friend of my father, volunteered to drive every blood donor to Baltimore in his 1957 Buick Century. Day after day, he drove the volunteers to the hospital and then bought them dinner on the way home. What a precious service Tommy provided to my family in our time of need.

Every day, after we both finished crabbing, Uncle Josh would drive me to Baltimore so I could check on Larry with my own eyes. He knew my car wasn't fit for long distance travel, so he offered to drive me to Baltimore as many times as I needed. And though his transportation assistance was needed, I really appreciated our drives over and back. Alone in his car, I could share with him how overwhelming this medical crisis was for me and how I feared that I might lose Larry. I didn't know it at the time, but God was working through Uncle Josh to keep me focused, calm, and positive about Larry's situation. I did realize, in spite of all the turmoil, that I was lucky and perhaps even blessed to have Uncle Josh in my life.

With a reliable supply of blood now pouring into Larry Jr, a large number of volunteers just stepped back a bit from the crisis and simply prayed for Larry, Dawn, Nancy, and even me. They stayed close, in case we needed some help, but they mostly just prayed for us. I must say it caught me off guard to learn that even complete strangers were pulling and praying for my little family and me.

In spite of the blood and a steady outpouring of love, Larry's health continued to fail and I watched him wither like a wrinkled soft crab. He looked like an old man to me. But the doctors and nurses kept experimenting with Larry and his blood systems while steadily pumping fresh blood into his veins. We remained in a wait-and-see status for a long time.

Thankfully, the doctors refused to quit on Larry and Larry refused to quit on life. Fighting hard, Larry regained his color and then his weight. I didn't know what part of his turnaround was due to the medical expertise or Larry's strong will to live. I was too naïve and headstrong at the time to know how (or if) to factor God into Larry's turnaround. Whatever forces were upon Larry Jr. and my family, Larry was released from the hospital and he thrived once he got home.

What a blessing it was to go crabbing again without stewing over whether Larry was going to live or die. Years later, I was pleased to learn that Larry's struggle helped the doctors develop better strategies to more effectively deal with this common blood disorder. Fortunately, the blood disorder is now prevented altogether by a simple injection prior to delivery. In spite of my rough ways, even I was moved by the way my hometown came together to help me when I couldn't help myself. I was also moved by the possibility that prayers offered freely by others (including strangers) could have played a role in saving Larry's life.

Chapter Twenty-Eight
Blisters on Ice

Larry Jr.'s health crisis rocked me to my core. It also drained me completely of my emotional energy. Surprisingly, it rocked my spiritual journey too and I started to question in earnest what parts of my life I could really control. Shaken up pretty badly by this medical crisis, I became even more driven to succeed at work as a waterman. I started to spend all of my time at work which immediately caused me more problems balancing my priorities between work, family, and my friends.

My friendships became my world. At some level, I believe I was trying to make up for all the social pleasures I missed by not going to college or the military. I also think I was trying to make up for my lost childhood since I never took much time out to play and just be a kid. I'm sure there were other triggers (including my age) that seduced me away from a good life, but this new wild streak in me just couldn't be tamed. Of course, sipping alcohol stripped away all remaining inhibitions that were bred into me to keep me safe.

It didn't take long for me to destroy my own marriage. I allowed a selfish, self-centered Larry Simns to emerge from within and take control of my life. Unbound by marriage or by faith, I let the good times associated with harvesting oysters, crabs, and fish define my success at work. And I let my great times to be defined by whom I socialized with and how many laughs we shared.

Like a fool, I pushed all sorts of wise counsel away from me, so my own immaturity was now directing my life. What a flawed model.

All through this messy period of my life, Captain Splint served as a true anchor. From listening to the Rock Hall grapevine, he knew my home life was in trouble and I was becoming increasingly wild around town. To his credit, he kept me on as one of his crewmembers from January through June anyway. Like a rock, he gave me structure and a foundation. He worked me hard physically, which proved to be good for my soul. Sometimes, he unintentionally worked me too hard for my own good.

In the winter of 1959, we were fishing for rockfish in deepwater using bottom nets (a type of drift net). This process involved sinking a gill net way down in the water column using weights. Once in place, the nets would be suspended just a few inches from the bottom. To keep the net tight underwater, large floatation corks were fastened to the top of the net to keep the net stretched in the water column. Once in place, the bottom nets would travel up and down the Chesapeake Bay with the tides.

Because this netting system was primarily underwater, we didn't have to deal with surface obstructions like floating debris or even other boats. Besides, Captain Splint knew the bottom of the Chesapeake Bay like the back of his hand, so we rarely lost a net to a rock pile or an old sunken workboat. Each section of the net was marked with large flags so we could find them in all kinds of weather or rough seas. In addition, the brightly colored buoys were clearly stenciled with Splint's license number so there was no confusion about who owned the net. Back then, no watermen with any sense would attempt to steal fish or nets from Captain Splint.

Pulling bottom nets was hard work when the seas were calm but was very hard when the winds and waves were rough. In fair weather conditions, we pulled the nets in over the stern while Captain Splint would reverse the engine on the *Mary C*. In this way, he took pressure off the backs of his crewmembers and let the workboat do the work. Usually, one crewmember would pull in the net using the hand-over-hand method. As the nets came on board, the second crewmember would pick the fish out of the nets and drop "the keepers" on the floor. The small fish or the off-target fish were thrown back overboard.

Making a profit with bottom nets was more about following good processes than it was complicated. As long as each man did his part right, we could fish all of our nets in about three hours. On the *Mary C*, Jackie Elburn and I usually set out and pulled in ten boxes of net which equated to about two miles of net. I liked fishing with bottom nets and I made a good living catching fish with this method for many years.

One sunny afternoon in early winter, Jackie and I were having a good day pulling in our bottom nets. We were fishing in about eighty feet of water and the nets were coming on board loaded with rockfish. It felt like one of those picture-perfect days on the water but our work turned ugly when a section of net became unbearably hard to pull in. At first, I thought the net was snagged on something deep underwater but the net was still coming up slowly so it wasn't hung up.

Regardless of what was causing the heaviness, we had lots of net to pull into the boat before this day would come to an end. Instead of finishing early, I now wondered if we were going to get home at all without leaving some net in the water. We still had over 1,200 feet of net jammed into one of the Chesapeake Bay's deep holes that could have been over 140 feet deep. Captain Splint backed down on the net as best he could but still had to make sure the net didn't get wrapped up in the propeller. We gave Splint the famous "woe this is hard" look but he paid no attention to our plea for empathy. As an experienced fisherman, he had struggled with deep holes before and he knew our only option was to pull in that net one foot at a time.

I nearly pulled my guts out trying to get the net up, but my real progress was minimal. After a few hard attempts, I told Jackie I couldn't pull this net out of this deep hole by myself. I told him if he wanted to get home tonight, he needed to help me pull, too. On the spot, we created a new process. I told him I would pull 10 corks first and then I would call for a "switch." We would then switch positions and roles and Jackie would then pull 10 corks. Neither of us felt we could pull more than 120 feet of net filled with fish without a break.

While I pulled and pulled, Jackie counted off the corks so that I would not pull less than 10 before calling a switch. Then Jackie would pull, and I would count off the corks so that he would not pull less than his share. With this counting method, we kept each other honest, but we also were able to encourage each other. It was a simple example of how watermen are expected to problem solve on their own with no direction from the captain. It also was a good reminder that two men working side by side is always better than one man trying to do it all alone.

As the afternoon wore on, we finally got the last nets into the boat and headed for Annapolis. My arms and shoulders were more sore than normal but my hands were "tore up" badly. Jackie hands were bloody and torn up as well. By the time we unloaded the fish and prepared our boat for the next day, our hands were swollen, aching, and loaded with blood-filled blisters. Once Splint released us from our duties, we went into the drugstore in downtown Annapolis and purchased iodine and Epsom salts.

Once back on board, we soaked our hands for hours in this time-tested mixture that would both ease the pain and prevent infections. We also hoped that our blisters would harden from the mixture and form calluses to protect our hands in the morning.

Soaking our hands helped a lot but I was not able to sleep that night because my hands hurt so badly. They were sensitive to the touch as several blisters were ripped open and raw flesh was exposed. Even touching the pillow and sleeping bag caused my hands to ache. To get some sleep, I wrapped my blistered hands around the cold chain holding up my bunk. The chain numbed the pain of my blisters enough so I could get a little sleep before we woke up the next morning to do it all over again.

Numbing the pain. *Courtesy of Ann Crane Harlan*.

Chapter Twenty-Nine
A Wrapped Wheel

Later that same winter, Captain Splint Downey, Jackie, and I were pulling in bottom nets in moderate seas south of Rock Hall. It was a cold and wet morning that Marylanders like me call simply "raw." Our nets were coming up empty, even though we set the nets just right to catch the tide shift. Without fish in the nets, I knew I was going to finish the day with no money in my pocket. As we pulled net after net into *Mary C*, our attitudes went sour and we all started grumbling to and against one another. Basically, we let our poor harvesting result grind against our good nature until we finally worked ourselves into a funk.

When there is no chance to make money, the physical work of fishing starts to feel more like punishment than a job. Having bad days is part of the business, but none of us wanted to come up short. For Jackie and I, we were not going to make any money. But for Captain Splint, he not only wasn't going to make money, he was actually going to lose money. Fish or no fish, Splint would have to pay all fuel, slip, insurance, and boat expenses waiting for him back in port.

Traditionally, once the captain loses hope for having a good day, the crewmembers generally follow and lose hope too. Once the crewmembers slip into a deep funk, it is more than likely going to be a bad day no matter what. When hard-charging men get frustrated onboard, tempers flare, unfriendly words sometimes slip out, and the camaraderie all but disappears for the day. Worst of all, however, an onboard funk creates an environment where watermen get lethargic and lose their edge to do their jobs right. Once a waterman loses his edge, he often makes careless and costly mistakes.

As for me, I was having a contrary day long before I even stepped foot on *Mary C*. I was lost in thought thinking about my growing troubles at home. In fact, I was miserable. Oh yes, I did my work, but I wasn't helping Jackie as much as I should have been. Like a mindless machine, I pulled the nets in while Jackie picked out the few fish we caught.

Jackie and I worked together without saying a word to one another. I was putting in the time, but my heart wasn't in it. In truth, I couldn't wait to get off *Mary C* so I could go out with my friends and forget the day. I kept pulling though, even though all traces of hope were now gone. As my self-induced funk worsened, I made a few stupid mistakes which slowed down the work for Jackie and Splint, too. Even the kinks and twists in the net that I handle every day were ticking me off.

Unfortunately, I was not the only waterman on the *Mary C* having a bad day. Apparently, Captain Splint was having an equally contrary day. Somehow, while backing down on the net, he either missed a gear or over-throttled which caused the boat to surge. In less than a second, Captain Splint Downey had backed down on his own net. Wrapped up in his wheel (propeller) and his steering system was a wad of nylon fishing net. He jammed it so tight that it locked up the propeller and forced the engine to stall out. On top of a poor harvest, Captain Splint had wrapped his wheel and that is never a good thing.

When Captain Splint realized what he had done, he exploded in anger. Apparently, this mistake was the last straw for him. His anger spiked from somewhere deep in his soul and he spewed out harsh words about *Mary C*, Jackie, and me. He was absolutely furious and screamed out words and images I am unable to write in this book. His wrath overflowed and he could not stop ranting. He tried to stop himself a few times, but he could not control his anger.

Jackie and I just stood still while he unraveled a few feet from us. I wasn't sure, but it looked like he was in a holy state of terror. In his rage, he told me to "grab the boat hook" which was stored near the front cabin next to me. I handed it to him though I didn't believe he could solve his problem with a boat hook. He jumped on the deck and tried to use the boat hook to tear away at loose pieces of net. But the net was wrapped too tightly around the propeller and the steering system. The more he tried to tear at the net, the angrier he became. He kept working with the boat hook even though he knew, and we knew, he was getting nowhere with his approach. Suddenly, his anger spiked and another blast of curse words spewed from his lips.

As his anger escalated again, I don't believe Splint even realized that Jackie and I were on the boat with him. It was just him and his anger battling alone on the *Mary C*. All of a sudden, this beautiful workboat was too small for Jackie and I to feel safe with Splint on board. Without saying a word to one another, we both eased up to the front of the cabin which was as far as we could get from him and still be on the boat.

Having been around hot captains before, Jackie and I just stayed up front in the cabin. Jackie turned to me, in a quiet but firm voice and said, "I'm done, Larry, that's enough for me." I paused for a moment and said, "Jackie, you can't leave me here with him in the middle of the season." Selfishly, I didn't want to work with any other crewmember and I also didn't want to stop working for Splint because he was making me good money. Under muffled voices so Splint wouldn't hear us, we kept talking between ourselves about what we should do and what we *could* do.

After one final attempt at freeing the propeller with the boat hook, in utter frustration and rage, Splint screamed out his final words at the top of his lungs. He said, "Jesus Christ, I would rather fall overboard and drown then get my net wrapped up in my wheel." While screaming, he threw the boat hook at Jackie and me, but missed us by a wide margin. It was a dreadful moment of anger and utter loss of control. Unsure what was to come, Jackie and I stood there motionless and speechless.

Immediately after Captain Splint threw the boat hook, his rage stopped. Somehow, Captain Splint managed to silence himself and then became absolutely still. I could visually see him settling down and regaining control of his senses, his composure, and his purpose. It took him a few minutes to find himself, but he came back. Now all alone in the back of the boat, I watched him start to think through ways to solve his tangled net problem. He was calm and steady now and was clearly thinking it all through.

In silence, he expertly started to work with the engine and the transmission to try and loosen up the net enough so he could at least get the propeller moving again. He kept at it without saying a word or without looking up at Jackie and me. In time, he managed to get enough forward and reverse thrust out of his engine where we could pull up our remaining (still empty) nets.

With limited power and steering capability, it took us many hours to get the rest of our nets in and limp our way back to Rock Hall. When Captain Splint moved up to the front cabin where it was warm, Jackie and I moved to the stern. We wanted nothing to do with him. We knew if we stayed in the cabin, we would get into a circular argument we could not win. We chose to stand out in the freezing cold air so we wouldn't have to speak or look at our captain. We were sure Splint needed some time alone to pull himself together. We also felt that if Splint stayed in the cabin, that God wouldn't try to wash him over the side (just yet).

As I looked out over the Chesapeake Bay, a number of thoughts ran through my mind. First, I realized I had just witnessed my first sighting of bay rage. It was terrifying to see my mentor display such an out-of-body experience over a stupid net. Second, this was the first time I had ever witnessed a God-fearing waterman blaspheme against God while on the water. I actually feared that maybe God might give Splint exactly what he asked for and be drowned. Third, and selfishly, I feared Jackie was going to leave me alone with Splint (and some new crewmember); I loved working with Jackie and I did not want to lose my comrade over a net.

On this contrary day, Captain Splint had snapped over a wrapped wheel and lost sight of himself in relation to God. It was an important time for me to fully witness how even a skilled captain can make one mistake that can lead to many others. It was also a good example of how anger can really get in the way of quality problem solving.

By the time we reached the harbor, I had made a number of important decisions about working alongside Splint in the future. I promised to never forget what it looks like when the raw emotions of an angry man eclipse his capacity to think or to control himself. Aware that I also had a hot temper, this was an example of how ugly a spike in anger looks to others. Sadly, I was now aware that Splint had the capacity to lose his temper completely. This time, he didn't breach our relationship permanently, but he did convince me to be careful around him. Finally, I admitted that I didn't want to work for Splint if Jackie wasn't by my side, but I didn't have enough guts or money to quit winter fishing with Splint since I didn't have another option lined up. With my home life falling apart, I needed the steady money that was a sure thing with Splint.

Once *Mary C* was tied up in her slip, Captain Splint came up to Jackie and me and looked us both in the eyes. In a soft tone, he said "I'm sorry, boys; I kind of lost it out there." Jackie looked Splint squarely back in the eye and said calmly, "Do that again and I'm quitting." I was proud of Jackie for telling Splint exactly how he felt and making it clear that this outburst not only breached his relationship with God but with him, too. Jackie defined exactly what his limit was and calmly articulated what he expected from his boss going forward.

Afterall, I got to keep my job and my friend with Jackie's clear message to Splint. A big part of me wanted to make him feel even worse by heaping on my own critique and then walking away from him for a while. But I didn't turn my back on him because he was already disgusted with himself for acting so poorly. I couldn't stay mad at a man who could muster the courage to apologize to Jackie and me. He totally disarmed my intent to make him suffer when he confessed his own poor judgment with his mouth, his eyes, and his heart. Splint, after all, was still the only true anchor I had left in my life.

Chapter Thirty
Green Water

Captain Splint Downey, Jackie, and I were fishing with bottom nets south off Annapolis. The morning had started out "ca'am as a dish" and all three of us expected an easy and profitable day on the Chesapeake Bay. After setting out our last box of net, I walked over to check "the glass" (barometer). To my surprise, the needle was upside down which meant a sharp change of weather was eminent. To be sure it was working properly, I tapped on the glass to see if maybe the needle was stuck. But the needle was working properly. Unfortunately, the harsh weather system that was forecast for later in the day was bearing down on us earlier than expected.

The smart move was to pull up our nets right then and go home. That's what every other captain working the fishing grounds decided to do. But the tide change was just about to occur and all three of us agreed to delay our departure just a few more hours so we could catch a load of fish. So while the other boats left for Rock Hall, we killed about an hour of time doing maintenance chores until the tide shift was finished.

By the time we finished pulling in our first box of net, I knew we made a big mistake. The nets were loaded with fish just as we had hoped, but the skies were also filled with angry, fast-moving clouds. The wind had already picked up and some of the gusts were excessive. Naturally, the waves were getting larger, too. We had made a big mistake, for sure, and now we were going to be out in deep water in a workboat with a low cabin and even lower sides. Our decision to gamble with our safety just to catch a few more fish was about to be tested by the forces of nature.

Failing to heed the warning of the barometer was our first mistake. Our second mistake was not pulling our nets in when other experienced captains aborted their efforts. The signs were all around us to get off the water, but we decided to gamble with our lives to make some money.

Now in a true predicament, Captain Splint had only bad options to choose from. He had already missed the window of opportunity to make the smart decision. He presented Jackie and I with the two thoughts that were swirling around in his mind. He said, "Should I leave the nets in the water and ride the storm out in Annapolis? Or should I take the time to pull in the nets (loaded with fish) and then work our way back to Annapolis or Rock Hall after dark? Wise or foolish, the three of us agreed that we would fish the nets. We had over two miles of net worth over $5,000 overboard in deep water and Splint didn't want to lose his nets. We decided to fish our nets bow in which would be safer but also slower. We agree to not pick out the fish or box up the net properly; we planned to haul everything on board the boat and clean up the mess when we got home. Using this approach, it took us three hours to get all of the nets and the fish into the boat. We caught plenty of rockfish that day.

By now, the storm was at full strength. Again, we were confronted with another decision. Should we steer the *Mary C* to Annapolis to ride out the storm? Or should we travel north against the wind and the waves to get back to Rock Hall? The smart move, again, was to go to Annapolis but we didn't want our nets and the fish to hard freeze on deck overnight. In Annapolis, we didn't have any place to warm up and empty our nets. In Annapolis, we would be safer, but we would lose another day of winter fishing which we didn't want, either.

After talking it over, we agreed to dead-head back to Rock Hall where we could straighten out our nets at Hubbard's Fish Pier and sleep in our own beds. We knew the fish house would stay open until the last workboat returned to the harbor. Wilkens Hubbard always kept his operation open until the "last in" call was made for the harbor. Unfortunately, Wilkens didn't keep the fish house open because he was sure that all other boats were riding the storm out in Annapolis. In fact, Wilkens asked Captain Woody Ashley if *Capistrano* was the last boat in. Woody acknowledged that his high-bowed workboat struggled in the storm and that no boats were behind him coming up the Chesapeake. He was sure that Splint played it safe and spent the night in Annapolis.

Right or wrong, we had elected to power north right into the winds and the waves. The moment *Mary C* turned north towards The Bay Bridge, I knew we were in for a dreadful trip. I knew Splint's workboat was impeccably maintained and seaworthy, but she was not built for this kind of water. She had low sides and no automatic cockpit bailer which meant she could take on water fast and not remove it quickly. Still, Splint was one of the finest boat handlers on the Chesapeake Bay and we all had been caught in bad weather before and lived to tell the story.

With these thoughts rolling around in my mind, I climbed into my bunk which was the only place where I wouldn't get pounded to pieces by the incoming waves. Jackie jumped into his bunk, too, and we left Splint to navigate and steer us towards Rock Hall since he had the only chair in the cabin. We hadn't been at rest for even ten minutes when Splint started screaming at Jackie and me. He told us to get out of our bunks, put on our oilskins and get out on deck. As I was rushing to put on my foul weather gear, I could see clearly what was causing Splint to get so intense.

The waves were too large for our workboat. Worse, the spacing between each wave was too tight. So instead of riding up and down each wave, *Mary C* was plowing into each oncoming wave. She was pounding violently every two or three seconds and that alone was unsettling. But as she plowed into each wave, water forced its way through the door and window seals and was squirting right into the cabin. Because *Mary C* was so well built, the water had no way of seeping into the bilge. Instead, water was now accumulating on the floor of the cabin. The water was already up to my knees.

Splint told me to bail the water off the floor and throw it out the back door of the cabin. I bailed like a maniac for a few minutes but the water was rising faster than I could bail. Not comfortable with my progress, Splint grabbed the axe and started chopping a hole in his own floor. Forcing the axe head through the water, Splint created enough of a hole so the water could drain into the bilge where it could be pumped overboard. Splint's quick thinking solved our immediate problem and *Mary C* was no longer heavy in the bow.

Not comfortable with the volume still pouring into *Mary C*, Splint ordered me to start pumping with our galvanized hand pump. My task was to suck the water out of the bilge and shoot it overboard. Splint knew that our bilge pump running off the engine was not getting the water off fast enough. Splint told me to do nothing else but pump water until he told me to stop. Using my arms and my shoulders, I started pumping water feverishly to keep *Mary C*, and, therefore, us, afloat.

Jackie was ordered to steer *Mary C* on a set course. He was told to keep her into the wind and to remain focused on keeping us from getting caught broadside by the incoming waves. Splint knew clearly that his thirty-eight-foot workboat was too small for these waters and this storm. With Jackie and I each charged with our respective tasks, Splint intended to serve as the utility man who would pitch in wherever he saw a need. If Jackie needed some help with navigating, he would be there. If the engine needed to be checked, he would do that, too. When the winds really gusted up, Splint even laid on the engine box to keep it from blowing off.

Jackie gave *Mary C* plenty of power, but our forward progress towards Rock Hall was minimal. In fact, it took us almost two hours just to get past the Chesapeake Bay Bridge. As we slowly made our way towards the mouth of the Chester River, the waves became large, steep, and very close together. They weren't ocean-sized waves, of course, but we also weren't in an ocean-sized boat. From where I was pumping water, I could see how effectively and expertly Jackie worked the controls and steering wheel to keep us safe and moving forward. I was impressed with how Jackie pushed the throttle forward going up the waves and how he eased off the throttle going down the waves. By aggressively revving up the engine at just the right time, Jackie managed to push a lot of water off the stern which probably kept us from sinking.

Slowly, we made our way past Love Point so Rock Hall wasn't too far ahead. But as soon as we reached this unique part of the Chesapeake Bay, our troubles became much more serious. A flood tide was pushing us north while the winds and waves were pushing against our bow. A strong current was also pushing due west out of the Chester River. And because we were so close to the Love Point shoal bar, the seas had become larger and steeper. Though we were close to home, we were in real trouble because these waters were so violent.

Now fighting every large wave head on, Jackie was unable to prevent the bow of *Mary C* from diving right into the incoming waves. Almost every wave forced the cabin of *Mary C* to go under water and all Jackie could see out the windows was "green water." From where I was pumping, I could see the water pressing against the glass which looked like an aquarium. But I kept my eyes mostly on the water rushing over the top of the cabin which had the power to knock me down and wash me right off the stern.

We kept diving into the waves over and over again and I wondered if *Mary C* could really take too much more. Suddenly, Jackie had to push into a massive wave and the entire cabin of *Mary C* went underwater. Every window turned green as the water poured over top of me and knocked me clear to the back of the boat. The time under the wave was so long that Jackie thought we were sinking and he ran right out of the cabin. Seeing his confusion, I said "Jackie, we are okay. We are not sunk. Just keep steering and throttle up even more when you are going up the waves." Jackie was shaken, but he managed to return to his post to keep steering. I was also shaken up, and I returned to the lonely job of pumping water over the side as fast as I could.

After seeing that large wave almost sink us, Captain Splint declared that his low-sided workboat was no match for this angry piece of water. He could see we were no longer making headway and he knew it was just a matter of time before *Mary C* would be swamped by another big wave or we would get rolled over by a wave that caught us broadside. Splint knew I couldn't pump enough water by hand and that Jackie couldn't protect us from every wave. I was amazed the green water hadn't already smashed in our windows.

Alone, Captain Splint decided he had seen all the green water he could stomach. He said, "boys, if we don't change our course right now we are going to lose her." He ordered Jackie to turn hard to starboard on the first wave that wouldn't roll us over. He then told Jackie to steer directly towards the Love Point shoal bar and find "the cut." Brilliantly, Splint was planning to use the high tide and Jackie's exceptional knowledge of this shoal bar to find the slice of deeper water that cuts across the sand bar. It was a gamble, for sure, but he was going to try and cross overtop of the shoal bar so we could reach the relative safety of the Chester River.

Splint's back up plan, I assume, was to have *Mary C* run aground on the Love Point shoal bar giving us a chance to wash ashore before the icy waters killed us. His decision was a counter-intuitive navigational maneuver and I would not have attempted this gutsy move had I been in charge.

As ordered, Jackie made the turn and steered right for the cut that he knew intimately from years of haul seining. I kept pumping. As we approached this narrow channel called the cut, two questions were swirling in my mind. Would *Mary C* break apart and swamp the second we struck the sand bar? And, how on earth would the old man (Captain Splint) make it to shore if the *Mary C* broke apart over the sand bar?

Jackie found the gap which enabled us to enter the shoal bar which was several hundred yards wide. But the water level was still too low and we bumped hard several times. At one point, we were actually hard aground but a following wave lifted us and pushed us forward a little ways. As I watched each wave come towards us, I was certain we were going to get swamped. Instead, a wide, full wave lifted *Mary C* over the final section of the sandbar and set us down at the drop off leading into the Chester River. I couldn't believe we managed to get off the shoal bar; it still is unbelievable.

We were afloat, and for the moment, away from the waves and winds that had nearly drowned us. But it was now dark and still stormy, so we used our flashlights to check over ribs and hull underneath the floorboards. Now back in deep water, we didn't want to sink in the Chester River because we had a loose board and didn't know it. Once we were certain *Mary C* was ready to go, we pushed back into the Chesapeake Bay for a few more miles. We pulled into the harbor at 10:30 p.m., long after the other watermen and the fish house had closed up for the night.

The inside of our boat look like a disaster area. Our fishing gear was scattered all over the work area. I was sure Captain Splint lost hundreds of dollars worth of nets, fish, flags, ropes, and buckets. To make matters worse, everything on board was now crusted over with an inch of ice and icicles were hanging everywhere. I was soaked to the bone and chilled badly, once I stopped pumping water. Jackie was exhausted and soaked as well. In our miserable state, we started the process of gathering up all the net, fish still attached, so we could get them warmed up inside the fish house to be sold in the morning.

The wrong way home. *Courtesy of Ann Crane Harlan.*

While Jackie and I were cleaning up the boat, Captain Splint Downey came over to us and spoke to us with sobering honesty. He said, "Boys, that was the dumbest move I have ever made. Surely I almost drowned you boys. I shouldn't have done it. I'm sorry." He was clearly upset with himself for choosing to plow directly into a bad storm in a river boat instead of making the smart move which was to steer west to Annapolis.

While we cleaned up the boat, I thought about the day and all the good and bad choices we made. I was embarrassed that I too wanted to stay and fish when all other boats were heading home. I was embarrassed that I thought we could out-muscle Mother Nature. Still, I was in awe of how Captain Splint never lost his cool and never stopped trying to improve our chances to survive. I was also amazed at how well Splint knew the waters, his crewmembers, and his workboat, and how he used each of our strengths to find a way home.

But more than anything else about that day, I was once again caught off guard with the way he spoke to Jackie and me at the dock. I was moved by his sincere apology and his unwavering accountability for the bad choices made on the water that day. Even though I had erred too, he accepted his role as captain to look out for the safety of his crew first and foremost. The way Captain Splint offered his public apology to Jackie and me spoke volumes about his role as a man, a waterman, and an American. I revered and respected him for the way he spoke to us that night.

With his words shared, we started in earnest to get *Mary C* and her gear in shape so we could leave in the morning to fish. We hung up the nets and iced down the fish so Wilkens could buy them in the morning. We left the docks after midnight and I crawled into bed with my sore arms and shoulders after pumping all that water. I was flat out exhausted but also thankful that I was alive and had a warm place to sleep at night.

Not a man to speak openly about his personal life, Splint never told me if (or how) our brush with death changed his life. But based on what I observed, I'm certain this trip shook him up badly. From the next day forward, Splint was a far kinder, gentler captain to his crewmembers. He treated his crewmembers like men instead of like machinery. He asked our opinions and thanked us for our hard work. On shore, he built a home next to his shanty, got married and built a bigger boat with high sides he appropriately named *Mary C II*. From my perspective, it looked like Splint's encounter with the storm helped him to become a better man which helped me to become a better fisherman. It also created an opportunity for me to sell *Sea Mite* and buy *Mary C*.

Part Three
Premiere Fishing
(1959 – 1971)

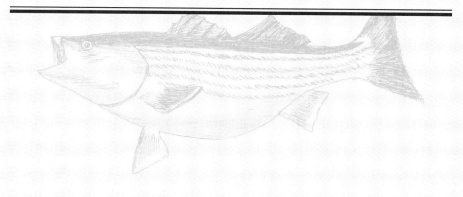

Chapter Thirty-One
My First Violation

The watermen culture was significantly different back in the sixties. To be a successful waterman, a man only needed a good boat, a strong back, a touch of pluck, and enough grit to survive the messy job of harvesting seafood. In this culture, there was an equal opportunity for white and black men to be successful. For working folks like me without a higher education, it was an American dream come true to be my own boss, define my own success, and spend full days out on the Chesapeake Bay.

To be clear, my goal every day was to harvest as much as I was legally permitted to take and still get home safely. I knew the regulations well and worked right up to the limit whenever I could. Though it may be hard to believe, I worked for many years when there were no harvesting limits on crabs, eels, fish, or oysters. The only reason I stopped harvesting some days was because I ran out of daylight or my workboat was already overloaded. We weren't breaking the fishing laws in place at the time.

In those days, our primary restrictions related to the size (therefore, the age) of each species. Legally we could not keep any oyster under three inches long and we were not allowed to have more than five percent "little ones." To remain within the law and still get the work done quickly, many workboats designated a crewmember as "the culler" who had the hard, tedious, and miserably cold job of handling every oyster that came on board.

My first violation was doled out by a newly appointed natural resource officer who was assigned to protect the natural resources of Kent County. One evening, as I was roaring into Rock Hall loaded down with oysters, he signaled me to stop in the mouth of the harbor. He informed me he was there to inspect my culling rate percentage and so I allowed him to come on board the *Mary C* to count my oysters. From a mountain of oysters over 150 bushels deep, he randomly selected a measured bushel and proceeded to separate them by size.

When he was done, he informed me I was in violation of the oyster culling laws on the books in Annapolis. Based on his single count, he told me I had over five percent little ones and I would have to return to the bar and dump my entire load of oysters. He didn't offer to recount his sample. He didn't take a second random sample to verify the accuracy of his first count. He did not pay any attention to my side of the inspection process. Now finished with me, he boarded his speedboat provided by the State of Maryland and shoved off. He waited there in the harbor until I returned well after dark to make sure I had dumped every oyster I had harvested that day.

As required, I did dump my oysters exactly where I had found them. When I got back to my slip in Rock Hall, I went out with my friends to share my story and vent some of my frustrations. I was furious, hurt, and humiliated by the way this officer had singled me out. I was also incensed that he made me dump the entire load instead of giving me a chance to cull the load again and return only the small ones. My sense of fairness had been severely tested that day. I had lost a day's pay, too, which always hurts. Mostly though, I lost some trust in an organization I thought was there to protect the natural resources and me.

That evening, I decided the "sting" from this one inspection and violation would not be wasted. I was still upset by the way this young officer counted my oysters, but I resolved to use this experience to protect other watermen from being unfairly singled out just because they were good at harvesting oysters. Almost immediately, I accelerated my service hours and intensity at the Kent County Watermen's Association. In fact, one of my first assignments as a leader was to work alongside fair-minded regulators in Annapolis to get the culling language improved. I wanted to amend the laws so law-abiding watermen could not be unfairly harmed by abuse of power issues from rogue officers. I wanted an appeals process which required law enforcement to provide written documentation of the infractions so a waterman would have a fighting chance to defend himself in front of a law-abiding judge.

Ironically, my first violation so inflamed me that I ended up spending the next fifty years of my life defending the livelihood of all watermen of Maryland. Funny how such a small incident so many years ago had such a lasting impact on my future.

Chapter Thirty-Two
Oyster Smash

I was making steady progress to become a professional waterman. I now had an exceptional boat in *Mary C* and because I lived in Rock Hall, I had easy access to some of the best fishing grounds in America. But I knew I couldn't find true success as a waterman until I found and retained a reliable, strong, and smart crewmember to help me do the work and share in the profits. In truth, I needed another waterman on board with me who would follow my lead, but also take over if needed.

In Kent County, I had access to many fine watermen who would have made fine partners. But I wanted Bob "Hoot" Gibson as my next crewmember. Having watched him serve as a crewmember for other captains, I knew he was eager to make money and could work like a machine. Though Bob was barely 16 and I was only 24, I was sure the two of us could out work and out-hustle every other two-man team in Rock Hall.

As a team, we regularly worked the T Tree Oyster Reef. I liked this particular bar because it was only a few miles away from Rock Hall and it was loaded with consistently large bay oysters. Harvesting these oysters meant a better price, less effort to cull down to five percent, and a better fill rate to fill one bushel basket. Unfortunately, working this bar was far from easy because it was prone to heavy seas. The oysters were also deeper into the water which meant we used a lot more rope. But what really made this oyster bar dangerous was the presence of many very large stones that were intermingled with the oysters.

To profitably harvest the oysters off the T Tree, I needed heavier tongs that could hold the stones and a load of oysters. So I turned to Martin Wagner and Alfred Jacquette, two of Maryland's best blacksmiths, and asked them to build me two heavy tongs made out of heavy gauge steel. When they were done, the tongs weighed 350 pounds each.

I loved working this bar because it consistently yielded good profits and was almost never crowded with other watermen. Back in the sixties, harvesting oysters with a drop tong system was nearly a perfect job for me. I didn't mind doing the repetitive work over and over. I liked working with my hands, too. I liked watching the piles of oysters build up around my feet as we worked. For me, harvesting oysters on the Chesapeake Bay was a perfect way for me to make a living.

Mary C was rigged up just right and our winder systems functioned consistently and safely all the time. A good waterman like Bob, in calm waters, could make three dips in a minute in eighteen feet of water. *Dip. Dip. Dip.* That's all we did from sunrise to sunset every day the weather allowed us to work the T Tree. I was sure that life couldn't get any better than what we enjoyed as fellow watermen harvesting oysters.

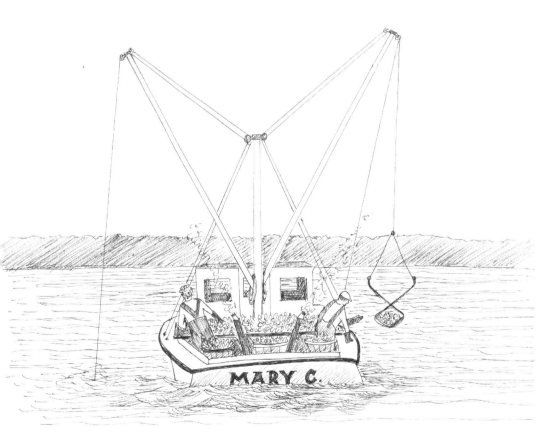

Drop tonging on the T Tree Bar. *Courtesy of Ann Crane Harlan.*

One rainy morning as the wind blew hard out of the northeast, Bob and I were alone on the T Tree Bar working our respective sides on *Mary C.* The rain didn't bother me because I was wearing my oilskins which kept me dry and warm. While I worked off the port (left) side, Bob was doing the exact same thing off the starboard (right) side. We worked so well, both as a team and as individuals, that our tongs almost never touched over the culling board. Trust me when I say that if you pick the right crewmember, life as a waterman is hard to beat.

I was working my side of the boat filling up the floorboards with oysters. I was in my zone where I was thinking about "everything and nothing." *Dip. Dip. Dip*.

While I was in a particularly nice rhythm and flow, two problems occurred simultaneously while I worked over the culling board. First, a massive stone had been dumped onto the culling board that was too big for me to push off by myself. Second, and far worse, the clutch on the winder failed which forced the tongs to climb over my head instead of falling back into the water. Consumed with moving the big stone off the culling board, I never even heard the sound when the tongs smashed into the block and tackle rig attached to the mast. Without a clue, my drop tongs released on contact with the mast and fell directly towards my head which was leaning over the culling board. In an instant, the tongs smashed my face down into the big stone before bouncing off the culling board and into the Chesapeake Bay.

Fortunately, my skull was not split wide open by the force of the drop tongs striking me. But I was knocked down on the floorboards of my workboat. Instantly, I was covered with blood and the rain splattered the redness everywhere. What Bob first saw must have been terrible. With blood everywhere, I had two bones sticking out of my nose. The roof of my mouth was split open which forced even more blood to gush from my mouth and nose. My cheek bones were broken and I had a gash in my back. I was bleeding like a stuck hog which must have been frightening to see on an all-white workboat.

What a situation for a young man of 16 years to witness! Following his gut instincts, Bob ran up to the front cabin to get a dry shirt to cover my face. But when he got close enough to see how badly my flesh was torn, he didn't want to use the shirt. Instead, he said "Don't touch yourself nowhere." He was concerned I might touch my wounds with my filthy oyster hands. The next words to flow from his mouth were, "Larry, don't look at me or I will pass out."

As I lay on the floorboards rolling back and forth in pain, Bob became filled with an adrenaline surge and pulled the tongs that had crushed me back into the boat by hand. He instinctively knew to not use the winder with the failed clutch system to pull in my tongs. He then pulled up the crankshaft drags being used to control drift while we were tonging. Though I was fading in and out of consciousness, I was amazed how Bob could pull those tongs up without using the winder.

Bob kept asking me what to do next but continued to follow his own good instincts. With no other workboats nearby to lend a hand, he had no options left but to get me back to Rock Hall and then to the emergency room in Chestertown. As he revved up the engine, he kept saying, "Don't look at me," and I kept telling him not to run the engine at full throttle or the engine would overheat. Once under way, the pain made it impossible for me to be still. And lying on the oyster filled floorboards made me feel sick to my stomach. After some trial and error, I found the least painful position for me was to stand up by holding the crossed ropes. As Bob steered us south towards Rock Hall, I looked north towards Baltimore so Bob wouldn't get sick.

Half way back to Rock Hall, the rudder pin pushed out of its housing which forced us to stop. Working side by side, we managed to get the rudder pin back in its post. While I was down near the engine, I smelled hot antifreeze indicating the engine was getting close to overheating. I told Bob not to overpower *Mary C*, but he disregarded my words, since I was in bad shape.

It must have been a frightening sight for my wife, Paula Sue, to see *Mary C* roar into the harbor at full speed in the middle of the day. She was working at the restaurant overlooking the harbor and I'm sure she was shocked to see my workboat in the harbor so early. Once *Mary C* was docked, Bob unloaded me quickly from the boat and then reloaded me into my '57 Ford Thunderbird. As Bob raced us down the stretch of Route 20 (locally called the Pat Leonard Highway), he told me he was having trouble keeping the car from drifting off the road. I told him he had to slow up or we'll both be dead before we get to Chestertown.

At the emergency room, I was in shock. I knew, for sure, I was covered with blood and I had much pain from my broken bones. I was unable to tell the doctor anything about the accident and Bob must have given him the details as best he could. Strangely, the only thing I seemed to be concerned about was my expensive watermen boots. I kept telling the people caring for me to keep an eye on my rubber boots. The doctor got tired of my asking about my boots, and finally told me to "quit worrying about your damn boots and let me stop some of this bleeding."

After studying the damage to my nose, the doctor informed me he couldn't make both the inside and the outside of my nose right without surgery. He asked which part I wanted to have right and in a daze I told him to fix the outside. He fixed my nose by shoving two probes right up my nostrils which hurt like the dickens. Then he covered my nose with a dark brown piece of clay to protect it from further damage. He sewed up the gash in my back and sent me home until I could recover enough to have surgery to fix my face.

For the first few days after my accident, I was so blanked out from the pain and the painkillers I didn't remember much. But when I returned to the doctor a few days later to discuss my options to heal fully, I was able to remember that conversation. After looking at each wound carefully, he told me I would be okay if I gave my wounds a chance to heal. He said my healing period could take three months, or much longer, if I didn't give my body a chance to rest. I was pretty upset with his plan, and I said, "Doc, I can't afford to be off the water for a couple of weeks, let alone months."

With no health insurance, no short-term disability, and no source of incoming cash to pay bills, I told him my recovery was going to be more harmful to my life than the accident. He listened to my whining for about two minutes and finally said, "Captain, you are grounded, so go home and heal." Stubborn as could be, I left his office fully planning to be on the water in less than two weeks. But as the last of my pain prescriptions ran out, I could clearly see that my body was severely damaged from the accident and a period of rest was upon me.

For the first time in my life, I was grounded physically, emotionally, and even spiritually. All I could think about was the money I was losing and the lost fishing days with my friends. I was miserable. At age 24, I was unable and unwilling to grasp how unfair and how unlucky I was to be the one waterman in Rock Hall grounded. I was so young and headstrong back then I couldn't possibly see how (or even if) God was guiding my life. Only years later, when I was in my sixties, did I realize that it was God who placed that stone and Bob Gibson on the *Mary C* to save my life.

Chapter Thirty-Three
Wounded, But Not Mortally So

Medically, I was in good hands. My face, neck, and back were badly torn up and required several surgeries to guide the healing process. Once the doctors were done with me, I was sent home to relax, read, and get some rest. At first, I hated to hear the words read, relax, or rest, and it nearly killed me to stay inside and patiently allow my bones and flesh to heal. But now, even I could see the only way I was going to get back on the water was to give it time.

After a couple of days of doing absolutely nothing, a serious case of cabin fever took control of me. I discovered that I had no skills or experience with the art of resting and relaxing. As a hard-charging waterman, I had no desire to be still. I was too beaten up and angry to socialize with my friends. Slowly, I slipped into a funk. And I stayed in this funk for about four weeks, which gave my flesh time to heal over and my bones time to set.

Fortunately, the community of Rock Hall found a couple of new ways to help me heal on the outside which also lifted my spirits. Mr. George Leary, who owned The Rock Hall Marine Railway, offered me a part-time job serving as a utility person to help his skilled craftsmen get their work done better. I myself wasn't a good enough carpenter to do billable services, but I was able to help the experts work more efficiently. Because my father had taught me so many skills, I was very adept at helping others. I required minimal instruction and less supervision, so I did not slow any of the full-time workers down. What a blessing it was for George to give me that job so I could keep my mind active and away from the boredom of sitting home alone.

Though my part-time job did keep groceries on the table, I was not able to keep up with my boat payments, house payments, and medical bills that were piling up at home. Without income from harvesting oysters and rockfish during the winter months, I was now flat broke and on my way to bankruptcy, which was not an attractive option for me as a waterman. To keep up with my bills, I decided to sell *Mary C* to Bob Gibson who was ready to upgrade. I knew Bob would take great care of her and I selfishly liked the idea that I would see her on the water now and then.

Between my day job and the revenues generated from the sale of *Mary C*, I held onto enough financial strength until my healing was complete. That spring, I bought the forty-two-foot gas-powered *Comet* from Captain Bobby Clark. Years before, Bobby had purchased her from the family of Uncle Josh, who died early from cancer. I was honored and thrilled to own the workboat once owned by Uncle Josh. For this special boat, I was willing to go into considerable debt to become its new owner.

It's funny how I had been dreaming about buying a larger workboat for a while, but couldn't find a way to make it all happen. For a while, I had wanted to convert some of my summer work to creating a charter fishing enterprise but I just couldn't find the right timing. Ironically, because of my oyster accident, events fell into place that helped me advance my dreams and the dreams of others at the same time.

As I had hoped, I enjoyed the charter fishing business because I liked to interact with the people. I took great pleasure in watching people catch their first rockfish, bluefish, and croakers and found real enjoyment in teaching young people the basics of fishing on the Chesapeake Bay. In many ways, my first years as a charter fishermen helped me reconnect with the world beyond Rock Hall. It also helped me get my strength and my confidence back after my accident on the T Tree bar.

Later that fall, I rigged up *Comet* to harvest oysters using hydraulically powered patent tongs. This was a new system that was far more expensive to set up than the drop tong system I had used for years. But, this harvesting system was worth every cent I borrowed from the bank to make *Comet* operational. With my new patent tong rig, I could dig oysters faster and deeper in mud or sand which dramatically increased my harvesting results as a waterman. Harvesting seventy-five bushels per day (the current daily limit per licensed watermen) was no problem with this new rig. Though I'll never meet the man who invented hydraulics or even the man who adapted this technology for marine uses, these two technologies revolutionized our capacity to harvest oysters on the Chesapeake Bay.

With *Comet* now fully geared, I roamed all over the Chesapeake Bay in search of the best public oyster reefs. With oyster buyers paying top dollar and plenty of healthy oyster reefs to meet market demands, I didn't even need to add a second rig or hire a third crewmember. All I needed to make good profits was to find and hire an experienced waterman to cull my oysters to, at, or below the "five percent little ones" rule seven days per week.

The crewmember who made my fall oyster season a complete success was a man named Willis Dashanay. Willis, locally known as Mighty Nice, culled our harvest quickly, legally, and profitably. He was a great asset to my business.

But even more important to me than just getting the work done, Willis brought his gift of laughter and a remarkable sense of humor. Willis recognized that I was a driven man trying to financially recoup from my oyster accident. Sensing my tendencies to push too hard, he provided just the right blend of strength and humor to keep me from relapsing physically by running at full throttle for too long. Willis was a blessing to me that fall and it made perfect sense to me when he left the water years later to become a preacher.

After missing out on the previous year's winter and spring fishing seasons, I was ready to make the good money again by working with an experienced captain. Captain Phil Perry hired me as a crewmember to help him catch rockfish, perch, and shad on *Sammy*. A superb waterman and even better friend, Phil got me back in the groove of fishing with gill nets. Through his friendship and his ability to catch fish, he enabled me to finish my healing process and declare myself healed. Phil helped me get back on track with my boat payments and clearing off the last of my medical bills.

Because of my accident, I lost almost a year's worth of income and momentum in the early sixties. With the help of these special people from Rock Hall, I financially survived my accident. Sadly, many watermen never recover financially from a physical injury like I had, so I knew I was either very lucky or somehow blessed. Now back in the game, I volunteered to serve the Kent County Watermen's Association at an even higher level.

Chapter Thirty-Four

Forward Thinking

In the early sixties, an ugly debate raged throughout Kent County over the future plans for a small piece of land we called East Neck Island. It was a true island with one gravel roadway (now Route 445) leading right to the water's edge. It was a special spot where about twelve families lived year round. They grew corn, wheat, fruit, vegetables, and all kinds of poultry and livestock. One of their specialty crops was asparagus. On this island, there were also a few elite gunning clubs. There were a number of places for watermen to keep their workboats year round with the most active spot being Bogles Wharf at the mouth of Durdin Creek. For a little island, it was an important part of Kent County commerce.

The rumor, and therefore the rub, was that this slice of heaven was "in play" among a handful of wealthy developers who wanted to carve up East Neck Island. At first, I naively assumed this was idle gossip among country folks and I mostly avoided the chatter around town. But the rumors persisted and slowly it dawned on the commercial fishing and farming communities that a land deal of significance was likely and imminent. For the longest time, I couldn't wrap my head around why anyone would want to pave over this prime marsh, timber, and farmland. In my wildest dreams, I could not see how this parcel of land could be improved by the hands of man. But as the debate raged on, I discovered that money and greed can make the best of men make awful decisions.

Selfishly, I had my own reasons for getting upset over this looming land deal. This was where I learned how to hunt with my father and his friends, so it was special to me. This was where Ame saved my life from the charging bull and also where he taught me about fresh drinking water. This was also a place where I earned a part of my annual income serving as a paid guide. Some of the best watermen, including Captain Splint, worked out of Bogles Wharf. Lastly, this place was like a sanctuary for my Dad and me, as we loved to watch the ducks fly around in the Eastern Neck Narrows. Like so many other folks in Rock Hall, I was both a stakeholder and part of a user group and I didn't want anything to change on East Neck Island.

Unfortunately, I had not adequately prepared myself to be an effective voice in this local battle. I was still young, around 26 years old, and I had a hot temper. I was also rough around the edges and was not an effective or considerate listener. I had a lot of trouble articulating my thoughts and frequently overused my emotions; these two weaknesses prevented me from receiving invitations to the many meetings about this land deal. It bothered me that I was not ready to influence the outcome of this debate. Unfortunately, neither the farmers nor the watermen of Kent County had a well-defined voice or message to properly engage in this debate. Apparently, this was not my battle to fight and wiser counsel would have to step up and tackle the issues on my behalf.

Because Kent County had plenty of strong leaders that loved the land, a handful of bright men and women volunteered to wrestle with this crisis until a good outcome could be found. From my viewpoint, I felt Senator Percy Hepbron did a superb job of insuring that every user group and stakeholder had a true voice at the table. It was his leadership that made sure that the largest numbers of people and natural resources would receive benefit from the final outcome. Contrary to what I had expected, the Federal Government actually demonstrated vision, depth, and practical wisdom on this issue as the debate bumped along.

In the end, the Federal Government purchased East Neck Island with the intent to create the Eastern Neck Island National Wildlife Refuge. Truthfully, I didn't see how the Federal Government could possibly steward the land as well as the private sector. So many times before, I had watched both the federal and state governments actually make things worse for the residents of Eastern Shore. I was fearful that the residents of Kent County were going to be burdened instead of helped by the Federal Government.

Though I personally was not a driving force in the positive outcome of this debate, I did learn some important lessons from this land deal. First, I was reminded of the potential greatness of our American political process when in the hands of capable men and women. Second, I learned that the Federal Government does have the capacity to create sustainable conservation strategies for America when they have access to the right information and allow a full dialogue to bloom. Third, there was no time like the present to learn how to articulate my positions and thoughts more clearly. Fourth, and importantly, when special interest groups are able to state their position clearly and truthfully without drawing a line in the sand, a positive outcome for many users and stakeholders is possible.

Once the land was transferred to the Federal Government, I saw many good things happen that were not wrong, but different from what I had initially hoped for. Today, much of the land is still tilled by farmers, which means the land is being stewarded by men and women who value the land. There is a beautiful public landing at Bogles Wharf where both commercial and recreational fishermen can access the waters free of charge. There are miles of trails for both residents and visitors to see the marshes and woods where I once hunted raccoons with Dad and Joe Downey. And though it is not as good as it was in sixties, a few hundred canvasback, redhead, and blackhead ducks still overwinter near The Eastern Neck Island National Wildlife Refuge.

Best of times on East Neck Island. *Courtesy of Ann Crane Harlan.*

Chapter Thirty-Five
Bring the Big Truck

The early part of the 1965 rockfish season was a disaster for the watermen that fished with nets. Oh, there were plenty of fish in the Chesapeake Bay and the waters were clear and clean. But we couldn't leave the harbor and access the fishing grounds because the upper Bay was clogged with ice. Even the Army Corps of Engineers' ice breakers were having trouble keeping the major harbors open and keeping the shipping channel open.

Though the fish were plentiful, it was not safe to go after them. We all lost a number of prime fishing days in January we simply couldn't make up later in the year. A lost fishing day is simply lost income, period. As the calendar rolled over into February, some of the less financially solid watermen like me were starting to get restless. The seasoned older captains could take the lost fishing days, but I could only stand so much. My fixed expenses including my boat payments, slip fees, and insurance premiums were all due and so were my child support payments. Almost as bad as the revenue loss, I was suffering from cabin fever, too. I was tired of hanging around with my watermen friends in the local bars and I found myself getting increasingly edgy and even more driven than normal. By early February, I was having trouble seeing a good outcome and I quietly nursed a fear that we might miss all of February, too.

One night over drinks and dinner, my best friend Glenny Edwards and I talked for hours about the abundance of ice and the scarcity of fish. Almost like a twin brother, he was also struggling with the cabin fever and a deficit of funds. As we talked our dilemma over, we kind of inspired each other into believing that we could go fishing in the morning. Maybe it was the alcohol talking some, but we hatched this crazy plan to go fishing north of Rock Hall where we were sure the rockfish would be schooled up. We knew that our boats would sustain some damage from the ice. We also knew we might lose a few nets under the ice (even with the use of ice buoys). We knew other watermen might judge us as fools. But at the end of this discussion, we both knew if we lost all of February locked in ice, we would both lose our minds with cabin fever. Armed with a surge of pluck, we parted to talk to our respective crewmembers about coming with us.

As I drove across town to meet with one of my crewmembers, I started to second guess the wisdom of our big idea. I knew full well that Glenny and I both had a tendency to "talk big" whenever we were together. I had this nagging fear that maybe this was one of those times when we egged each other on just to be macho. I didn't want my good judgment, or his, to get blinded by our natural tendency to one-up the other. To myself, I wondered if maybe this time we were planning to take too big of a risk. I'll never know for sure, but I bet he was second guessing the wisdom of the trip too but didn't want me to know he was having second thoughts.

As soon as I presented the idea with my crewmembers, they both signed on immediately and so did Glenny's crewmembers. They were all fed up with "doing nothing" and agreed to meet us at our workboats prior to sunrise all ready to go. For several reasons, we all agreed not to tell any other watermen we were going fishing in the morning. Serving as crewmembers on my workboat *Dawn* were my close friends Frankie Jester and Billy "Scratch" Ashley. Earlier that year, I had purchased *Dawn* from Captain Calvin Kendall after I'd sold *Comet* to Captain Finey Sewell. Serving as crewmembers on Glenny's boat, *Candy,* was Robert Wagner and Lester Baker. Our plan was to stay together while traveling in the ice and only spread out once we were at the fishing grounds. We agreed to never be out of sight of one another during the trip.

We left the harbor by following in the ice track created by the ice breaker the night before. Once we reached the Chesapeake Bay, we immediately encountered large chunks of partially submerged ice that we simply had to avoid. As expected, our progress was slow and we burned up most of the day just grinding our way to the mouth of the Sassafras River.

Though we had plenty of net on board, we decided to set only five anchor nets per boat. We didn't know exactly where the fish were nor could we anticipate how many problems we would encounter locating our markers among all the ice. Five nets was the most expense I was willing to gamble on our first day of fishing. It took almost till dark, but we managed to find enough open water to set five nets apiece.

We used ice buoys to give us the best chance of finding the nets in the morning. This amazingly clever invention enabled watermen to fish with nets under the ice with minimal net loss.

With our nets set, we made our way back to the landing at Betterton where we cooked dinner and crawled into our bunks to rest. But, none of us got a good night of sleep because of the sounds caused by the shifting ice. The noise of the ice grinding against the pilings and our own workboats was pretty intense. But so were the groaning and cracking sounds we could hear out on the river.

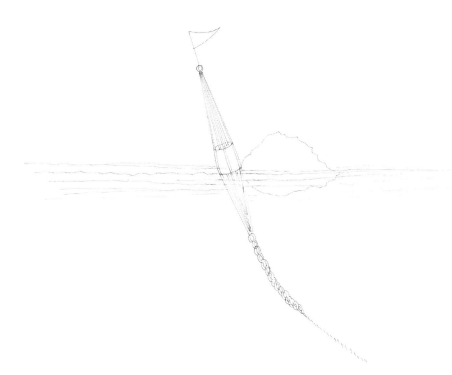

An ice buoy. *Courtesy of Ann Crane Harlan.*

In my sleepless state, my mind started to wander again about the wisdom of this fishing trip. Even though *Dawn's* hull was protected by a sheath of steel, I worried her wooden hull would get damaged or destroyed. I worried I might lose all of my nets. I worried *Dawn* might get iced in for the rest of February and cause me to miss even more fishing days. I worried we might not find any rockfish and then be forced to endure ridicule from my friends for taking such a big risk – for nothing. For me, it was a dreadful night of second guessing and I was so glad when the alarm went off and it was time to go fishing. Nothing calms my fears better than doing something.

After breakfast, we eased out through the ice to find our nets. Surprisingly, it was easier than what I had dreaded during the night. As we hauled in the first section, I swelled up with excitement as our nets were loaded with fish. Using the hand-over-hand method, we pulled each net into the boat and picked the fish out as they came on board. In the stern, we created a massive pile of rockfish. Using only five nets, both boats landed several tons of fish and our attitude skyrocketed from cautious to almost giddy. We set out five new nets apiece and returned to Betterton to re-box the wet nets and sell the fish.

I was excited and pleased with our big catch. We had taken a huge risk to come up here and already we were being rewarded for our pluck with a huge harvest. Within myself, I still nursed a quiet fear about the risks taken to catch these fish but I didn't say a word to Glenny or the others. I didn't want to spoil the enthusiasm of the others as I too was pretty pumped up about our great first day.

Once both workboats were unloaded and the fish were ready to be picked up, we called our fish buyer Al Woodfield from the pay phone at the landing. We told him, "Al, bring up the big truck because we were all over the rockfish." Desperate to fill fish orders at restaurants and retail fish markets, his driver came to Betterton in less than an hour to take every fish we had at a premium price. After one night of fishing, the six of us received the first money we had earned in weeks. Later, I heard from my friends that when Al's truck rolled into Rock Hall, there was quite a stir among the other watermen. Naturally competitive, I'm sure a few of them were green with envy that we had taken the risks and caught the fish. But I'm sure others feared we were pushing our luck by fishing around all that ice. In hindsight now, I probably had more courage than good sense back then, but I was too young, at the time, to know the difference.

That evening, we stayed up and talked about our great day on the Sassafras River. We knew we were on the rock fish in a big way and felt sure no other watermen would be crowding us or our nets in the morning. Almost like magic, the power of fresh money in our wallets had created some confidence in our souls and we soaked up the special feelings that had eluded us for all of January. It's funny how a little good luck can change a man's attitude and his vision. That night, I did sleep better, but I never lost sight of the dangerous ice surrounding us.

When we checked our nets the second morning, again we found them full of fish. We followed the exact same processes we had the day before, and again set out five more nets before we went back to Betterton for the night. When we fished our nets the third morning, they were filled with fish. In total, after just three nights of fishing with only five nets apiece, *Dawn* and *Candy* both landed 13.5 tons of rockfish. In just four days, the six of us had shifted from a position of scarcity to one of abundance.

With the net profits from almost 27 tons of rockfish, this trip had been a once-in-a-lifetime success for all of us. We had been financially rewarded for taking a big risk and we swelled up with pride and happiness for the great pluck we had demonstrated. Though excited, we all knew even good things must come to an end. So, we packed up our gear and headed for Rock Hall so we could beat the incoming winter storm forecast to hammer Kent County.

Chapter Thirty-Six
Too Much Pluck!

As predicted, the winter storm pushed the ice against the Western Shore over to the Eastern Shore. It was a mixture of slab and chunk ice that gave the Chesapeake a very uneven and frigid look. The winds piled up the ice on our shoreline and also pressed hard against some workboats that weren't fully protected in the harbors. Looking at the dangerous nature of this ice, Glenny and I delayed our next fishing trip by three days to give the ice a chance to break and spread out. As soon as we thought the Chesapeake was passable, we gathered up our crewmembers and slipped out of the harbor early in the morning. Since we sustained no real damage from our last outing, we felt our chances of being safe were pretty good.

After our recent success on the Sassafras River, I was sure other boats would follow us but no workboats left that morning which concerned me. Looking out on the harbor from his loft, Captain Harry Carter saw the fading images of *Candy* and *Dawn* easing out of the harbor that morning. As he worked on his nets, he turned to one of his young crewmembers and said, "There they go; they may not get them, but they will get close. Them boys have pluck."

The term pluck was regularly used by watermen in reference to a man's work ethic combined with his willingness to take risks. Having pluck meant a waterman was willing to venture out into dangerous waters and expend a lot of effort just for the chance to catch fish. It meant a man was willing to give a whole lot of push (sweat) to create a little bit of luck (success). Being labeled as a waterman with pluck was a compliment about a man's nerve though it didn't necessarily speak about a man's judgment or intelligence. Captain Splint and Captain Cope both had pluck and so did Glenny and I.

The moment we pushed our way out of the Rock Hall harbor and turned north, that nagging feeling returned to the pit of my stomach that this trip was a bad idea. It bothered me how no other captains came to set nets with us. I mulled this over all the way up to Betterton but the bad feelings didn't fade away. Finally, with an unsettled feeling too clear to ignore, I shared my concerns first with Frankie and Scratch and then with Glenny by radio. As it turns out, Glenny was having second thoughts about the wisdom of this fishing trip as well. In addition, both of us were mindful that another winter storm was expected in the next forty-eight hours (give or take).

When we reached our prime fishing spot, the waters were clear of ice so we set a few nets about a half a mile from each other. Right after we set our last net, I got this intense vibe that fishing in this water was not smart. My inner soul was screaming that it was time to get off the water now. In a moment of pure honesty, I realized that my own greed and a self-induced confidence had led me to go fishing instead of staying home in Rock Hall like the wiser Captain Carter. It wasn't pluck I was demonstrating at all; it's was an ugly blend of stupidity, arrogance, and defiance. By radio, I told Glenny we were in a bad spot on the Chesapeake Bay and it was time to go home.

Frankie, Scratch, and I got our nets back in first so we eased over near *Candy* as they pulled in their last net. While Lester and Robert pulled in the nets hand over hand, Glenny slowly backed down on the nets to make it easier and faster for the men to get the nets in. But large slabs of ice were accumulating around the transom as he backed up which was fouling up the nets. To help clear the ice, Glenny stood up on the back deck to push away a big chunk with the boat hook. I told Glenny, "Be careful," but he leaned way out to make it easy on his crewmembers.

Glenny leaned out too far and the ice he was pushing gave way. Glenny fell head first into the icy water. He went all the way under and disappeared for a second. When he came up, he blew a spray of water out of his mouth like a porpoise. He screamed for help the moment he broke the surface and told his crew, "Get me out." Lester Baker, a hard as nails watermen with a dry wit, quipped, "Ain't this a hell of mess? We are out here trying to get our nets and now you are overboard." Still screaming, Glenny said, "Yeah, but I don't want to be in the water, so get me out."

Lester and Robert lifted Glenny out of the water immediately. He was probably in the water less than twenty seconds, though it seemed to take forever. Glenny ran into the cabin and stripped off his wet clothes and dried off with a towel. He put on every piece of clothing he could find and cranked up the heater. He stayed in the cabin for over an hour trying to regain the heat he'd lost while in the water.

It was a terrifying moment for us all. Had Glenny become entangled in his own nets or somehow gotten trapped under a slab of ice, we could have lost him, even though he was only three feet from the boat. Had he stayed in that icy water much longer, he could have lost his arm strength and been unable to swim back to the boat. The shock of the cold water could have triggered a heart attack on the spot. Even inside the cabin, he could have still lost his body heat and died of hypothermia. Fortunately, luck was with Glenny and the rest of us that day.

Seeing Glenny in that water scared me to death. Though we spend a lot of time near the water, few watermen actually go overboard. No waterman intentionally enters into icy waters unless they are properly equipped with winter diving equipment. With Glenny's near-death experience, I had all the proof I needed that we had pushed the luck part of our pluck too hard. Fish or no fish, our good luck was now gone and it was time to get home.

We lost precious time getting Glenny out of the water and ready for travel. Immediately, we steered directly into a strong headwind that had pushed in acres of thick, broken ice. Though we only had a mile of water to travel to reach the landing, the thick ice made our progress very slow. Inch by inch, we used the bow of our boats to break up the ice and then push it away. The steel sheathing protected the wood from getting bruised up, but the ice was too thick to count on sheathing to protect our hulls. To make real headway, we ultimately had to force our workboats over top of the ice and allowed the weight of the hulls to break a path in the ice. This ice-breaking technique was not optimal for boats like ours, but it was the only technique to get us through the thickest part of the ice pack. As we pushed our way forward, I could feel and hear the ice making direct contact with the boards of *Dawn*. I feared her boards and ribs were taking an excessive amount of pounding and crunching. I feared that structural damage was occurring inside the hull, too, as both boats were twisting and grinding in the ice. Mostly, I felt responsible for getting us into this mess in the first place.

It took us two hours to go a few miles, but we finally made our way to the Betterton landing where we could offload some equipment and drop off Frankie to drive home in the truck. We unloaded *Candy* first and off she roared for open water to lead the way home. By the time I got under way, Glenny was just a mile ahead and still in sight. Scratch seized the moment to catch some sleep in his bunk while I steered for Rock Hall. Now relieved the worst part of this failed trip was behind us, Glenny and I started talking over the radio. We talked about everything from our amazing haul of rockfish earlier in the week to the nearly tragic moment when Glenny fell overboard. After thirty minutes of "fish tales," our discussion shifted to where we felt we could try to find more fish after the incoming storm passed through. One way or another, Glenny and I always got back to talking about the fish.

While I was talking, Glenny interrupted me and said, "Larry, why are you talking to me so strangely?" In response, I said, "I don't know what you are talking about." I was sure, as usual, he was pulling my leg, so I just kept talking. But Glenny persisted and said, "No, I mean it, Larry; you are slurring your words worse than normal and I can barely understand you." Before I could respond again, our radio contact abruptly stopped as I was nearing Howell Point.

I didn't think twice about Glenny's comment as I steered down the Chesapeake Bay. I kept my eyes focused on the waters ahead so *Dawn* wouldn't strike a rogue slab of ice laying flat on the water. I could see *Candy* clearly up ahead and since Glenny had nearly talked my ears off, I looked forward to a little quiet time alone. With the radio now silent, however, I noticed a very strange sound coming from the engine box. Something wasn't quite right back there and I listened for a few moments to try to figure out what it was.

I couldn't figure out the sound, so I opened up the cabin door to hear it more clearly. It was a muffled noise that sounded way off to me. I didn't trust that sound, so I yelled over to Scratch to wake him up. I wanted him to get up and go check out the noise while I focused on the waters ahead. But Scratch was in a deep sleep and I was unable to wake him with just my voice. So, I eased off the throttle and walked over to his bunk. I shook him and told him to get up, but he was unresponsive. Normally Scratch would get up fast and be out the back door on the first request. Finally, he sat up in his bunk but seemed uninterested in me or my concerns.

Still groggy, he instinctively reached for his cigarettes and matches. As I was telling him to go out and check the motor, he struck his first match which ignited fast but then went out. He lit another match and it went out, too. Not a smoker, I grew very impatient with Scratch and told him to forget the matches and go check out the noise. I didn't understand why Scratch wasn't budging, even though I was now yelling sternly. Finally, I got so frustrated with Scratch that I pulled way back on the throttle and walked to the stern of *Dawn* myself to see what was wrong.

Once I was standing aft of the engine box, my eyes instantly locked in on the problem. As a result of all of the grinding and twisting in the pack ice, my exhaust pipe had cracked wide open and was leaking carbon monoxide directly into the bilge system under the floorboards. The asbestos wrapping around the pipe had concealed most of the crack and was the reason why the sound was muffled. I now understood what was causing the weird noise; I was also relieved to know there was nothing wrong with the engine.

In that moment, however, I put two and two together and realized we still had a serious problem on board. I thought about Glenny's comment about my garbled words. I thought about how hard it was to get Scratch up from his bunk and how he couldn't light his matches. In that moment, I realized Scratch and I were silently being poisoned by carbon monoxide fumes that had seeped into the cabin through the bilge. I rushed back to the cabin to find Scratch out cold in his bunk. When I saw him lying there motionless, I thought he was dead. Now driven by a boost of pure adrenaline, I dragged his limp body right across the floor and out the back door.

The second my nostrils hit the fresh air, I was knocked out cold. I have no clue how long the two of us were out. Gradually, the cold fresh air worked its way into our lungs, and brought me back first and then Scratch. By the time I had regained part of my senses back, I was covered with spray water and my fingernails had that purple tinge to them. I have no clue how *Dawn* didn't strike a chunk of ice or run aground. All I know, for sure, was neither Scratch nor I saved ourselves while we were out cold.

I managed to get up off the floor and idle *Dawn* down and took her out of gear. I opened all of the windows and left the back door open. It took Scratch a while longer to come around enough for him to be able to sit up and take in air on his own. Once stable, I covered him with blankets and forced him to stay out of the cabin where he could suck in fresh air and also vomit as needed. I hung my head out the window to get fresh air as I steered Dawn towards Rock Hall.

As we pulled into our slip, Glenny helped us tie down the boat. He said we looked terrible and was shocked to learn that just a mile behind him we'd nearly died of carbon monoxide poisoning. He felt bad he didn't double back to help us, but he had no clue we were in trouble. He insisted that we both go to the hospital to get our lungs pumped with fresh oxygen but I said no. I was cold and wet and I wanted to go home and warm up.

In hindsight, Glenny should have made us both go and not let me override him in my dazed condition. As the captain of *Dawn*, I should have insisted that Scratch get checked over carefully but I wasn't thinking right. I learned from that nearly fatal lapse in judgment that a poisoned man should not be making his own health care decisions.

Bad air. *Courtesy of Ann Crane Harlan.*

Chapter Thirty-Seven

S. Glyn Edwards

Throughout the sixties, the Maryland watermen endured very few problems with the fishery that I would classify as a crisis. We endured no massive fish kills or chemical spills (at least that we were aware of). Certainly, we continued to clash with the swelling numbers of recreational fishermen. We also suffered through long periods of low dockside prices due to the abundance of seafood available. But truly there was nothing "hot" that required vigilant leadership in Annapolis. Even the gradual decline in water quality was so subtle that many user groups, including the watermen, failed to raise the warning flag.

With no real battles to fight and no heinous polluters to call out by name, most of the fishery problems were handled by the county watermen's associations. For the most part, local watermen solved their own problems. In Kent County, I had become plenty active in The Kent County Watermen's Association which gave me a place to meet with my friends, talk about issues, and learn more about pending regulations in Annapolis. I liked attending the monthly meetings for the information exchange and its social benefits as well.

Though we didn't scream and shout about it, there was an underlying concern that the once pristine Chesapeake Bay was not as clean or as clear as it used to be. Though she was still producing massive quantities of fish, crabs, clams, and oysters, something below the surface wasn't right. In the Maryland Legislature, a wad of bills was starting to get some real airtime and attention by the leading politicians. Sensing that water quality was a growing and looming concern, a leadership call was sounded within our county organization. There was a leadership call for new blood and new ideas to insure that our association remained relevant and forward thinking. But no one from Kent County was willing to step forward and take charge. Like me, every other waterman wanted a venue to air their concerns, but nobody wanted to take the lead.

On the surface, agreeing to take on a leadership role in a non-profit trade organization seemed like a dumb idea. Why would any waterman want to give up their personal income to work for free? Why would anyone, in their right mind, want to lead a hundred rowdy, rough-handed commercial fishermen? (It would be easier to herd cats). Why would an uneducated waterman want to engage in a complex fishery debate with world class PhD scientists? Why would any waterman drive to Annapolis after dark to have an open discussion with an environmentalist that had already publicly vowed to eliminate all watermen from working in Maryland? On the surface, serving as a leader in a county watermen's association didn't make a lot of sense to me.

So when it was my turn to accept or decline the call to leadership within Kent County, I quickly said no. I used my well-honed excuse that I was too busy making a living so I could feed my three children. I even admitted, publicly, that I was not comfortable speaking in public and I had trouble articulating when I got too emotional about an issue. But the real reason I didn't want to lead other watermen was because I was still young, hot tempered, and self absorbed with making as much money as I could. I was afraid to speak in public but not because I sounded rough. I was afraid to speak in public because I didn't have my thoughts all ordered and logical, which meant I lacked the confidence I needed to be successful. In truth, I lacked the poise and depth to speak clearly and convincingly in the world beyond Kent County.

Though I was not ready to be the leader, I knew my friend, S. Glyn Edwards, could lead The Kent County Watermen's Association. With his great people and organizational skills, I knew he could take our organization to the next level. With his nearly perfect photographic memory, I knew he could run with the big dogs in Chestertown and even Annapolis. So, like a true friend, I proceeded to arm twist and even manipulate him from behind the scenes to get him interested in the job. I wore Glenny down with my persistence until he agreed to serve as a candidate for president of The Kent County Watermen's Association. I promised that I would be his right-hand man if he was voted in as president. With ease, he was selected to lead our watermen.

Almost overnight, Glenny emerged as a competent, credible force within the association. He got things done and made a lasting impact on leaders in Chestertown (county seat) and in Annapolis (state capital). As his point man, I gained a great deal of exposure, wisdom, and experience simply by watching him work with others on issues. Professionally, he was a master with people and I knew he would always achieve great things for the watermen and for Kent County. And he did, without ceasing.

Politically, Glenny was a dominant and important figure in Kent County politics (and he remained so for years). But far more important to me personally, he was my best friend. We fished together, led together, and always socialized together. Most of the time, we remained furious with each other for getting in each other's way. But, like the mark of a true friend, we could never stay mad at each other for very long. Our desire to be together always trumped our willingness to irritate each other. We had learned early in our relationship to never let a fishing hole, an argument, or a woman come between us as friends.

On the water, however, we fought like twin brothers to be the number one waterman each and every day. Without fail, we would talk by radio on the way home every day to see who caught the most fish or who had the best story of the day. We were very competitive and that helped us become and remain very sharp, driven fishermen. We took great pride in beating each other and then spreading our momentary success all over Rock Hall.

One winter, I was preparing to set my nets over top of a nice school of rockfish. I was right on top of them when, suddenly, a full box of net became entangled and messed up. I had to stop setting my nets and straighten out the mess. Hearing my plight over the radio, Glenny eased over to offer his assistance in getting my nets in order which, on the surface, I thought was very kind. But when he could see that I had a pretty bad mess on my hands, he shoved off and proceeded to set his own nets right in my prime spot. I was furious with him for being such a hog. And the madder I got, the harder he laughed which drove me crazy. He netted a nice catch of rockfish that day, and once ashore, he dragged our story all over Rock Hall to win some laughs at my expense. That was Glenny and I miss him and his antics so much.

Chapter Thirty-Eight
The Unsettled Sixties

A small cluster of credible scientists and conservationists from Maryland, Virginia, and Delaware started expressing concerns about the deteriorating water quality of the Chesapeake and Delaware Bays. These were bright men and women who spoke about their concerns with respect and compassion. They were not extreme activists who generically detested commercial fishermen. They spoke calmly using non-offensive or divisive language to make their points clear. They were not using the plight of the Chesapeake Bay to gain fame or recognition for themselves. All they wanted was to improve the quality of Maryland waters.

Fundamentally, their fears were rooted in the belief that any further decline in water quality would one day destroy the natural resources of the Chesapeake Bay. Going a step further, they also feared that the Eastern Oyster was showing serious signs of health and habitat problems and were at grave risk. Valued as an indicator species, a filter feeder, a robust fishery, and simply a beautiful creature in nature, these experts considered the oyster to be the foundational species upon which the Chesapeake Bay would either thrive or fail. Their message was clearly articulated and prophetic, but many user groups and stakeholders were too busy, or uninterested, to heed the warning.

Unfortunately, Americans throughout the sixties were angry and distracted by a number of problems beyond the issues facing the Chesapeake Bay. Sadly, we were embroiled in a messy war in Vietnam which proved to be lethal and expensive, and without a clearly defined endpoint. In addition, several highly public, charismatic leaders striving for peace and equality were assassinated during those years. Close to home, in Washington, D.C., Baltimore, and small towns like Rock Hall, racial tension between the white and black communities ran hot and occasionally turned violent. The sixties were a tough time for America, as I recall.

When I reflect back on the complexity of these issues, I can understand how the plight of the Chesapeake Bay didn't garner enough attention in Annapolis. Compared to a war that was killing thousands of young people, protecting the oysters did seem to be a rather small cause at first. For the record, the scientific community did warn us all how an unhealthy Chesapeake Bay would someday become an economic issue, which was usually a good way to get America's attention. At the moment in time when our country knew the Chesapeake Bay was in trouble, we all should have dropped our selfish agendas and come together to save the bay when it was within easy reach. Instead, we faltered and failed to unite as user groups, stakeholders, and special interest groups. Instead, every individual and organization got defensive and "turfy" about plans and desires for the waters of Maryland and we grew apart. Instead of working together to solve the water quality problems, we broke out into a war filled with grungy infighting, and we have never fully stopped.

Without a common goal or a crisis to inspire all the opposing groups to work together, we became divisive. With no leadership to bring us together, we splintered into hundreds of little organizations filled with small, selfish agendas. Though not intentional, we collectively made it possible for the Chesapeake Bay and her tributaries to be harmed by some kind of trigger or event. Sensing a vulnerability, our nation became vigilant in preventing catastrophic events like chemical spills, nuclear meltdowns, and human diseases caused by the presence of raw (human) sewage.

In my worst nightmare, I never imagined that the catastrophic wound that would send the Chesapeake Bay into a tailspin would be Dermo or MSX.

Chapter Thirty-Nine
The Oyster Collapse

Since the 1800s, the Maryland Seafood Industry had evolved to a point where it was nearly perfect in handling and shipping massive volumes of oysters. The producer (waterman) was geared up to harvest oysters and his sole focus was yield. For years, we didn't waste space on board by using bushel baskets. Instead, we allowed the oysters to accumulate on the floorboards and used grain shovels and industrial-grade elevators to move oysters. The middle man (seafood buyer) was geared up to process, handle and transport tons of oysters fast, so they were all about efficiency and maintaining freshness. And the end user (consumer) wanted large quantities of great tasting, fresh oysters to enjoy in the cold weather months.

Almost every waterman from Crisfield to Cecilton valued the oyster fishery as his "bread and butter" income stream. The oyster fishery had been so strong and steady for so many years that many generations of watermen have cut their teeth harvesting oysters with tongs or dredges. No matter how bad things got with the economy, a lone waterman could always pay his bills by tonging for oysters. Maryland, after all, boasted to have one of the most robust oyster fisheries in the world.

I had an unsettled feeling when I first heard the scientists talk and write about MSX and Dermo. For years, I had been listening to bits and pieces about these two diseases but I wasn't really worried. The hotspots showed up randomly and no counties in Maryland were completely affected by an outbreak of the disease. Of course, we didn't have cell phones, texts, or Internet technologies to spread information around about the disease either, so most of us saw this as a "spotty" problem.

My view changed significantly when our Maryland scientists revealed that two oyster diseases, Dermo and MSX, had wiped out highly productive oysters beds in the lower and central parts of the Chesapeake Bay. From Cape Charles Virginia north to the Choptank River, thousands of acres of historically fertile oyster bars were killed off. The oyster bars closest to the Atlantic Ocean were damaged the most, due to their higher salinity levels (salt content). Significantly, these outbreaks followed a number of dry years where salinities were well above normal for the lower Chesapeake Bay.

The severity of this oyster collapse created an immediate concern among all stakeholders and user groups associated with Maryland waters. Since the oysters were a significant source of Maryland's tourism and tax revenues, busy politicians in Annapolis found time in their schedules to work on (show concern for) the oyster crisis. From the onset, I envisioned three possible good outcomes that might result from this catastrophic assault on Maryland's most stable fishery. First, I hoped the issue of water quality would receive due consideration in discussions about saving this fishery. Second, all of the user groups seemed to grasp that this particular species was a key component of the estuary loaded with interdependencies and complexities. Third, because this was a statewide issue impacting all watermen, I hoped this issue would unite us into a common user group of Maryland watermen.

The issues associated with the Dermo and MSX outbreak were too large and complex for Glenny and The Kent County Watermen's association to fix on our own. This was a monster-sized issue that was going to take many minds and many months to even understand, let alone solve. A window of opportunity had revealed itself for the watermen to work with leaders in Annapolis, instead of around them, to find a sustainable solution. We instinctively knew that if watermen tried to fix this problem on a county by county basis, we would likely do damage to both the oyster fishery and our own livelihoods. I was thankful that Glenny was firmly established as president of The Kent County Watermen's Association when this oyster crisis occurred. This would have been a bad time to be operating without a strong leader at the helm. From day one, he guided us brilliantly and kept us focused on finding solutions instead of searching for someone to blame.

As Glenny's right-hand man, this oyster collapse changed the direction of my life both personally and professionally. There was so much raw emotion over this issue that I was repeatedly asked to travel to Annapolis and share what our county's views and recommendations were. Armed with nothing more than a few talking points and a pickup truck, I was asked to represent the association on a wide range of topics (some of which I had never heard of before). Certain questions, like addressing the human safety aspects of consuming infected oysters, were beyond my understanding at first, but I went to Annapolis and did my best.

Glenny expected me to work alongside natural resource managers who had the statutory responsibility for protecting the natural resources. These men and women were dedicated to conserving stocks while keeping the watermen in business (as best they could). He also asked me to work alongside political leaders who wanted to solve problems but only through bills that were properly funded by the state of Maryland or the federal government. Further, I was expected to represent every fishery and every waterman in Kent County while in Annapolis without giving up an inch of fishing income or changing the watermen's way of life.

Ironically, the science community that warned all user groups about the risks associated with declining water quality was treated harshly by political powers for failing to anticipate the outbreaks of Dermo and MSX in our home waters. They received sharp criticism for not having an immediate fix or solution to the two diseases as well. I felt both charges against the scientific community were unfair.

As an emerging leader within the watermen community, I had my own theory about what caused the outbreak of Dermo and MSX. I believed the poor water quality had destroyed much of the food sources oysters required to reproduce abundantly. Unprotected by a weakened immune system, I believe the oysters were much more susceptible to an attack by Dermo and MSX. Once the environmental conditions were favorable for the two diseases to explode, the diseases flared up and attacked vast acreages of traditionally healthy oysters.

Though it has been over forty years since our oyster reefs in Maryland collapsed, I still believe my theory is the likely cause of the disease outbreaks. Tragically, because pollution sources are so hard to trace once they are released in the water, very few (if any) chronic polluters were held accountable or responsible for triggering this oyster collapse. This time, the watermen of Maryland were not solely blamed for causing the oyster fishery to fall apart. Because the disease outbreaks were so widely scattered and so effective in killing off entire populations of oysters, the charge of overfishing was not used to explain the oyster probleme. The high number of dead oysters convinced us that something was wrong with the oyster, not the oystermen.

Chapter Forty

Desperate Measures

As this biological crisis unraveled over a two- or three-year period, every stakeholder and user group scrambled to find a solution, or at least a stop-gap measure to prevent the oyster fishery from dying away. Two groups, in particular, were launched head-first into trying to deal with this oyster crisis. The first group to feel pressure was the watermen because their bread and butter fishery was no longer paying the bills. Our mission, selfishly, was to save the Eastern Oyster so we could save our way of life. The second group to feel the pinch quickly was the fishery regulators who were responsible for saving arguably one of Maryland's most precious natural resources from disappearing altogether from Maryland waters. The general public, who in this situation were also the consumers, wanted to preserve the oyster reefs as nature had intended, but still have access to plenty of fresh, cheap oysters to eat.

Southern Maryland counties were in deep trouble over this oyster collapse. Watermen in Dorchester, Somerset, Wicomico, St. Mary's, Charles and Calvert counties no longer had access to quality, healthy oyster reefs, so their problems were immediate and severe. Watermen in Cecil, Kent, Baltimore, Harford, Carroll, Queen Anne's, Talbot, and Anne Arundel had enough oysters to have a successful season, so their problem was more "down the road." For the first time in my memory, there was a new division among the watermen. No longer was the dividing line between eastern and western shore watermen (split by the Chesapeake Bay). Because this disease outbreak was primarily determined based on salinity levels, the new division among the watermen was more south and north. Naturally, the watermen without oysters wanted access to them and watermen with oysters did not want to share them.

Watermen from Somerset, Wicomico, and Dorchester counties were hit very badly by this disease. For these men, the oyster fishery represented a larger proportion of their annual income so they had more at stake. The fact that the diseases hit the southern oystermen harder was like rubbing salt in a wound; they felt singled out.

To address their crisis head on, they formed new relationships across county lines and mapped out a wise strategy to gain access to northern oysters currently unavailable to them based on the laws on the books. Led by the Tangier Sound Watermen's Association based on Smith Island, legal counsel helped these men gain access to surviving oyster reefs in the north. Had the situation been reversed, I'm sure the northern watermen would have pursued the same legal recourse if they were left with no ability to harvest and sell oysters.

Starting with this initiative, a favorable state court ruling was granted in 1971 and watermen still refer to this law as the Bruce Decision (sometimes called the Bruce Case). With the stroke of a pen, harvesting zones requiring watermen to stay inside their home county waters were lifted. For the first time in my lifetime, watermen could legally harvest oysters anywhere in Maryland as long as they had a valid, commercial fishermen's license. County boundaries no longer meant anything to oystermen. In practical terms, if a waterman from Rumbley, Maryland wanted to run his boat all the way up to Tolchester to harvest oysters, he was legally permitted to do so.

To be fair, the lawmakers and regulators responsible for protecting Maryland's natural resources were confronted with a very difficult challenge. Analytical methods in the 1960s were marginally accurate compared to the instruments we use today. In 1971, other than reviewing annual harvesting results dating back to 1840, none of us knew exactly how many oysters were on the bottom or how healthy they were. In the wild, it was (and remains) hard to know exactly what was wrong with the fishery.

From a practical perspective, the Bruce Decision changed the Maryland oyster industry in a big way. As expected, southern oystermen traveled great distances by boat and truck to harvest oysters from still productive bars. It was hard to watch watermen from all over the state converge on a solitary oyster bed and pick it clean. It was also hard to watch oyster beds that Kent County had been stewarding for decades get picked clean in a few weeks. Between the tongers and the dredgers, every public oyster bar with live oysters received full harvesting pressure until most legal oysters were caught.

As the oyster season progressed towards March, bar after bar was ultimately picked clean. There was some tension among the watermen, but the real heat was between the watermen and Annapolis. Regulators were tasked with establishing a daily limit per licensed waterman that would preserve the oyster fishery. Ideas considered included rezoning the Chesapeake Bay (again) and lowering the daily limit to ten bushels, which was below the break-even point for southern watermen incurring high fuel and meal expenses while sleeping on their boats.

At Glenny's request, I worked alongside the watermen in Calvert and Anne Arundel counties to formulate our best recommendation to get us through the end of the season. Representing The Kent County Watermen's Association, I was sent to attend a number of meetings in Annapolis to make it clear that a 25-bushel daily limit (per licensed waterman) with strong law enforcement would keep us in business, but a 10- to 15-bushel limit would lead to our demise. I believed a 25-bushel limit would hold the oyster fishery and all stakeholders at bay until a working group could cobble together a long-term solution to protect the fishery. In time, the 25-bushel limit was established to finish the season.

With a reasonable harvesting limit and some open dialogue, I believed we could start and build a state-wide watermen's organization capable of supporting all watermen of Maryland.

Chapter Forty-One

One Voice

The demise of the oyster fishery forced each waterman to rethink his own values, processes and beliefs about oysters. It was a painful mind shift to endure, but it had to happen if we hoped to have any kind of oyster fishery. Within our Kent County fleet, I saw three major shifts occur. First, I realized that our lawmakers and regulators were trying to manage the oyster fishery without fully understanding how we harvested oysters. Second, I realized we were sending mixed messages to Annapolis by shouting out our narrow opinions at the county level. Because Annapolis heard so much conflicting and often off-setting information from the watermen, they had learned to ignore us, instead of understand us. Third, I could see that if we didn't cultivate lasting relationships with the leaders in Annapolis, we would have no voice and therefore no role.

The oyster crisis scared the watermen community into working together. Our traditionally valuable can-do attitude and hard work ethic was ineffective in battling against Dermo and MSX. Our relationship with our end user, the oyster consumer, had changed, too. Consumers no longer seemed in awe or respectful of the dangers and the pain watermen experienced to bring in the harvest. For some reason, the consumers were showing a greater concern for the oyster than they were for the oystermen, which was a hard concept for us to accept. Still is today.

Down, but not beaten, the watermen from each county started to change and grow in new ways. Every existing county association started to build in terms of numbers of members and willing leaders. And in the few counties where no formal organization existed, a few watermen stepped in to get it started. Following a grass-roots approach frequently modeled by the smaller environmental groups, situational leaders started to emerge from within each association. Men untrained in public speaking mustered up their nerve and spoke from the heart about these issues. Every county organization now had a willing spokesman armed with a credible, simple set of talking points and recommendations.

Fortunately, the watermen's associations within both Anne Arundel and Kent County were already well established and were powerfully led by Captain Rodney Gross and Glen Edwards respectively. In addition, these two organizations worked well together because we shared two important realities in common. First, these two counties were home to the largest reserves of healthy oyster reefs left on the Chesapeake Bay. Second, both organizations had established sustainable relationships with the right political leaders who believed that both the oyster and oysterman were good for Maryland's future.

Working side by side, our two organizations requested the opportunity to work closely with (then) State Delegate Clayton Mitchell to create a non-partisan committee. Once formed, we felt a committee comprised of experienced watermen would be able to draft up new oyster regulations that all Maryland lawmakers could support. Using the county ballot process, the plan was to create a small group of watermen (less than a dozen) who could speak objectively about their fisheries, waters and the unique needs of their fellow watermen. As the number two man in The Kent County Watermen's Association, my name was placed on the ballot so Glenny could remain focused on the needs of Kent County.

In due time, I was elected to represent Kent County in Annapolis which was both an honor and a challenge for me. In spite of the fact that I was still rough around the edges and a pretty awkward speaker, I went to Annapolis anyway so I could do my best to work with other watermen to strengthen our oyster fishery.

In addition to watermen, there were a half dozen regulators and research experts present at the meetings to give our commission balance and depth. Our tasks were to share relevant facts we knew about the oyster fishery, draft practical solutions that would protect the oysters and the oystermen and to keep our respective associations informed of our progress and our obstacles.

The first meeting in Annapolis remains one of my favorite moments of my professional career – because gathered together in one room were men from many backgrounds, races, and accents. In terms of fishing expertise, we had gill netters, trotliners, clammers, eelers, and pound netters. Naturally, we had every kind of oysterman there too including hand tongers, patent tongers, power dredgers, and sail dredgers. I can't recall for sure, but we probably had some watermen who harvested oysters on privately owned beds (aquaculture).

With the help of quality moderators and driven by a common need, the watermen in that room found our rhythm and our focus. In time, we ironed out a set of recommendations to manage all of the natural resources involved with fisheries including the vulnerable Eastern Oyster. Written with a surprising level of detail, the recommendations included specific catch limits, culling specifications, fishing times, and seasons. It wasn't perfect, but it was surely a blueprint that regulators and lawmakers could use to finalize the upcoming fishery laws and regulations that would guide the behaviors of the watermen and influence the sustainability of the fisheries.

As I walked out of the meeting room for the last time to return to my real job as an oysterman, I realized I had grown significantly by serving in these meetings. I made a number of true friends who have remained exceptional friends over forty years later. I also developed some solid contacts with lawmakers, regulators and even an environmentalist or two. Importantly, I learned some leaders in Annapolis actually craved accurate and unfiltered information about the ways and thoughts of watermen. Even as a newcomer to Annapolis, I found I could help elected officials make better decisions simply by sharing what I had observed about the fisheries as water quality declined.

Most of the watermen who participated in these meetings were equally changed and inspired by the process and the results of the meeting. We all came out feeling more positive about Annapolis and gained a much deeper appreciation for this cumbersome but effective concept called democracy. I was still plenty hot headed and stubborn, but I gained some real energy and passion by serving in this leadership role on behalf of Kent County. For the first time since the oyster collapse, I sensed a ray of hope emerging from me about the future of the oyster fishery. It took a while, but I realized that preserving a small oyster fishery was far better than enduring an indefinite moratorium.

Even after our working group ended, the twelve of us continued to talk across county lines by telephone almost every week. Once a quarter, we also met in person at a couple of central locations to stay connected, exchange ideas, and look forward. In these informal meetings, we moved past the day-to-day struggles of the watermen and focused on strategic issues like water quality, access to new markets, and how to remain profitable in spite of new regulations. It was remarkable to see how many fresh ideas and solutions we were able to generate simply by sharing our candid thoughts with one another.

Gradually, this small cluster of men recognized that our individual voices had plenty of value. We believed that if we could harness our collective thoughts and speak with one voice in Annapolis, we were certain we could accomplish good things for the watermen and the fisheries. Organically, the idea had emerged that it was time to create a new, statewide association to serve the needs of all Maryland watermen. We believed that a member driven, non-profit trade organization could accomplish good results in Annapolis, Baltimore, and Washington, D.C.

Further, we wanted each county and each fishery (including gear differences) to be represented fully. We did not want to be financed, and therefore controlled, by a handful of private donors who might shrewdly insert their desires in with our needs. We agreed to run lean so we would not lose track of our real purpose which was to serve and strengthen the watermen of Maryland.

From the demise of the oyster fishery, a seed was formed in Annapolis to one day create a statewide association of watermen uniquely dedicated to the interests of all who derive beauty and benefit from Maryland waters. Strategically, we believed that each waterman could best steward his home waters. Likewise, we felt each county association was ideally suited to handle local water, fishery, and users' issues that would flare up now and then.

I was asked to serve as the face and voice of the association in Annapolis when controversial issues arose. This time I answered the call to leadership and agreed to serve as president of the emerging statewide watermen's association to help get the organization off the ground. At the time, I had no idea that I would spend the next forty years of my life working for and with watermen from around the state.

Chapter Forty-Two
Wise Counsel

As vice president of The Kent County Watermen's Association and now president of the unnamed, but fast -growing statewide watermen's association, the trajectory of my life changed exponentially. On a daily basis, I was immersed in statewide issues that involved every fishery and every state within the Chesapeake Bay watershed. On any given day, I might be working with Delaware watermen to better understand the life cycle of the horseshoe crabs that eelers used for bait. On the next day, I might be working alongside a member of the Potomac River Fisheries Commission so we could both conserve the stocks and preserve the watermen's way of life on the Potomac River. Every day was different and every issue was of interest to me.

By adding the role of president into my schedule, my work life took on a whole new dimension and intensity. By day, I maintained my aggressive efforts to harvest oysters, crabs, and fish on *Dawn*. At night and on weekends, I joined the social and political world where folks wore neckties to discuss fishery issues over drinks and dinner. Almost overnight, I had become an executive of sorts, spending time thinking through issues in my mind instead of trying to solve everything with my hands.

Now burning the candle at both ends pretty hard, my new life as president was causing me great hardship and problems at home. Truthfully, I wasn't home much and spent far too little time with Dawn, Larry Jr., and Robby than I would have preferred. I was absolutely fascinated and enjoyed working alongside politicians, lawmakers, regulators, and fellow watermen from around Maryland. By working with these men and women from all over Maryland, my sphere of influence had grown significantly beyond the boundaries of Kent County and I enjoyed learning so much about the rest of Maryland. I discovered really quickly that the rest of Maryland was a great place to work and live also. As it has always done in the past, I assumed my body and my lifestyle would adjust to my job as president, but this time it never did.

I never found my new normal because Glenny Edwards won the Kent County Commissioner seat for the 5th District which included serving as the chairman. I was proud of my friend for winning this race with a wide margin and was also pleased that he was willing to continue to fish commercially and serve as president of The Kent County Watermen's Association. I could be a much more effective president knowing he was guiding my home county. But Glenny saw my needs differently, and he tendered his resignation as president. He explained that he couldn't do all three jobs well and refused to under serve his fellow watermen.

Reluctantly, I agreed to serve as president of the Kent County Watermen's Association while simultaneously building the framework for a new statewide organization. I hoped there would be enough overlap (now called synergy) between the two jobs that I could "kill two birds with one stone" and still make good money on the water. Besides, our board of directors had already laid plans to bring in a full-time executive director to run the show at the state level. All I had to do was hold the new group together until we picked up some momentum and critical mass.

Always a good friend, Glenny recognized long before I did that I was in complete overload and was going to kill myself by working so hard on all of these projects. Over drinks one night, he told me I was on a collision course with burnout if I wasn't careful. I got very defensive and told him that hearing him say that was "like the pot calling the kettle black."

For a little while, I remained mad at him for judging me so harshly. But, I knew my friend was speaking the truth, which is why I got so defensive about it. Later that week, Glenny confided in me that he was in the early stages of joining the Masonic Order in Kent County. He told me why he was seeking membership and asked me to look into it also. I asked him how and why he started down the road of joining the Masons without telling me. He said, "Larry, I'm not allowed to tell you." Once again, I got defensive for being left out and was hurt.

As I worked on *Dawn*, I thought about our conversation and decided to do some checking around to see what was involved with joining the Masonic Order. Having watched my father and his friends actively serve in this brotherhood of good men (sometimes called a secret society), I was hopeful that I might find a spot in the organization, too.

As required, I completed my petition to become a member and secured three signatures of quality men who agreed to sponsor me. I submitted my petition exactly as spelled out in the guidelines, but my petition was rejected almost instantly. I was crushed with the speed in which I was turned away and even more incensed that no one from the Masons told me why I was rejected. That didn't seem fair to me. And to know my best friend was in and I was out – well that frosted me in a major way.

Back working on *Dawn*, I tried to analyze why the Masons might have rejected my petition. In this period of self reflection, I discovered that there were several reasons why I might not have been chosen. Barely into my thirties, I had been married three times and divorced twice (so far). I had never taken any time away from my work to recharge and rest, so I looked haggard and tired. My reputation around town revealed a streak of wild, including a tendency to get into fist fights. I had also drifted away from church and my own family. Once I was finished with my self-analysis, it wasn't hard to see how the Masons could reject me.

Still, Glenny was in and I was out, and that drove me crazy. Glenny told me to learn from the experience and resubmit the same petition in six months. He told me to show them that I really wanted it and to use the time to think about what I really wanted in my life. He told me that men with far fewer gifts and talents had already become members, so I should be patient and not despair.

I did submit a new petition with three signatures and was accepted into the candidate's program. Like clockwork, I received a call from a Mason who proceeded to tell me that he was now my mentor and would teach me everything I needed to know to become a Mason, and also a better man – if I wanted to be a better man. His name was Captain Pek Downey and he was known throughout Kent County as an even, steady, and fair waterman who was highly respected by everyone in Rock Hall. He lived a simple life. He never owned a truck, but walked or rode his bike wherever he needed to go. He loved to grow plants in his garden. His passion in life was to help younger men find their purpose in life and to help them build a good foundation. In some ways, Pek reminded me of Captain Willie, which helped me be receptive to his wise counsel.

Pek taught me the history, vision, and degrees (levels) of the Masonic Order so I could reach the first degree of membership into the Masons. After crabbing all day, he spent hours with me talking in his garden or in his workshop, going over the material. Patiently, he taught me every word of the catechism (Masonic guiding principles) and made sure I could recite the words clearly and in order. Pek made sure I understood the meaning of every word. With him guiding my pace, I was amazed that even I could remember and recite large amounts of this Old English information back to him.

By working with me one on one, Pek filled me with confidence, which helped me to become a more impactful and interesting speaker.

He didn't try to change my accent or rate my speech; he wasn't there to fix me. Rather, he simply encouraged me to find and then use my natural talents to draw out good thoughts and behaviors in others. He insisted that I look and speak directly into the eyes of my audience and therefore never allowed me to use notes or a written speech. He urged me to avoid clichés at all costs. Instead, he asked me to use my dry, and often pointed, sense of humor to engage the audience. He told me it was my responsibility as a speaker to share information that would help those who received it. Pek convinced me that I could speak effectively even in large groups as long as I was passionate about my subject. From that day forward, I stopped dreading the thought of speaking in public and started to look forward to it.

On my first attempt, I achieved my goal of reaching the first degree in the Masonic Order. (Ultimately, I would become a thirty-second degree Mason). My time with Pek had a profound impact on me. As a humble mentor, he helped me see my imperfections as a man without being overly critical or crushing my spirit. He helped me see where I was actually blocking my own progress as a human being and inspired me to mature just a little bit every day.

Once my initial work with Pek was done, I missed the regular contact with my mentor and friend. I liked having an older gentleman looking out for me and guiding my thoughts. But, I knew it was time for me to solve my own problems. I already knew of two areas of my life that needed immediate attention. First, I needed to find and spend time with a few quality men who would lift me up and steer me away from temptations. Second, I needed to choose whether drinking alcohol would play a role in my future.

To be clear, Pek did not fix many of my weaknesses overnight and I still was a hardened, driven waterman with a mean streak. But, my time with Pek led me to become a Mason. And my time as a Mason inspired me to spend time with higher-quality men. And my time with a few good friends led me to find my way back to God. Over many years, I realized that God didn't leave me behind at all. It was me, not Him, that walked away from the simple path to a good life, and only I could find my way back to Him.

The Masonic Symbol.
Courtesy of Ann Crane Harlan.

Chapter Forty-Three
Annapolis, at Her Best

I have always loved the look and feel of Annapolis. Home to both The Naval Academy and The State Capitol, I liked the feel of cobblestones beneath my feet and seeing all the brick architecture around State Circle. I have always considered Annapolis to be a special town just like Chestertown, only larger. For years, Annapolis had a raw bar right at The City Market where anyone could walk in off the street and slurp down a dozen salty oysters on the half shell. I loved how I could step off *Dawn* and walk right up Main Street to have drinks and dinner with my friends. To me, that was as good as it could get for a working waterman.

Historically, Annapolis has served as a significant seafood hub for the East Coast. For decades, the inner part of the harbor was preferentially set aside for use by watermen for overnight docking. During the oyster season, the boats were so tightly packed in the harbor that a man could walk across the decks of the various workboats without even seeing the water. There was time, not so long ago, when the Severn River had enough oysters to keep every hand tonger from Anne Arundel County in good money through March.

As both the county seat and state capital, Annapolis served as the primary meeting place for the business end of the Maryland Seafood Industry. It was the one place where political, regulatory, and industry leaders would come together and hash out real solutions to fishery problems. Countless meetings were held in Carvel Hall (now called the William Paca House) where leaders like Captain Splint would meet directly with lawmakers and regulators over a nice dinner to speak candidly about the issues facing watermen. These dinners were not just "photo ops" to help convince the public that politicians valued watermen. Instead, these were working meetings with roots dating back to the fifties when Captain Frank Beck and Captain Irvin Crouch were leaders.

In spite of the social and political importance of Annapolis, I could never leave Rock Hall and make Annapolis my home. I could have saved a lot of gasoline and tolls had I lived full time in Annapolis, but Dawn, Larry Jr., Robby, and *Dawn* were all back in Rock Hall. Instead, I viewed Annapolis as my place to cement relationships that could help the fisheries and the fishermen thrive. In the seventies when I became president of the organization, I was certain the Chesapeake Bay could be saved.

It took a great deal of heavy lifting to get our statewide organization off the ground. Maybe if we had all been trained executives it would have been less difficult, but for us fishermen with marginal writing skills, it was not easy. As with all important projects, many hands came together to build our organization. I know I can't list and honor them all in this book. But there were a couple of men who went above and beyond the call of duty to insure that our state organization would survive and grow.

The strongest leader in the early days was a poised, mature black waterman named Captain Rodney Gross from Shady Side, Maryland. He was part of the original group of watermen who met in Annapolis to hammer out the new regulations after the Bruce Rule was inked into law. Rodney was head and shoulders above the rest of us in terms of leadership, maturity, and wisdom and he shared his gifts freely. He taught us how to get along, in spite of our differences, and to look only forward. He was the epitome of gentleness, confidence, and compassion. He insured we stayed calm instead of allowing our anxieties about the oyster crisis to consume us. As the lone black watermen in a leadership role, he artfully made sure every man in Maryland, regardless of his skin color, had a voice in Annapolis.

A few years after Captain Gross retired, a resourceful, driven white waterman named Captain Bob Evans from Shady Side, Maryland stepped in to backfill this critical leadership spot. Bob used his gifts of leadership, decision making, and can-do spirit to advance the Anne Arundel County Watermen's Association. Bob would regularly testify at hearings in Annapolis without complaint for his lost fishing income. In terms of credibility at the microphone, Bob could deliver our messages spot on every time. Had Bob not stepped in to keep the Anne Arundel County Watermen's Association strong behind Rodney, I believe the statewide organization would have imploded.

By providing a constant, professional voice within earshot of Annapolis, Rodney and Bob made it impossible for lawmakers and regulators to ignore or dismiss the watermen of Maryland. Because Rodney was so respected by both the black watermen and the white watermen, we never lost momentum or energy wrestling over racial tensions that were rampant and ugly back in the sixties and early seventies. Rodney always managed to take the high road which inspired us all to follow his lead as best we could.

I personally owe Rodney and Bob a huge debt of gratitude for making me more effective and successful as a president than I would have been without them. They gave me lift and helped me achieve things I wouldn't have attempted alone.

Significantly, Rodney's son, James Rodney Gross, Jr., followed in his father footsteps to serve in leadership roles within Anne Arundel County Watermen's Association and our statewide organization. JR was a magnificent leader and follower. He demonstrated a pure love for his fellow watermen and the Maryland Seafood Industry. He loved to

work on the water. JR was born on August 31, 1967 and passed away on July 9, 2011. Prior to his death, JR wrote down a few of the people who helped him succeed as a waterman and a leader. To his credit, JR modeled wisdom and respect when he listed DNR (Department of Natural Resources) along with his family and friends.

I have truly seen Annapolis at her best. I have forged many life-long friendships there. I have won, and, in some cases, lost some important battles in Annapolis and will always cherish those struggles. For me, Annapolis will always be that all-American town that honored the Maryland watermen for risking much to put great tasting seafood on the table. Without question, Annapolis has always been and will always be a part of my best of times on the Chesapeake Bay.

Annapolis in her prime.
Courtesy of Ann Crane Harlan.

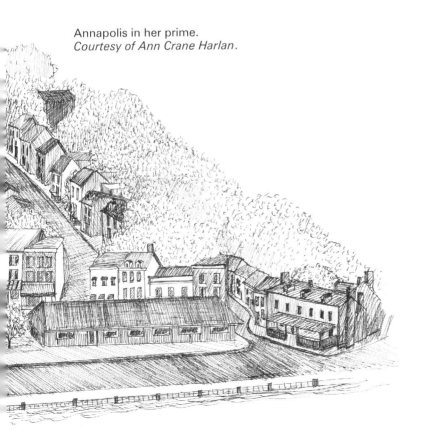

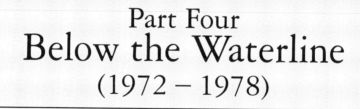

Part Four
Below the Waterline
(1972 – 1978)

Chapter Forty-Four
A Winter Tragedy

I still remember the night my cousin, Kenny, called me to talk about the new "used" boat he found for sale in Virginia. As he dreamed for many years, he found a classic Virginia-built deadrise workboat with a rounded stern and a high bow. For years, he had been searching for just the right boat so he could take his fishing enterprise to the next level. He was simply calling me to see if I had the time to go with him so we could ride back up the Chesapeake Bay together.

Unfortunately, it was late February and I was deep into the winter fishing season. I was also busy keeping the momentum going with our fledgling watermen's association. I couldn't afford two days away from it all and I declined his invitation. He told me he understood and said his father and his son were planning to ride back with him so he would not be alone.

Kenny Stevens was my cousin and a direct descendent of Captain Willie Stevens. Kenny was a fellow waterman too so we were always talking about crabs, oysters, fish, and water quality issues whenever we were together. Beyond work and family connections, Kenny was also my friend and we spent many hours at the rifle range and in the duck blind. We were like brothers, since we both loved Captain Willie and the Chesapeake Bay.

Our relationship tragically ended on March 1, 1972 when his workboat failed to arrive in Rock Hall. None of us knows for sure what happened on that first, and last, trip up the Chesapeake Bay. The workboat was never found so the experts were unable to inspect the engine or hull to determine possible reasons for the loss. When a workboat goes down with no survivors to tell the story, the pain of the loss remains fresh for a long, long time. Losing Kenny left my family upset and unsettled for many years.

Like most watermen, Kenny didn't leave a written float plan with his family or relatives but we all knew what his plan was. Rescue team leaders did share some of the details they discovered during the investigation. We knew he left Virginia waters in the afternoon under clear skies and moderate seas. We knew a freak winter storm raged up the Chesapeake the night he went down. We knew that Kenny's father and his son were found lashed together by the strings of their life jackets. We knew there was no winter ice, but the waters were too cold to survive. We knew Kenny's workboat was traveling alone and that no other fishing vessels (f/v) reported seeing his workboat go down. We knew that no "mayday" was recorded by the United States Coast Guard. We knew Kenny's body was found a few days after his father and son were found.

We'll never know, for sure, what really happened to the three men from this family. As an experienced and strong master scuba diver, Kenny certainly had the skills he needed to save his family if the situation had afforded him more time. Maybe a rogue wave rolled them over. Maybe the engine lost power and his workboat was swamped and was sunk by a following wave. Maybe an old plank (or board) broke loose below the waterline. Maybe they hit an underwater obstruction or smashed into a navigational marker. Maybe they were struck head on or run over by a freighter transiting the Chesapeake Bay. Maybe they were struck by lightning. Only God knows for sure what happened and maybe that's the way it should be; I never know for sure what is best for the family. Either way, the families are devastated.

Personally, I can't imagine the pain Kenny must have endured in the seconds before his death. I have this feeling he lashed his father and his son together so rescuers could find them. If that was the case, what a tragic moment to endure before losing one's own life to cold water. For the surviving friends and family members, it was an absolute nightmare to lose three generations off the same branch in one day. To help the family and the watermen community start the healing process, a special service was held at VFW in Grasonville, Maryland where Tiny, a superb singer, sang as watermen from across Maryland came to pay their last respects to their lost brothers.

As my roles in the two watermen's associations pulled me further and further into the business of commercial fishing, I became an active board member for the Coast Guard Commercial Vessel Safety Advisory Board. This was a nationwide body of forward thinkers who worked together for a number of years to find more and better ways to protect commercial fishermen while at sea. Our focus was in developing practical and affordable equipment that would significantly save lives. I was asked to join the board at a time when excessive human losses were accruing throughout North America. It was one of the most important, and meaningful, opportunities that came my way, simply because I was willing to lead fishermen. For me, it was a good way to honor Kenny's life.

Chapter Forty-Five

Hurricane Agnes

In preparation for the arrival of Hurricane Agnes, I followed the preventative steps I had learned from earlier storms including Hazel, Donna, and Ginger. I canceled all of my booked charters because I knew the waters would be churned up pretty bad and the rockfish would be scattered. Fishing has never been good after a hurricane rips through. Unfortunately, I also had 100 crab pots overboard scattered from Rock Hall all the way to the mouth of the Elk River. I was working on a blue crab migration study with researchers at the time. Though Agnes was a slow-moving storm, I didn't have enough time to get the pots hauled out and still protect my family and workboat. So, I left them in deep water and hoped for the best.

As the storm approached Maryland, it was downgraded to a tropical storm, which from my perspective didn't change anything I was doing. I was taught to plan for the worst, so I secured my home and made sure my extended family was ready to weather Agnes, too. Then, I concentrated my energies on securing *Dawn*. I fueled her up and loaded her with fresh water and food. When I felt the storm's arrival was imminent, I cruised out of the Rock Hall harbor and pushed deep into Swan Creek where I would ride out Hurricane Agnes near (but not too close) to other watermen protecting their boats.

When the full impact of Agnes pressed down on *Dawn*, I knew it was going to be a long, sleepless night. Between the howling winds and the torrential rains pounding against the cabin, there was too much noise to sleep. During peak gusts of rain-filled wind, I could not see anything outside my cabin windows. Once in a while, I opened the back door just to watch and hear the rain dance on the water. The rain was coming down so hard I couldn't even hear my engine idling.

My boat was a rock solid forty-six-foot wooden workboat that had seen plenty of bad weather and angry seas. I was completely confident of this workboat and all of her systems, and so I never doubted her ability to handle this volume of rainwater. Both her automatic and manual bilge pumps worked beautifully throughout the storm.

With nothing to do on *Dawn* except kill time, I sat in my chair and talked back and forth on the CB and VHF radios to my fellow watermen within radio range. As required, we kept the Coast Guard emergency channel (#16) free of watermen chatter especially on this night.

During the storm, watermen up and down the Chesapeake Bay did not seem overly concerned about the high winds, high waves, or even a bad storm surge. Mostly, we were concerned about the volume of rain that was falling for such a long period of time. Another concern voiced was how early in the summer this storm was striking the East Coast. As a lifelong resident of the Eastern Shore, I wondered how much flooding and water damage the homes and businesses would encounter.

All night long, I sat alone in my chair eating crackers and listening to the radio. In the morning, the rains just kept on coming and never let up. In fact, they poured all day long and into the night so I decided to stay right there another night. I felt helpless there in Swan Creek, but it was the only way I knew that *Dawn* would be safe from heavy seas breaking into the harbor. It served as a good test of my mental strength to be alone for thirty-six hours with no control over anything. Other than feelings of total boredom and some loneliness, I didn't have a sense that this storm would change the direction of my life.

Chapter Forty-Six
The Aftermath

The following morning after the storm was over, I eased out of Swan Creek at dawn to return to Rock Hall. A mixture of curiosity and fear had a grip on me, so I wanted to get home and make sure everyone was all right. As I entered the harbor, I immediately could see the physical damage to the marinas and boats had been far less than previous storms. This storm did not push a wall of water and wind a quarter mile into Rock Hall like Hurricane Hazel did in 1954. However, many boats were swamped or sunk at the moorings and there was lots of physical damage to the docks and bulkheads.

My dock had been ripped from its pilings and was unusable, but my pilings were still standing so I was able to dock and tie down *Dawn*. I rushed over to check on my kids, parents, neighbors, and my hunting dogs; and all, fortunately, were fine. Then I began a preliminary scouting mission around town to check on my friends and fellow watermen. When I was certain all human life in Rock Hall was spared, I returned back to *Dawn* to listen to the accounts of other watermen talking over the radio. All telephone lines were inoperable so all reports came by word of mouth.

On the first morning back on dry land, I was relieved the physical damage was less than expected. So far, I felt our community could weather the aftermath. We expected a mild storm surge but nothing extreme. We also knew that lots of rain would be flowing from New York, Pennsylvania, and Northern Maryland down the Susquehanna River and into the Susquehanna Flats. Again, I had seen lots of fresh water before, so I wasn't too worried. Up until 1972, the Chesapeake Bay always had the capacity and strength to bounce back.

After a couple of hours of milling around, I started to pick up wood and debris that had accumulated near my slip. I wasn't really enthused about the first couple of armfuls, but gradually I got my mind around the task at hand and cleaned up my whole area. I piled up the debris next where I normally parked my truck. This small clean-up effort helped me focus on looking forward instead of dwelling on all the property damages. I knew I was fortunate to still have my family, my home, and my workboat after Agnes. I knew there were many families and homes less than a hundred miles away that lost everything. I was reminded how a severe weather event often helps me appreciate what I have been blessed with.

On my second day on dry land, however, I no longer felt optimistic or lucky. As I listened to the radio reports of the devastation still occurring in Pennsylvania and New York, I felt bad for their misfortune. Selfishly, I also started to worry that maybe the full aftermath of Agnes was not fully upon us yet. Reports of widespread flooding of both branches of the upper Susquehanna River concerned me. But what really got my attention were the public safety announcements focused on residents and businesses close to the Holtwood, Safe Harbor, and Conowingo dams.

When I realized the engineers at Conowingo Dam were considering opening most or all of the flood gates, I was alarmed. What a difficult choice to make with no time to gain input or feedback from others. On the one hand, the volume of water backing up behind the dam would surely cause widespread flooding and property damage. Hypothetically, if too much water was held back at one time, maybe even the integrity of the dam would be compromised. On the other hand, prematurely releasing too much water too fast could wipe out towns where the Susquehanna River narrows in places like Port Deposit or Perryville. Had I been the engineer forced with choosing between saving human lives and preserving the American Shad, I would have opened the flood gates, too.

After hearing this trauma over the radio, I felt my worries about the fisheries and the watermen were rather small.

Seeing how fortunate we were (at the moment), I resolved to do my best to get the watermen back on the waters as soon as possible. I convinced myself that "this too shall pass," but my optimism was short lived! When I drove out to the Rock Hall Community Beach to see how the Chesapeake Bay looked at sunrise, I was almost sick to my stomach. Right there before my eyes, my beloved Chesapeake Bay was turning into a brown, murky mess that can best be described as "beef gravy." The waters off Rock Hall were now opaque and were filled with all kinds of floating objects. And this was just the beginning of what was to come.

By my third day on dry land, the full aftermath of Tropical Storm Agnes was clearly visible to anyone who chose to see it. Floating in the water, I saw a little bit of everything. Plastic and glass bottles were everywhere. There were tons of flotsam floating on the surface that was filled with litter. I saw whole trees including their roots floating in the water. I saw many propane, fertilizer, and gasoline tanks in the water. I also saw a workbench, a ladder, a sofa, and dozens of beer coolers. I saw an entire roof, a barn door and a picnic table...

The two objects that really upset me were a dead Holstein cow and an empty chemical drum. For a long time, I couldn't get these images out of my mind. Seeing that chemical drum made me wonder what else was now suspended in the water column. Though I didn't know what to do with this knowledge, I was certain that an unwelcomed toxic chowder full of man-made stuff like animal waste, human waste, chlorine, pesticides, industrial chemicals, gasoline, diesel, and fertilizer was now part of the Maryland's water system. Fortunately, I didn't see a human floating in the Chesapeake Bay, nor did I see any pets floating in the water. I think that would have pushed me to sickness.

Though I knew the waters were brown like gravy, it took me a while to realize that "dirt" had become a major part of the water column. Prior to Agnes, I had always viewed the slight browning of the waters after a storm as "just a little runoff." Truthfully, I never gave it another thought because it never impacted my ability to harvest plenty of seafood. Naively, I allowed the belief that the solution to soil pollution was dilution with fresh water. But looking at the dirty water coloring the entire Chesapeake in front of me, I realized that even soil can be a toxin if it is not stewarded just right. It took me thirty years of living to grasp that plain old dirt was one of America's most precious natural resources just like fresh water, fresh air, and native plants. Ironically, I still didn't believe that dirt was more precious than oil or natural gas. Today, of course, I know that soil, water, and air give life while oil and natural gas make me comfortable.

I became somewhat fixated on the downstream issues associated with dirt, and gradually I developed some new concerns about all this misplaced dirt. First, I feared that tons of silt were released into the Susquehanna River when the floodgates at Conowingo were opened. I feared that the gunk piled up in front of the dam was toxic enough to qualify as a superfund site. Second, I feared that thousands of miles of unprotected shoreline was getting scoured out and the sediment was washed into the Susquehanna Flats and beyond. Third, I feared that hundreds of construction sites were left uncovered and unprotected when the heavy rains pelted down. I envisioned that tons of loose, virgin topsoil were literally hosed off the job site which then poured into the water systems. Fourth, I feared that pesticides freshly sprayed on fields prior to (or at) planting were washed off (or with) the soil particles that were now suspended in the Chesapeake Bay. For sure, all of these four concerns were rooted in practices that were legal and encouraged back in 1972.

It may seem odd to be reading about dirt in a book that promised to talk about water. But, in my opinion, it was actually the volume and toxicity of this soil that caused the most damage to the fisheries of Maryland. Acutely, the dirty water scattered the fish and crabs as they scrambled to find clear water to feed in. It also injected tons of excess nutrients into the water column which triggered massive algal blooms that used up all the oxygen the fish, crabs, clams, eels, oysters, and bay grasses needed to live.

As the waters settled down, however, the sediments sank (fell out) to the bottoms of the river and the Chesapeake Bay, which unfortunately killed thousands of acres of prime submerged aquatic vegetation (SAV). Now covered with silt and sediment, the SAVs were unable to receive the sun rays that they needed to grow through a process called photosynthesis. Tragically, the plants died before they could produce the next year's seeds. Ironically, I didn't have a worry in the world about bay grasses before 1972, and now not a day goes by when I don't wish for their full return.

Relative to the Chesapeake Bay's most important keystone species, Agnes severely upset the delicate ecosystem of the Eastern Oyster. The volumes of fresh water forced into the oysters all over Maryland proved to be toxic. In the lower Bay, salinity levels were lowered for many weeks which reduced the disease pressure but also reduced spat sets. In the upper Bay, the salinity levels were so low that the oysters simply died. In the central part of the Bay, the critical "salt wedge" was moved fifty miles south of its natural range which upset the chemistry of the water and the physiology of the oysters. Little did I know, back in 1972, that this biological event was actually revealing why oyster aquaculture in Maryland is different than Virginia and why seeding and replanting results vary so widely through the Maryland part of the Chesapeake Bay. Sadly, it wasn't until the Oyster Recovery Partnership was established in 1994 that I fully grasped the long-term implications of the salt wedge being forced so far south for so long.

Before Tropical Storm Agnes ravaged the East Coast, I was sure I could remain a good waterman and serve in leadership. I was only thirty-five years old and was doing all right. But once I grasped how extensively Agnes assaulted Maryland with excess volumes of fresh water and dirt, I instinctively knew that the plan for my life was about to change. With all of the problems caused by Agnes, I could no longer fish as much as I wanted to. It was time, ready or not, to lead the Maryland watermen first and allow my needs as a waterman to default to second place. With this shift in my life's plan, I diverted my time and financial resources away from myself and my family – a decision I periodically regret as I age in Rock Hall in hard economic times. One day, I hope my family understands why I made this life-altering choice after Agnes hit Maryland.

From a prophetic perspective, Hurricane Agnes gave the watermen from my generation a unique look into the future. What we thought was a "once in a lifetime" water quality crisis that would pass turned out to be a real indicator of what was to come. In 2012, our water quality problems are similar to what we encountered in 1972, only worse. Who among us would have ever believed that the muddy waters that caused hardy watermen to cry in 1972 would become our daily reality in 2012? Personally, I was not able to see that far forward in 1972.

Today, of course, our fisheries are more fragile and the vulnerability of the Chesapeake Bay is far greater. For that reason alone, I am no longer satisfied with the goal of saving the Chesapeake Bay "as is" because it will not survive. Now, we have to go the extra mile and restore the waters of Maryland back to prime. It is important to use what we have learned in the past forty years so the fish and the fishermen can survive the next tropical storm like Agnes. Perhaps the passing of the 40th anniversary of Agnes will usher in a new level of commitment, urgency, and accountability. It's possible.

Chapter Forty-Seven
A Rock and a Hard Place

Because of the unique timing of Hurricane Agnes, several fisheries were not acutely damaged by the storm. The shad season had just closed. The oyster season was still three months away from starting, though it was already in big trouble before Agnes. The rockfish season remained open for the pound netters, charter fishermen, and recreational fishermen, though the fish scattered like wildfire trying to find enough baitfish to survive. The entire blue crab fishery (basket, peeler, soft) also stalled out for about a month while the waters settled down and cleared up. The crab season was never officially closed though the trot-liners and crab-potters dealt with a big harvest drop off and all sorts of gear loss.

In the short run, the first fishery to suffer immediate consequences was the soft shell clam market. Natural resource managers and regulators were concerned about the clam's ability to survive in the dirty water. They knew as key filter feeders, this species would be at risk and would need time to recover from the storm. Unfortunately, most of the prime soft clam bars were covered with silt and were exposed to levels of solids beyond what their internal systems could handle.

The fishery managers within the Department of Natural Resources had a tough decision to make as to whether the clams were healthy enough to survive the sediment and toxins released by Agnes. It was a hard call, I'm sure, because every clam bar in Maryland was affected differently by Agnes depending on its location, salinity, and exposure to pollutants. Afforded little time to mull over the issues, they really had few options to choose from. Clearly, their safest move was to install a harvesting moratorium against the small number of active clammers and keep the bars closed until the clams fully recovered. They knew the Maryland clammers would pitch a fit but they could rightfully argue that they were taking a conservative approach so there would be plenty of clams to harvest in the future. Establishing harvesting restrictions based on fishery stocks and health was a primary role in their department and they had decades of precedent to compare with.

The much harder call for the Maryland Government was the decision facing the Department of Health. Naturally, they too were concerned about the health of the clams for estuarial reasons. But, their primary concern related to human health risks associated with eating raw clams contaminated from raw sewage releases. It's hard to even write this on paper, but as a result of Hurricane Agnes overpowering our waste-handling systems in Maryland, Pennsylvania, and New York, millions of gallons of raw human sewage were released into the Chesapeake Bay. Our Chesapeake Bay, known to millions as a national treasure, was awash with human feces, urine, and prescription drugs because our waste-handling systems had not kept pace with our human population growth.

So the Health Department had a real human health risk to manage without causing unfair or inappropriate harm to user groups like watermen and recreational fishermen. To be fair, these professionals were terrified that an unsuspecting seafood consumer would inadvertently eat a raw clam contaminated by the presence of raw sewage and get what my mother called "food poisoning." Historically, there have been significant cases of human sickness and death from eating clams contaminated with human sewage.

Without question, the Health Department of Maryland had a time-sensitive decision to make and they had to be right the first time. Again, the safe move for this department was to close down the clam fishery and keep clammers away until the clams were tested to be safe for human consumption. Had I been the executive responsible to protect the health of humans, I would have shut down the shellfish industry until the bacterial testing proved the clams were safe. And that is exactly what they did. To protect human health and to preserve the image and culture of the Maryland Seafood Industry, an indefinite moratorium was placed on harvesting all shellfish in Maryland until further notice.

But I wasn't responsible for making that particular decision. Rather, I was in charge of protecting the image and markets of the Maryland Seafood Industry which necessarily meant I also wanted our seafood consumers to eat only healthy, safe clams. So, this well-intended shellfish moratorium placed me between a rock and a hard place. On the one hand, I did not want any one in America getting sick by eating one contaminated clam from the State of Maryland. On the other hand, I did not want perfectly healthy clams to be left unharvested by Maryland clammers while watermen from other states filled our orders. Furthermore, I was totally disgusted with the idea that our waste management systems in America legally allowed human wastes to reach the Chesapeake Bay at all.

When word spread among the active clammers that an indefinite shellfish moratorium was in place, I was bombarded with a stream of hard questions that required fast but true answers. How long will the moratorium last? What bacterial count levels must be achieved before the moratorium is lifted? Which department has trumping power relative to reopening the clam bars? Are Virginia clammers under a moratorium too? Did the Health Department seek your recommendation on this moratorium? Will we lose our preferred status as a reliable supplier of clams to New England? In short, the full-time clammers were asking their new board at the statewide organization what we were going to do to get the moratorium lifted.

These were all good questions, and I now realized that my grace period as an incoming president had come to an end. It was my time to help these clammers get answers and find some hope at the other end of the moratorium. Though I didn't own a clam rig at the time, I knew over 300 watermen had invested a hunk of money to gear up their workboats to only clam.

As a first step, I encouraged each board member (who were mostly county leaders) to speak directly with their respective clammers to get ideas. Later in the same week, the board convened in Annapolis to triage our few options and create a strategy to preserve some part of the 1972 clam fishery.

Our strategy was to make sure that no matter what, we planned to get some portion of the Maryland clam fishery open in 1972 so we could preserve our spot in the distribution channel. We agreed, in principle, that human health would not be compromised nor would we do anything to harm the very strong branding of our Maryland clams.

With this simple strategy to guide us, we implemented three action steps to achieve our objectives. We hired an attorney to help us understand the finer print in Maryland's moratorium laws. Based on his interpretation, a harvesting moratorium was not appropriate without testing the clams and the waters. Armed with a better understanding of the law, we met with the Health Department, DNR, and a few pro-watermen lawmakers to explain our view. The fact that we hired an attorney in spite of our meager financial strength spoke volumes about our commitment to the clammers.

Next, we provided practical amendment language to the recently issued shellfish moratorium. Fundamentally, we wanted to protect human health and protect the strong image of the Maryland clam fishery. We did not want to skirmish with DNR over this point, nor did we want to be at odds with the critical work of the Health Department. What we wanted was to keep the southern part of the Chesapeake Bay open unless testing proved the clams to be unsafe. It made no sense to us that a waterman in Crisfield, Maryland was under an indefinite moratorium while another waterman a few miles away in Marsh Market Virginia could keep harvesting clams. We also didn't believe a clam bed near Fishing Creek (Dorchester County) would be as adversely affected by Agnes as a clam bar off Kent Island (Queen Anne's County).

Last, we offered the use of our workboats to transport all technicians and scientists directly to the clam bars all over Maryland. We wanted to make it easy and fast for the experts to access the bars to take their readings. In the process, we made many trips for the state of Maryland which enabled us to form lasting relationships that increased the trust level between the watermen and Annapolis.

There were a lot of hurt feelings over the issue, but ultimately the Departments of Health and Natural Resources agreed to reopen the clam bars in the southern part of the Chesapeake Bay until bacterial counts tested by experts deemed the clam bars to be unsafe. We were not able to get the shellfish moratorium lifted for the entire Chesapeake Bay – nor did we want to. All we wanted was to keep a slice of the Maryland clamming fishery open so our markets would remain viable and strong for the years ahead.

One by one, the clam bars throughout the rest of Maryland were opened based on testing principles. Science, not emotion and fear, was now protecting the consumer from harm and all the watermen were satisfied that our amended process was an improvement over an indefinite shellfish moratorium. Because we were able to help the southern watermen hang on, our statewide trade organization gained some credibility among watermen who previously saw no value or purpose in working together. To some degree, we also improved our public image because we demonstrated maturity, balance, and backbone.

In Annapolis, we sent a clear message that the watermen of Maryland refused to be ignored or marginalized for any reason. In our own way, our board of directors endured our second crisis (first being Agnes) and came through for the clammers. I was pleased that some clamming income was still being infused into the counties that were hit hardest by Dermo and MSX. Mostly, I was proud of the watermen who held their heads up high and focused on creating solutions instead of blaming others or Agnes for their losses. I respected the maturity they demonstrated and believe they helped me learn to be a more effective president.

Chapter Forty-Eight
The Maryland
Watermen's Association

The oyster collapse in the late sixties created a reason for the watermen of Maryland to work together. But Hurricane Agnes provided the final proof that watermen were unable to stand alone and still be heard in Annapolis. Fortunately, the foundation for a statewide association of watermen was well under way when Agnes attacked Maryland in 1972. We weren't incorporated and established, but the vision was already set and the board members and county leaders were all in place and functioning. After more than three years of heavy lifting, the Maryland Watermen's Association was incorporated in 1973. From the start, we intended our organization to remain dedicated to the interests of all who derive beauty and benefit from Maryland waters. From the beginning, we called ourselves MWA.

Starting a trade association from the ground up was one thing, but successfully operating and leading a membership-driven organization was something else. As simple fishermen, we had plenty of backbone and bite to get MWA started, but we did not have the organizational and leadership skills to make it grow. Even with a solid dream and a dedicated board of directors, we didn't have the skills to take us to the next level. As president, I was well prepared to serve as the spokesperson on fishery issues, but I was not trained to run a trade organization and still work full time as a waterman.

To help us grow, we hired a special man named Les Belcher who proved vital in getting us organized, operational, and moving forward. From day one, Les grasped our vision and helped us develop strategies we could implement on a practical level. He helped us refine our talking points so we could speak clearly to our members around the state. Equally important to MWA, Les helped us reach the political, regulatory, and environmental leaders who would play a role in our future. Les created *The Watermen's Gazette* which became our primary method for getting information to all MWA members. He also spearheaded the creation of The East Coast Fishermen's Expo which has run without interruption for over thirty seven years. Additionally,

Les managed the office and staff superbly, which gave each staff member an ongoing place to seek direction and encouragement.

Recognizing the challenges of keeping remote watermen current and connected, Les created a platform within *The Watermen's Gazette* called "The Podium." "The Podium" was my place to share my ideas, thoughts, and concerns to the people. Here, I could communicate hard and sometimes problematic thoughts to others without being diluted or contorted by the media or our critics. Over the years, "The Podium" has helped watermen understand our issues at a deeper level. Naturally, it has also created some angst and tension between me and a handful of people who truly dislike watermen in general and me in particular.

With Les inside and a strong board by my side, I found my stride as the MWA president working on the outside. I could use my strengths and my energy to initiate and advance relevant dialogues with leaders in Annapolis. Through our monthly meetings, I was able to provide strategic guidance to our board members and remain listed as the point person for rockfish and shad fishery issues. I regularly testified at hearings and public forums to get our messages delivered and entered into the record.

Though less pleasant, I served as the MWA "lightning rod" and was responsible for delivering our more intense messages as deemed appropriate by our board. In this role, I was moved to go toe to toe with individuals and organizations that had their crosshairs affixed on MWA. Long ago, my father taught me not to be distracted by the noise created by critics. His counsel was to "mend my ways" if the critics were right, and to forget them if the critics were wrong. Ironically, I have become close friends with many men and women who initially attacked MWA (and therefore me) over some fishery issues or diverging viewpoints.

Finding Les Belcher was a blessing for MWA and me. MWA would never have survived the early years if he had not been there to give us a foundation and road map to follow. He was a gifted, high-level executive who worked amongst us so MWA could survive. We knew from the beginning that his skills and experience were suited for a larger, more progressive purpose, so we used his expertise as long as it was available. To his credit, Les stayed on with MWA so we wouldn't backslide without him and fall apart.

With a foundation to hold us and a purpose big enough to sustain us, we created a physical presence in Annapolis which increased our credibility and our effectiveness. Finally, we didn't have to hold our board meetings in restaurants or standing around the tailgate of my pickup truck. With some critical mass to prop us up, we were able to attract and hire the right staff members who knew how to deliver quality benefits and services to our members. As a result, our membership bloomed.

Like many not-for-profit trade organizations, we struggled daily with growing pains and the hard work of serving the diverse needs of our members. Because we initially set our membership dues low to encourage membership, we never had enough funds to promote our seafood, finance large initiatives, or pay our staff enough. In fact, MWA survived the lean years because of the generosity and enthusiasm of a few watermen and their wives who sacrificed much of their time to fundraise for MWA. Only God knows how many fish, crabs, clams, and oysters these families cooked to keep MWA alive. Because MWA had no major sponsors or donors to keep us flush with cash, we regularly struggled financially. In hindsight, we should have charged much higher dues in the seventies when our profits were good and we should have been more fiscally tough on the members who were chronically slow to pay.

With Les no longer driving the operation on the inside, my functional role shifted to be more like a general manager. I continued to serve as spokesperson for the shad and rockfish fisheries, while working myself to the bone on my boat. At first, I thrived on the challenge of serving as a general manager, president, and full-time waterman. I liked being in the thick of things. I felt productive and effective since I had control over the major parts of corporate MWA. And I truly loved the work and found the interaction with people to be priceless.

But the personal cost of serving in this high-flying role started to burn me out. With my home and my boat in Rock Hall and my office in Annapolis, I was pulled in many directions and failed at times to deliver quality work or be there for my board members. Even maintaining an apartment in Annapolis didn't improve my effectiveness. I struggled everyday to keep my balance as I tried to fish, lead watermen, and still be there for my children. The fact that I also had an active social life simply made a bad situation worse.

Increasingly, I resented that I was losing many prime fishing days so I could serve the Maryland Watermen's Association for free. Because *Dawn's* daily income stream was inconsistent, I had trouble attracting quality crewmembers and back-up captains. By the late seventies, I informed the board of directors of my plan to resign so I could get back on the water to fish full time. I confided that I had over-invested my own personal energy and equity to get MWA started and I was now exhausted. I told them it was time, probably past time, for another waterman from Maryland to take the lead spot at MWA. In a moment of pure candor, I also told them that I was tired of enduring the divisive behaviors of a few members who used the platform of MWA to grandstand for their own gain. One of my regrets as president was my inability to get these bright but highly corrosive men to put their energy to good use at MWA (instead of against us).

The board rejected my plan to resign. Instead, they insisted that I receive a small stipend to offset some of my lost fishing income. Their logic was that the shad fishery, my passion, was in peril and that my experience and voice was needed on that issue without interruption. They also knew, as did I, that no other waterman was willing to sacrifice their prime fishing income to serve as the next MWA president. Driven purely by a sense of obligation to my board members, I agreed to stay on until the shad fishery improved or until the board found a better leader to guide MWA into the 1980s. Right or wrong, I was unable to walk away from the loyal board and staff members who had given so much to get MWA off the ground. Regretfully, I caused undue hardship and struggle for my family by agreeing to stay on as president.

To help me be more effective, the board empowered me to find and then hire Betty Duty to run my office, write grants, and drive our fundraising efforts. Gifted with amazing business development and relationship skills, Betty transformed our fledgling organization into a credible, professional force. Without the day-to-day responsibilities for running the operations at MWA, I was once again free to either fight for or take a hit for MWA.

Since MWA never had a war chest of funds to outspend high-priced lobbyists, we relied on ourselves and our skills to make things happen in Annapolis. By day, MWA and its respective county associations worked hard to defend against unfair or mean attacks against the fisheries and the watermen. After all, it was a daily chore (like pumping out the bilge on *Dawn*) to spend time and money to defend against attacks from our critics. Like a persistent mosquito that buzzes around the cabin while a waterman tries to get a few hours of sleep, we always had to remain vigilant and aggressive to ward off nuisance attacks. No matter what, we always had to maintain our daily balance so we could stay in the fight for the watermen.

By night and on weekends, almost all MWA board members and county leaders would work hard to advance our cause while the lobbyists rested in their plush hotel rooms. Driven by our passion to serve watermen, we cultivated deep relationships with lawmakers, companies, trade organizations, regulators, and even a few moderate environmentalists. Over dinner and drinks, we told them what we wanted and what we needed. We were pretty transparent with our intent.

We also listened to what their constituencies and customers needed so we could find the common ground between both parties. We worked hard to avoid getting backed into a corner where "a line in the sand would be drawn." As a small organization with little money, we knew that forcing our views on leaders too many times would ultimately harm all watermen. We always tried to remember that a handful of powerful people were lurking in the shadows whose purpose was to eliminate the watermen of Maryland.

Often, I would endure severe pushback and even rejection during the day from leaders while they were on stage in front of their employees and the public. But when the crowds were gone, those same leaders and I would talk one on one about the same issues and often we were able to solve the problems. I understood they had obligations and desires of their own, so I tried not to push them too hard in public. But in private, I expected them to shoot me straight and I offered the same. For this reason, I was usually careful about who and when I used rough words in public venues. It was never my first choice to intentionally cause a firestorm of attention. I knew, more often than not, that aggressive words from MWA (or me) would not be presented to the public in a favorable light.

Though I worked many hours for MWA during the day, most of my best results were generated after hours. Several high profile leaders in Annapolis took me under their wing, told me who to look out for, and invited me to meetings that I couldn't possibly get into using my own credentials or MWA funds. They knew I didn't have money to run with the big dogs, but they invited me to come along with them as their guest.

I wondered, at times, why these leaders would help me and the MWA when they didn't have to. The reason they supported us, I believe, was because we showed up every day, worked hard and passionately believed in our cause. I believe they viewed us as people and not just another grouping of voters to win (or buy) them over. Because they spent time getting to know us, they genuinely liked us in spite of our flaws.

I will always cherish the time of my life while the board members, staff, and I built the Maryland Watermen's Association. I am proud it has endured the test of time. Even now, in 2012, I still wonder what might have become of the watermen if the Maryland Watermen's Association and it's ancillary working groups had never been created.

Maryland Watermen's Association logo. *Courtesy of Ann Crane Harlan*.

Chapter Forty-Nine
The Water's Edge

In 1973, United States Senator Charles McCurdy "Mac" Mathias traveled extensively through the Chesapeake Bay watershed. He wanted real answers to hard questions that his constituency was demanding him to solve, but he didn't want the information about the Chesapeake Bay filtered by others. Apparently, he was not confident he was receiving a holistic picture from his own team.

As he made his way around the watershed visiting people from all kinds of backgrounds and experiences, he came to visit me in Rock Hall. Senator Mathias boarded *Dawn* where we began a frank discussion that took several hours. As the host, I served him my traditional meal of cheese crackers and a soda so he would feel welcome. Together, we shared an unscripted, unrecorded private discussion between one lawmaker and one waterman. I told him how the water quality had changed since I first observed it in the early forties. I also told him all the major issues that fellow watermen from across the state had shared with me as the MWA president. Surprisingly, he did not interrupt me nor did he get defensive when I told him less than flattering truths about his (and my) beloved state of Maryland. He did ask me questions to further his understanding, but did not try to reverse or change my beliefs.

He asked me why these problems identified by watermen had not been solved before now. Because he asked this important and relevant question, I chose to answer him fully without sugarcoating my response. I explained how the views of watermen are frequently discounted and even dismissed in Annapolis because we collectively lack scientific and educational credentials. I told him that much of our practical wisdom and experience was rarely considered by decision makers in Annapolis.

I went on to explain, and admit, that most watermen were different than the folks we were trying to work with in Annapolis. Most watermen were not raised in families of great wealth or privilege. Most watermen were hard working, blue-collar-type entrepreneurs who were simply trying to live out their American dream. If a waterman was wealthy, it was only because he had worked hard all of his life and managed to retain his earnings by living within his means like Uncle Josh. Though Senator Mathias knew much of this already, it was refreshing to share these facts about watermen with him. It helped him understand why watermen are sometimes left off the invitation list when key discussions are being held about the Chesapeake Bay.

To give him a true and balanced perspective on this issue, I did acknowledge that a portion of our perception problem was of our own making. Our visibly successful harvesting results in the 50s and 60s gave the general public an impression that watermen were greedy takers of the sea. When a tourist standing on the bridge at Knapps Narrows sees a workboat so loaded down with oysters that it looks like she might sink, the impression gets imprinted that watermen are pretty aggressive.

Our perception problems were sometimes aggravated by opinion columns written by skilled, but also biased, writers in local, state, and national newspapers. Particularly back in the seventies, watermen were unprepared to talk wisely to the media. Instead of talking with their heads, many watermen would speak from their hearts about an issue. Speaking directly into a microphone, a tape recorder, or a video camera, watermen spoke emotionally and simply about their concerns. Sometimes, the public would see only the rough side of the watermen and not see their wisdom, compassion, or common sense. I must admit that I, too, as president of MWA, was often too direct and too intense about the issues to be effectively heard by leaders in Annapolis or understood by the general public.

After I answered his questions as best I could, Senator Mathias thanked me for my candor and started to share what he had learned so far. He revealed that Maryland's water quality problems were serious. He explained his views on point-source problems including storm water drainage, sewage treatment plants, and permitted releases of toxins. He explained why he was planning to demonstrate, through a major research study, how poor water quality was the real problem affecting the fisheries.

He urged me to be patient and to not lose faith. He told me that he would call me when the report and the recommendations were complete. He reminded me how progress in Annapolis and Washington, D.C. takes time, and periodic setbacks and diversions were part of the process. He cautioned me to get my house (MWA) in order and urged me to make sure a few rogue watermen didn't spoil the image of the fleet.

He stepped off my boat and returned to Washington, D.C. to fight for a clean, clear Chesapeake Bay. The Senator's efforts were widely reported by the media, so it was easy to track his progress and his regressions as he pursued this research project with vigor and maturity. It was fascinating, and inspiring, to watch this great man work inside both beltways and in Annapolis to make things happen. I watched him break down political barriers and personal agendas of others so he could get the research project approved and funded.

Many times, I watched him stick his neck out politically to help save the Bay. I watched a few of his "friends" support him privately, but crush him in public. More frequently though, I watched a number of leaders support him in public but then judge his intent and approach him harshly when away from the microphone. By watching this particular senator, I learned the difference between feel-good politics and clean, clear policy that often leads to lasting, positive change. From him, I learned to look carefully at the voting records of a lawmaker instead of getting swept up in the charismatic rhetoric. By watching him work, I learned that a strategy or tactic was not going to accomplish very much if there was no money or laws attached to it. I learned that Senator Mathias had an enduring optimism about nature and his fellow man that he reflected in his visions about the Chesapeake Bay. Sadly, I watched him endure massive amounts of criticism for choosing to spend taxpayer dollars on research instead of pouring it into more entitlement programs. In my opinion, Senator Mathias was good for Maryland and for America.

After several years, I received a direct call from Senator Mathias. He informed me of the report and that the recommendations were done and that the watermen of Maryland were spot on with their assessment. He was shocked how simple watermen like me could see the problems of the Chesapeake Bay so clearly. He asked me how we knew so much about the waters of Maryland without doing all the research. I told him how we see the day-to-day changes right at the water's edge. We detect subtle changes by observing the fisheries and the waters each day. I admitted that there was nothing magical or complicated about what we know. To cement my point, I told him that if a waterman can't read the waters, then he will fail as a commercial fisherman.

With this research project complete, all of the stakeholders and key decision makers had credible proof that the Chesapeake Bay was in trouble. This proof gave a much-needed jolt of awareness and focus to the plight of the Chesapeake. All sorts of special interest groups fell into line behind the Senator now that the project was deemed a worthy endeavor. Years later, when Governor Harry Hughes was elected to office, in 1979, he embraced the study as written instead of commissioning more research in his own name. As Governor, Hughes effectively used his authority and leadership skills to advance the momentum created by Senator Mathias. He made sure that practical actions were implemented at the local level so water quality could really be improved.

Without Senator Mathias, I believe we could have lost the fisheries of the Chesapeake Bay by 1980. Today, I fear our political leaders don't even realize they have been entrusted with the same powers to improve Maryland waters just as Senator Mathias once had. I trust Maryland history will record Senator Charles McCurdy "Mac" Mathias as one of the best stewards of Maryland's natural resources. He gave much of himself so that all future users and stakeholders of the Chesapeake Bay, including the watermen, could still have a bay from which to derive beauty and bounty.

Chapter Fifty
The Last Oyster

If Senator Mathias was willing to go to battle in Annapolis and Washington to clean up the Chesapeake Bay, then I knew it was only right for me to follow his counsel and get the MWA in order. Admittedly, there were a number of watermen behaviors that were tarnishing our image in small and large ways and I did proceed to work on some of them.

In towns with deep harbors liked Annapolis, Solomons, and Rock Hall, watermen like to congregate in bars and restaurants after work to talk, drink, and sometimes fight. This alone complicated our relationship with the public. But we also irritated the public by making lots of noise in the morning, some of which was avoidable. Even the way some watermen named their boats caused the public to frown at us at times. As the leader of MWA, I didn't attempt to clean up this part of my house because I knew it would be harder to fix than herding cats. Truthfully, I had my own rough edge.

Fortunately, "poaching" as has been experienced in the past few years in Maryland, was not a real concern of mine in the seventies. There were plenty of fish, no daily limits on most species, and the seasons were long. There was no reason or desire for a waterman to go outside of the law since most fisheries were doing great at that time. In addition, serial poachers were easily caught by the natural resources police if the brotherhood of watermen didn't stop them first. I didn't spend much time on this issue since it represented a small fraction of the total harvests for most species. In hindsight, perhaps I should have spent more time on this issue.

Where I did spend time my time and my energy was in dealing with the thorny problem of overfishing (a.k.a. overharvesting). For as long as watermen have worked the Chesapeake Bay, we periodically are pigeon-holed as greedy takers of the sea. Certainly, there have been times when this has been true, though many times it is just legend or myth being repeated in new circles. Without being too defensive or offensive with my words, I hope to share a couple of points with my readers about the issue of overfishing. To make my points as clear as I can, I'll refer only to the oyster fishery.

Watermen harvest oysters to make money. They invest in many types of gear and take significant risks to make that money. When oysters are plentiful and operating expenses are low, they can make good money if the dockside price is good. If the harvest is poor, operating expenses are high and the price is low, it can be very hard to make a profit. A hand tonger will work his shoulders to the point of pain to catch his limit. But when an oyster bar has been fully harvested of legal oysters, he will not stay on the bar to find the last legal oyster. If he can't catch enough oysters to cover his break-even point and make a profit, he will leave the bar. If he can't find another bar nearby, he will move to a new area. If there are no productive bars nearby, he will stop oystering completely. For years, the oysters left behind were sufficient to restock the ones that were harvested by the watermen.

The "homework" I have wrestled with for nearly forty years has to do with regulatory compliance. Our primary role, as I see it, is to stay within the boundaries set by the Department of Natural Resources. Once the fishery managers receive approval on their fishery regulations (commercial and recreational), then it is our collective job as watermen to stay within the limits, times, seasons, and designated fishing grounds so they can keep the overall fishery from being overharvested.

When we exceed the regulations dictated by DNR, then we are contributing to the overfishing of a species. So, the primary role of the MWA board was to convince our members, one by one, that fishing "outside of the lines" hurts not only the fish, but also the fishermen. I recognize and dislike the fact that increased regulations usually means more costs and less fish, but it is a better alternative than to be denied access to the fishery altogether. Obviously, I am often "twixt and between" on this issue because I know the regulators are only trying to sustain the fisheries and I know the watermen only want to make a living. Ironically, I receive more heat and resentment from my own members on this point than I do from all other issues combined. Their charge against me, as their leader, is that "I'm giving in to the regulators and not looking out for the watermen." In my defense, I feel like I am looking out for the watermen – all watermen.

Relative to this overfishing issue, my job is not near as tough as the role of the regulators and fishery managers. Using the best scientific instruments available to them, they are required to determine a finite population count for each species (by sex, age, and health) that either lives or migrates into Maryland waters. Without the ability to see what they are counting, they must come up with a baseline target so they can properly establish harvesting targets for commercial fishermen. Like the rest of us, they have no capacity to see into the future, so they are unable to factor climate, water quality, and other factors that can dramatically impact each fishery. I'm sure it is hard to calculate what a fishery response will be to both the laws of nature and needs of man.

The most important point I hope to make here is that projecting fishery numbers is not a perfect science. Even when the fisheries are robust and thriving, they are hard to manage properly. Over time, I have learned that good science is good for the watermen. In fact, without it, I don't believe watermen can stay in business. The system works best when the scientists and the waterman exchange their observations and knowledge freely and then select the best path based on the information we have at the time. The system is least effective when a user group or stakeholder has too much influence and overrides the science. When politics trumps science, everyone loses a lot.

I will continue to encourage all watermen to stay within the laws established in Annapolis. I will also encourage us to clean out our own bad apples so quality watermen can keep harvesting crabs, fish, and oysters for the Maryland seafood lovers. Naively, I'm hoping in return that the leaders who arbitrarily use the term "overfishing" will only use it when it is warranted and true.

A hand-tonger on Eastern Bay. *Courtesy of Ann Crane Harlan.*

Chapter Fifty-One
Below the Waterline

From time to time, research organizations would reach out to MWA to advance their projects. With approval from the MWA board, Georgy Rail, Perry Como, and I were commissioned to use *Stacy*, *Sandy C* and *Dawn* to test alternative substrates to serve as cultch for baby oysters. (For the curious, Perry Como was the nickname of the Crisfield watermen helping on the project. He picked up the nickname from his baseball coach as a child. For the life of me, I can't remember his real name. In our culture, watermen often "earn" a nickname early in life and often it follows them for life.)

The goal of the project was to see if discarded tires could serve as a good substrate to attract and hold baby oysters (called spat). To accomplish this research in deep, rough waters, we built heavy racks capable of holding heavy tires suspended in the water column. We tested two prime oyster breeding spots in the Hooper Straits (Dorchester County) and a third one in the Potomac River (St. Mary's County). After almost a year of testing, we learned that rubber does not attract or hold baby oysters though it does attract barnacles and moss. The experiment was a bust and I was disappointed that we couldn't solve part of the oyster crisis by finding a use for the tires.

Even though the research project was a bust, we still needed to go out in late winter and recover those spat racks. It was now early April and all three workboats were fully loaded with the testing gear we used to conduct the experiment. The equipment was heavy and bulky and we used our oyster booms to hoist the racks on and off our boats. Fortunately, we were paid a small stipend for our troubles so we didn't lose any money by helping out with the research. But now we were ready to go back home and get our workboats ready to run crab pots all summer.

Since my boat was already fully loaded, I eased *Dawn* up to full power so I could get there ahead of *Stacy* and *Sandy C*. As project leader, I needed to get to our destination first so I could make sure the trucks were staged and ready to take these spat racks to the landfill (this was before recycling was logistically feasible). Just to be sure, I radioed ahead to make sure someone would be at the dock to meet us. I had a strong wind pushing down on me from behind and there was no ice on the water.

With white caps all around me and just a little bit of sunlight left, I ran her at full speed all the way into the Potomac River. One by one, I passed the lighted navigational markers which guided me into the river. My visibility was good but I was having trouble finding the next marker in the sequence. I could see one way ahead, but not the one I was looking for. Suddenly, *Dawn* struck a submerged day marker right below the waterline. In a split second, the hull of *Dawn* was pierced by the steel shaft of the day marker and it impaled her like a toothpick going through a scallop.

The force of the crash shoved me up against my steering wheel and my front window. By the time I regained my balance, cold water was pouring into the cabin. I grabbed the radio mic and told Georgy, "Come get me; I'm sunk," and then rushed out of the cabin door. I instantly climbed up the mast of my oyster rig and clung to it like a child for thirty minutes. Luckily, Georgy heard my call for help and came to me as quickly as possible. Because of the way the water filled in the cabin, I didn't have time to don my lifejacket or deploy my life raft.

Soaking wet and cold as the dickens, Georgy plucked me off the mast and got me into the cabin. My arm strength was almost gone and my skin was as cold as ice. But, I peeled off my wet clothes to get that cold water off my skin. I put on every piece of clothing Georgy had in his cabin, wrapped myself in blankets and got as close to the heater as possible without burning my skin. I was only alive because of Georgy's alertness and responsiveness to my radio call. In icy cold waters, seconds matter.

That night, *Dawn* spent the night out in the cold water alone. I hated to leave my boat unattended and unsecured there in the channel but it was too dark and too rough for a salvage crew to work safely. I should have gone to the hospital to make sure I was not losing body temperature due to hypothermia. But, full of pride, I stayed in a local hotel to wait for daylight and calmer seas to refloat *Dawn*. That evening, my bones and my joints ached from my exposure to the cold water and cold night air.

The next day, a commercial diver was on site to help me free *Dawn* from the underwater obstruction. He was a highly experienced diver and he used an underwater torch to cut the steel beam that was holding *Dawn*. Once the steel was cut away, the salvage crew floated *Dawn* by inserting flat inner tubes inside her hull and then filling them with compressed air. Once afloat, she was placed in a loose sling and slowly hauled back to St. Mary's County where she was repaired. Mr. Harry White, a first class Rock Hall boat builder, came down with his tools to make *Dawn* right.

As it turns out, this "little" experiment cost me a small fortune. But, had I not been commissioned to do this work, I would have surely sunk anyway. Ironically, while I nearly froze to death in the Potomac River, three of my closest fishing friends encountered some bad luck of their own. While tied up at the Betterton Landing that same spring, a freak storm ripped through northern Kent County and swamped the workboats of Captains Cope Hubbard, Ronnie Fithian, and Buffalo Strong at the public landing. Had I not been with Georgy and Perry Como on the Potomac, I would have probably sunk right alongside my friends on the Sassafras River.

Chapter Fifty-Two
Equal Partners

With the Maryland oyster fishery in trouble, most marketing and tourism resources in Maryland were into the blue crab brand. Through excellent seafood marketing and some natural assistance from Mother Nature, the widely abundant, low-cost steamed crab market evolved in a big way. Now, independent restaurants all over the East Coast were selling large quantities of freshly steamed crabs along with their traditional menu items made with lump crab meat or soft crabs. Maryland (and certainly Virginia) watermen were now catching millions of hard crabs to supply a seemingly unstoppable demand for the sweet, white meat. The Maryland blue crab fishery became the growth market for watermen and seafood buyers.

By 1974, my wife, Ginny, and I created and ran a thriving blue crab enterprise in Rock Hall. Though we had vastly different roles, we were equal partners in every way. Our dream was for me to harvest hard crabs and peelers on *Dawn* while Ginny ran the profitable soft crab business in the space next to our boat slip. Our physical assets included *Dawn*, 700 crab pots, a dozen sloughing tanks, a pickup truck, and an old milk truck. To the partnership, Ginny brought patience, an even temper, multi-tasking skills, good customer relations, and the commitment to be the primary care giver to our children. To the enterprise, I brought the ability to catch many hard crabs and a good understanding of how the basket trade and soft shell business could work in harmony and be profitable.

By the mid seventies, water quality on the Chesapeake Bay was showing obvious signs of decline but the hardy blue crab fishery remained strong. At the time, the blue crab fishery looked resilient as the crabs seemed to be reproducing at a sustainable and healthy rate. Like me, many watermen ramped up their business to catch hard crab (instead of oysters) as their "bread and butter" fishery.

To thrive in this crowded, competitive market, Ginny and I worked hard to deliver an excellent soft shell crab to our customers. On a continuous basis, from late April through August, Ginny would carefully check every sloughing tank every few hours to remove the freshly molted crabs and discard the old "sloughs" (shells) and dead ones. As soon as the crabs were out of the water, she would cool them down immediately to stop the hardening process. If the soft crabs were headed for the fresh market, she would grade them by size, wrap them in wet newspaper and place them in cold storage until they were sold later that day. If the soft crab was headed for the freezer, then she would cut out the eyes and mouthparts, tear out the "dead men" (lungs) before they were placed in the freezer.

My role was to harvest hard crabs by running a long set of crab pots from Turkey Point to Bloody Point on the east and west sides of the Chesapeake Bay. Working before dawn till late in the afternoon, my crewmembers and I fished hundreds of steel and mesh crab pots to catch enough crabs to sell to our seafood buyers. Though our daily harvest would vary based on the time of year, I regularly expected to harvest between 30-50 bushels of hard crabs daily. There were no harvesting limits on blue crabs in the seventies, so being accused of overfishing was not a concern of mine. My only focus was to catch as many legal-sized hard crabs as I could.

Though there were many exceptions, I'm sure, most of the watermen I worked with relied heavily on their spouses to make a good living. Working on the water is too hard to do it all by yourself, unless you choose to stay in the rivers and keep your operation relatively small. Ginny did more than her share to run the soft crab business, run the family, and operate a bus company during the school year. Had Ginny not been there as my equal partner, I would not have entered into the profitable soft crab business.

What many people don't realize, or understand, is that running a soft crab enterprise is a twenty-four-hour commitment, seven days a week.

There are no days off, no vacation days, and no sick days. Crabs molt according to their biological clocks and the water quality they are exposed to. To deliver the best product, Ginny and I took turns checking the crabs at night so our crabs would always be soft and fresh. Ginny had a keen eye in determining when a peeler was about to molt; she could read the red and pink sign on the back fin as well as anyone on the water.

Though I worked like a dog every day, I made my fair share of mistakes, and one of the most memorable involved Ginny. Technically, I was responsible for buying and maintaining all mechanical equipment needed to run our operations. So, I purchased an old milk truck and converted it to a cooling shed for our soft crabs. For several years, this system worked real well because it had a side and back door which made it easy to load and unload. All day and night, Ginny and I would go in and out of the truck either loading or unloading our crabs.

One day, while I was a dozen miles away on *Dawn* hauling crab pots with my crewmembers Danny Elburn and Larry Jr., Ginny went inside the truck to wrap up the soft crabs for sale. Somehow, the latch on the side door failed and she could not get out. Now in complete darkness, she eased her way to the back door to try and get out that way. But, the rear door was jammed too. Wearing only summer clothes, Ginny was totally trapped in the truck and no one in Rock Hall knew where she was – not even our kids. No one could hear her screaming from inside the icebox and she knew I wouldn't be back for hours.

Fortunately, an alert waterman noticed that Ginny's car was parked in her normal spot but he didn't see her anywhere near the sloughing tanks. Thinking that maybe she had fallen overboard, he walked over to the shedding tanks just to make sure she was all right. As he came near, he heard Ginny pounding on the side of the truck and quickly let her out. She was as cold as ice when she stepped out of the truck.

Though she had a few hours to calm down before I got home, she was mighty irritated with me. When I eased back into my slip, she gave me a good currying (waterman slang for cussing) for not keeping those doors in good repair. That night, I fixed both doors so they would never lock on her or our children again.

Chapter Fifty-Three

Danny

With the number of pots we had overboard, I always had two crewmembers working alongside me to get the job done. Larry Jr. was one of the men who helped me. He was (and remains) a hard working, tough waterman who could do every task on our boat, including my job. He was one of those tough watermen who could work without resting; he could even work while enduring seasickness which is quite rare even among watermen. The other crewmember on board was a strong teenager named Danny Elburn. He was the son of Jackie Elburn who crewed alongside me for years on the *Mary C*. When all three of us were working well, I felt we were as able and capable as any three-man team on the Chesapeake Bay.

There were days, however, when Danny and I would butt heads on the water. Though we were both motivated by making money and getting the job done, Danny had a certain way he liked to do things. Unfortunately for Danny, so did I and I was the lone captain on *Dawn*. Danny and I were both headstrong. Whenever we clashed over an issue or an idea, sometimes I had to trump his good judgment just so he would remember who was in charge which infuriated him. When he was mad at me, he would display his anger in three ways. His first move was to grumble under his breath just enough so I could hear his voice but not make out the words. If that didn't get my attention, he would give me the silent treatment and wouldn't answer me when I spoke to him. But if these first two approaches didn't get my attention, he would start rough handling my crab pots which always ticked me off.

One morning, we were crabbing close to Rock Hall and all three of us were having a contrary day. After fishing over a hundred pots, we knew the crabs had "dropped off" which meant the rest of the day was going to be a bust. As captain, I could see I wasn't even going to cover my bait and fuel expenses for the day. As a crewmember working on shares, Danny could see he was going to make nothing that day and therefore he was almost working for free. As Danny pulled in empty pot after empty pot, I could see his frustration growing. I also could see his irritation with me was growing. As his captain, he expected me to figure out where the crabs were moving and to keep on them so he could make money. Obviously, the crabs outfoxed me this time, which was irritating both of us.

Over the course of an hour, we went from small talk to no talk. Danny just went quiet on me and then started to rough handle my pots as he pulled them from the water. He dragged the pots along the side and then banged them against the culling board as he dumped the few crabs. Even while baiting the traps with menhaden, he was shoving them in rougher than was necessary. I asked him what was bothering him, but he didn't say a word.

Well, I do not like to see my pots get rough handled. It makes me more contrary and it makes the work day drag. Steady and sure is the only way to last all day on a boat pulling crab pots. But I also don't like to see my pots get banged round because it makes the steel weak. Once the steel (or wire mesh) gets weak, the pot loses its shape which means it won't catch as well, nor does it handle or transport properly. Over time, a rough-handled pot will not last as long and that creates an expense for the captain, but not the crewmember.

I tried to give Danny time to work through his own funk, but finally I warned him by saying, "Danny, take it easy on my pots". As one of the best crab pot pullers on the Chesapeake Bay, he bristled up big time and gave me *the look*. My first warning did not accomplish anything good, and Danny proceeded to be even rougher with my pots. I was sure he was irritated with me and he wasn't going to tell me why. Now, I am irritated with him too and all of sudden my forty-six-foot workboat seemed crowded. Larry

Jr. focused his efforts on culling the crabs and wisely stayed clear of the brewing tension. We didn't need a father-son dynamic to further aggravate the situation.

Speaking as his captain and not his buddy, I warned him clearly to take it easy on my pots, but he kept on banging them. I now realized he was not going to honor my role as his boss at that moment. Now boiling over with irritation, Danny started back talking to me which was pretty unusual for him. Right then, I decided I had endured enough and I quietly hatched a plan to make my point of who was in charge and who was not.

The strategy rolling around my mind was simple, but I knew it would work if I executed it properly. I had decided to cool him off by throwing him overboard. Without saying a word, I started to stop just a little farther away from the floating cork so Danny would have to stretch a bit to snag it with the boat hook. At first, I was subtle about it and Danny didn't even know I was intentionally making it harder for him. Cork after cork, I always pulled up close enough for Danny to grab the buoy but each time he would have to work just a little harder to get it. When he barked at me for making him reach too far, I told him the current was pushing me hard and I was having trouble lining up with the cork. At that point, I didn't care if he was inconvenienced by my steering or if he believed my story about the current. All I wanted now was to throw him overboard to cool him off.

I carefully picked my moment and placed *Dawn* a full body length away from the cork. Danny looked at me with a *what are you doing?* look, while he extended his entire body over the side to get that cork. Once he was hyper-extended, I slipped up behind him, grabbed his boots and flipped him out of the boat. In full gear (sunglasses, oilskin apron, and boots), I threw one of the best crewmembers I had ever worked with out of my boat.

I was so mad at him I didn't care if he quit on the spot. I had decided, no matter what, that if he was going to work on *Dawn* for shares, he was going to follow my lead. Not for one second did I worry about Danny's safety. He was a superb swimmer and strong as an ox and I knew he could tread water for hours as long as I kept him clear of the propeller and rudder.

When Danny swam to the surface, I could see and hear that he was not pleased with my decision to throw him overboard. In fact, he was furious with me. He cussed me up and down and thrashed around in the water like a shark on a feeding frenzy. In his raw anger, he told me he was going to "beat the devil out of me" when he got back on board. I told Danny, "Well that's fine, so don't expect to get back on this boat".

For a brief moment, I had the upper hand on him which was what I had been angling for. So, I circled around him for over a half an hour while Danny sorted out his options. We were a half mile off shore so swimming to land was a possibility. But Danny knew that if he swam to shore, he would lose a day's pay and probably his job. He knew I was serious and was going to fire him if he didn't get in line. I knew he could get a job with another captain easily, but not during the summer when all the boats and crews were set. So, he continued to tread water while trash talking directly at me. And I kept circling around him.

At this point, all I could do was wait him out to see if (or when) he would cool down. I knew he wouldn't want to stay in the water all day. And he knew that I was not going to pick him up until I was sure he wouldn't beat me up. Slowly, he acknowledged he was not going to beat me up and that he was sorry he had been rough on my pots. He admitted that I got him this time. He told me he wanted to come back on board and finish pulling the rest of the pots.

As we talked about ten feet apart from one another, I could see his anger had melted away and so had mine. Gradually, we both started to smile and then we started to laugh hard. Sure that he was done, I eased alongside him and we plucked him out of the water. We didn't talk about his mid-day swim or the fact that the fishing was poor. I did notice that Danny had become gentler with my crab pots. It was nice to have my full crew following my lead, even if the crabbing that day was terrible.

Later that summer, Danny, Larry Jr., and I had just fished our last crab pot off Turkey Point so I revved up the motor to head back home. We had enjoyed a good day on the water with a decent harvest, but I was hot, sweaty, and tired and I wanted to get home. I was not in the mood to horse around – but Danny was. He told me he wanted to ski all the way back to Rock Hall with the pair of skis that Larry Jr. had left in the front cabin. I told him, "No way, because *Dawn* doesn't have enough hull speed to pull you right. Besides, if your arms give out, then I don't want to waste time picking you up".

As always, Danny persisted and against my better judgment I agreed to pull him to Rock Hall. I was clear that if he couldn't hold on, he would have to swim to shore and hitchhike back to Rock Hall. I promised him that I was not going to turn around and retrieve him if he fell. Larry Jr. and I laughed hard as he jumped overboard and put on the skis. *Dawn* was plenty powerful enough to plane off on the Chesapeake Bay, but she wasn't fast enough for Danny to ski easily. To his credit, this brute of a teenager stayed up all the way back to Rock Hall. When we stopped at the harbor, his arms and shoulders were so tired, we had to lift him into the boat. Like a true waterman, Danny said he could do it and delivered on his promise in spite of his pain.

I could share a dozen more "fun and funny" stories about my work experiences with Danny as we worked together on the Chesapeake Bay. But, Danny was not simply a piece of machinery on board my boat to get the heavy lifting done. Like his father, Danny was (and remains) an integral part of my life on many levels.

One evening after *Dawn* had returned to port with a load of hard crabs, my younger son, Robby, was checking the pilings to see if he could catch any jimmies or doublers. Not more than 5 years old, Robby was reaching around the back side of a piling, trying to catch a "doubler" when he slipped. With the crab net in hand, Robby fell head first into deep water. I was working on the engine and didn't hear him fall. Larry Jr. was loading bushels baskets on the pickup truck and didn't see him fall either. Ginny was inside the milk truck tending to her soft crabs and didn't even know Robby was crabbing. Without saying a word, Danny dove in head first and fished Robby out of the water and saved his life.

Robby scraping for a doubler. *Courtesy of Ann Crane Harlan.*

Chapter Fifty-Four
The Highliner Award

Overall, the seventies were not great but still good for the watermen. Certainly, the oyster and shad fisheries struggled a great deal, but the rockfish and perch fisheries did very well. The eel fishery came on strong and so did soft shell clams. The undisputed success story in the seventies was clearly the blue crab fishery.

As president of the Maryland Watermen's Association, I was pleased with our progress as an organization. We survived Hurricane Agnes and her aftermath. We had a well-functioning board of directors who were willing to sacrifice everything to keep their watermen in business. With almost ten years of experience as a leader, I had hired some special people to help keep MWA sharp and growing even with limited resources.

At the national level, several important initiatives and milestones were accomplished in the seventies. Notably, the Environmental Protection Agency (EPA) was created and assigned the task of protecting the environment from human progress. Armed with massive powers and resources galore, this giant bureaucracy was intended to be the first line of defense against corporations, municipalities and individuals that were unwilling or unable to steward the natural resources of America. Though EPA mandated many regulations that would ultimately complicate the lives of watermen, I still found it reassuring that some governmental agency was going to watch over the soil, air, and water.

In this decade, The Clean Air Act (amendments), The Safe Drinking Water Act and The Clean Water Act were all inked into law. Though enforcement and accountability measures proved to be marginal, it was a start in the right direction. In hindsight, I wish our government had also enacted the Clean Soil Act, but in those days, soil was not considered a natural resource at all – it was just dirt and America seemed to have a limitless supply of topsoil. Significantly, EPA banned the manufacture of PCBs and also banned all registrations for DDT in the United States of America.

With water quality clearly declining throughout the seventies, the environmental movement really came on strong in Maryland. Dozens of grass-roots organizations sprouted up all over the Chesapeake Bay watershed. Some of these were nimble special interest groups with a single purpose like cleaning one river or working with their bare hands to remove an invasive species from a threatened marsh. Other organizations grew in strength and size and were able to create a huge level of awareness. By using a "boots on the ground" kind of approach, they peacefully shined their spotlight on many issues that warranted attention. Though these groups would periodically cause MWA and me angst, I credit them for doing important work over a sustained period of time. Without question, if organizations like the Chesapeake Bay Foundation (CBF) and others had not been proactive and "in the fight for clean water," I am not certain the Chesapeake Bay would have survived at all.

I personally enjoyed a bright moment in 1978 when I was selected to receive the Highliner Award sponsored by *National Fisherman*. This award was annually presented to three commercial fishermen from across America who had demonstrated an over-arching contribution to their industry and their communities. Enjoying the spotlight with me that evening in Boston was Captain Daniel A. Arnold of Marshfield, Massachusetts (*The Frances Elizabeth*) and Captain John Joseph Ross of Biloxi, Mississippi (*The Colonel O'Keefe*). I was humbled by this recognition and will always cherish receiving the Highliner Award.

In Boston, I had a great time talking with previous recipients of the Highliner Award. I also met a number of high-level industry leaders for the first time, which helped me see the importance of the industry beyond the Chesapeake Bay. Though I didn't expect it, receiving this award opened up all kinds of doors for me as president of the Maryland Watermen's Association.

As a fisherman from Maryland receiving this level of recognition, I started a professional relationship with publishers, editors, writers, and staff members at *National Fisherman*. For over fifty years, *National Fisherman* magazine had been mailed to thousands of commercial fishermen and their families throughout North America. It was also mailed regularly to a large number of paid subscribers who simply enjoyed reading about fish, fisheries, and commercial fishermen. As a Highliner Award recipient, I was now able to share the ideas and issues important to MWA with a much larger audience.

Closer to home, the Highliner Award allowed the MWA members to see that my passion for the commercial fishing industry was real. It enabled me to form great relationships with fishermen from Alaska, Massachusetts, Louisiana, Florida, Alabama, and many other states. Now, I had a broader group of peers to check in with to test an idea or share a concern. In time, this award also opened doors for me so I could join boards, commissions, forums, etc., which I value tremendously. I'm sure the recognition from this award helps me even now, in 2012, as I serve as Secretary of The Commercial Fishermen Association of America.

National Fisherman Highliner Award.
Courtesy of Ann Crane Harlan.

Part Five
Full Throttle
(1979 – 1998)

Chapter Fifty-Five
The Shad Moratorium

The last great year I would ever experience as a shad fisherman was 1972. After that season, I witnessed my seasonal harvest drop off considerably each subsequent year. By 1978, I had stopped shad fishing altogether because I was no longer able to make a good profit harvesting shad with gill nets. As much as I loved to go "pretty fishing" each spring, I was not willing to fish at a loss just so I could enjoy my passion. To recover from the lost shad income, I poured my heart and soul into crabs, eels, rockfish, and soft clams.

By the time the state of Maryland finally declared a harvesting moratorium on the American Shad in 1980, most of the progressive watermen had already left the fishery. A few watermen tried to get regulators in Annapolis to keep the shad fishery open, but the shad stocks had crashed too far down to receive any serious consideration. To me, the timing of the announcement was "too little too late," for sure.

But what really hurt me personally was when the general public was informed that the primary reason the shad fishery failed was due to "overfishing" by commercial fishermen. Specifically, it was the gill netters like me who were singled out as the driving force that caused the shad fishery to collapse. I didn't like this accusation for two reasons. First, I didn't think it was true and so I was naturally defensive for being falsely accused. Second, by assigning the blame for the shad decline on the gill netters, it gave the general public (including the recreational fishermen) the impression that the shad would return once the nets were removed from the waters.

I never did embrace the charge that gill netters caused the shad collapse and probably never will at this point in my life. It was clear to me that the shad intended to migrate into Virginia, Pennsylvania, Delaware, New Jersey, and New York waters were having trouble, too, so something bigger than a Maryland gill netter seemed to be working against the shad. In addition, we all witnessed a massive die off of SAV's (submerged aquatic vegetation) in the Susquehanna Flats where the majority of Maryland shad generally spawned. As a fact of life, if newly hatched shad can't find food in the first one to two days of their lives, they will die off in massive numbers. Finally, I was familiar with the reproductive capacity of this wild fish and was sure that something big was preventing the shad from spawning or developing properly.

It has now been over thirty years since the watermen of Maryland were banned from shad fishing with nets. One might expect, with such a long break from commercial harvesting pressure, the shad would return in abundance. But they have never come back in numbers even close to what I witnessed as a young boy. The American Shad never bounced back. Had the real cause of the shad decline been overfishing, the shad would have returned. With the benefit of hindsight as my guide, I have developed my own theories about what caused the shad to drop off so sharply back in the seventies.

More than any other single event, I believe an entire generation (or more) of fingerling and young shad were killed in the summer of 1972 when the Susquehanna River washed millions of the fragile fish away from the food supply and sheltered waters. The timing of Hurricane Agnes couldn't have been worse for the shad (and the rockfish, for that matter).

Equally important, I believe that surviving generations of shad returning to Maryland waters in 1973 found few good places to lay their eggs. Their traditional spawning habitat had been destroyed by rushing waters and excess sediment. Because the submerged underwater grasses were either smothered or killed, there wasn't an adequate supply of food to feed the 1973 brood of fingerlings once they hatched. Something was keeping the bay grasses from reseeding and developing properly under water, though I was not sure what.

Because only a few shad could successfully spawn north of the Conowingo Dam, there was little genetic diversity in the Maryland shad population. Sadly, most of the shad migrating in Maryland waters were forced to spawn in massive numbers where disease, toxins, or sediment could clobber large populations with one harsh weather event. If Hurricane Agnes truly wiped out several generations of native shad in 1972, 1973, and 1974, then it's possible that there were insufficient numbers of shad to offset the populations blocked by the dam. Again, these are just my theories after thinking it over for thirty years.

In my lifetime, I do hope to see large schools of American Shad migrate up the Susquehanna, Elk, and Sassafras rivers to spawn successfully. I am encouraged by the results the user groups and stakeholders have generated to bring back the native shad on the Delaware River. Of course, these fish don't have three hydroelectric dams to swim past before they deposit their eggs and milt, but I think their unified efforts to clean up the Delaware River have been inspiring and successful.

Because of the high volume of boat traffic and underwater obstacles now in the upper Chesapeake Bay, I don't expect to see top nets used to harvest shad in Maryland in my lifetime. In time, I could envision a small, tightly controlled, hook and line fishery. But not until the upstream access issues are solved at Holtwood, Safe Harbor, and Conowingo dams. There are many watermen, myself included, who believe the Chesapeake Bay and her shad fishery will never recover until the Susquehanna River is restored.

The Conowingo Dam. *Courtesy of Ann Crane Harlan.*

Chapter Fifty-Six

Headwaters

By the mid seventies, scientists and natural resource managers started to observe a slow-but-steady decline in the rockfish populations feeding and spawning in Maryland waters. Since these waters serve as the prime spawning grounds for most of the Atlantic striped bass in America, this decline was significant. As fishermen, we were not seeing a drop off in our seasonal harvests and were somewhat skeptical about the observations. For centuries, generations of watermen before me had always observed periodic ups and downs in every fishery, so I assumed, and hoped, that this downturn was nothing more than a cycle.

The concern over the rockfish decline never did subside. In fact, by the late seventies, there were ongoing talks in Annapolis about reducing commercial harvesting activities. In certain circles, there was even a discussion about banning the use of commercial nets altogether. These discussions in Annapolis had the board members at MWA very concerned, so we met regularly to learn more about the issues. We were uncomfortable having only folks in Annapolis making decisions for us.

Sensing a need to do something about the problem, we identified things we could do with our own resources to strengthen the rockfish fishery. Mostly, we wanted to learn more about the fish and its relationship to the water. We believed we could lower the mortality rates of larvae and fingerling rockfish by adjusting the timing and rates of chlorine in water treatment plants near the headwaters. We also believed we could do something to increase the food supply for young rockfish until the submerged aquatic vegetation (SAV's) recovered from the siltation caused by Hurricane Agnes. Finally, we wanted to see if we could boost the native population of rockfish by utilizing an old hatchery in Elkton, Maryland.

At first, these ideas might seem more like research projects than activities normally completed by watermen. It was a stretch for us, but it was also time for us to learn more about our prize market. We were motivated to learn since this was the first time my generation ever was at risk of losing this fishery. In my worst nightmare, I couldn't have envisioned proceeding into the winter months without a robust, profitable rockfish season.

Since most of the rockfish spawning areas were in the upper Chesapeake Bay, the watermen from Cecil and Harford County Watermen's Association took the lead on this MWA project. With their close proximity and intimate knowledge of these headwaters, they provided the lion's share of the planning and organization. Spearheading the project for MWA was Captain Steve Bristow from Elkton who had the right mixture of skills and temperament to make this project move forward. We also hired a biologist named William "Skip" Bason to conduct the tests and help us analyze the information generated by the project.

There was a great deal of hard, physical labor required to get the old hatchery ready for the project. When Steve put out the word he needed "all hands on deck" to get this site prepared, more than sixty-five watermen from Tilghman to Havre de Grace volunteered their equipment, time, and sweat to get this project on schedule. Watermen converged in Elkton in pickup trucks loaded down with chain saws and bush axes to clear brush and clean out ponds. As president of MWA, I was impressed and inspired by the way these men came together to pitch in.

Restoring the Elkton Hatchery. *Courtesy of Ann Crane Harlan.*

Once the site was prepared, we began testing our theories about fish mortality. We wanted to know if native rockfish were still able to lay (release) enough eggs to survive in Maryland headwaters. We also wanted to make sure the eggs that were released were actually getting fertilized by the males. At the time, there was a lingering concern that PCBs could be reducing egg deposition counts and fertilization success rates.

We transported live native cow (female) rockfish and buck (male) rockfish to the hatchery and spawned them in tanks filled with clean water. We squeezed the eggs out of the females and then squeezed the milt (sperm) out of the males. After meticulously counting the number of eggs in each sample, we blended the eggs and sperm together and allowed them to develop as if they were in the wild. We then carefully measured and calculated the numbers of eggs successfully fertilized by counting the hatched larvae. To our satisfaction, we proved native rockfish egg releases were still normal when spawned in waters pulled from the Elk River. We further proved the eggs developed properly into the larval stage when quality water was present.

To better understand what role chlorine played in the development of small rockfish, we conducted a side-by-side comparison using a 500-gallon tank with water and another tank with water plus chlorine. We measured two drops of commercial grade chlorine and placed them in the second tank. Our findings were definitive; two drops of chlorine killed all the larvae in the second tank. We verified that chlorine in small quantities can be lethal to rockfish larvae. In hindsight, I wish we had tested the impact of chlorine on the fingerling stage as well but we didn't. It would have been helpful to know if well-fed, fast-growing fingerlings could survive a similar dose of chlorine.

Our research was already helping us better understand the life cycles of the striped bass, but we had more to test and learn. After the larvae hatched, we released them into the hatchery ponds so we could observe and learn more about their nutritional needs. To make sure there was plenty of the right food at the right time, we covered the bottom of each pond with bales of hay purchased from nearby farms. We thought (and hoped) the bales of hay would biologically react with the water and create enough plankton and zooplankton to feed the rapidly developing larvae. To some, throwing bales of hay into a hatchery pond might sound overly simplistic but, over the years, I have watched scientists, regulators, and watermen walk right by a practical solution in search of something more complex.

We didn't attempt to prove that chlorine was toxic to plankton and zooplankton in our experiment. We also did not try to figure out what percentage of the larvae was killed directly by the chlorine versus those that died of starvation caused by the chlorine killing the food supply. Intuitively, we believed chlorine at some concentration was toxic to these microorganisms, but we did not attempt to validate these beliefs. We didn't stray far from our mission which was to identify factors that might be limiting the survival and growth of new generations of rockfish in the headwaters.

With our preliminary results in hand, we shared our findings with several experts. Our first visit was with the Maryland Department of Health in Elkton where we shared what we had learned. They listened to our findings and shared them within their teams. After much discussion and a thorough review of their own research files, the department agreed to delay chlorination treatments in the upper bay, where appropriate, during the cold weather months when rockfish were spawning. They changed their chlorine treatments to something more akin to "as needed" instead of "as scheduled." Their decision to use chlorine only as needed decreased their water treatment costs with no measurable decline in human health.

Our second visit was with DNR in Annapolis. Our objectives in this meeting were two fold. First, we wanted to share what we had learned from our use of hay in the ponds. We wanted them to fund wide-scale dumping of hay bales directly into the Susquehanna Flats to help promote phytoplankton and zooplankton growth. Unfortunately, our hay distribution concept was dismissed as too expensive and too simplistic. We were told there wasn't enough hay in Maryland to make a biological difference to the rockfish in such a large body of water.

Not deterred, we made a second request of DNR. We wanted the state of Maryland to use the Elkton hatchery we had just cleaned up to create a surplus of wild rockfish until the native fishery recovered naturally. Because the Elk River was a natural spawning river for rockfish and less impacted by the downstream flow of the Susquehanna River, we thought this was a good idea. Though we had proven that wild rockfish could be raised up in captivity and then released into nature successfully, this idea was also rejected. Lack of resources to pay salaries, utilities, feed, equipment, etc., were cited as the primary reasons why the Elkton facility would not be established as a permanent hatchery. Later, DNR did operate a state-run hatchery in southern Maryland to boost rockfish numbers, which was good, but it was not close to the rockfish spawning areas.

As I reflect back on this Elkton Project, I remain proud of the MWA and its watermen for taking on this science-oriented challenge. It was right for us to invest our time and our money to learn more about the fish we had built our livelihood around. Though it has been over thirty years now, I still am appreciative of the hard work, expertise and commitment MWA received from Captain Bristow, Skip Bason, and the members of MWA.

Chapter Fifty-Seven
Crystal Blue

With a large influx of recreational crabbers and part-time watermen crabbing on the Chesapeake Bay and her tributaries, I gradually found that my beloved Chesapeake Bay was too crowded for me. More and more, I saw trotliners competing with one another (and recreational crabbers) for the best "lay" (crabbing spot). Likewise, the Chesapeake Bay had become an absolute sea of brightly colored corks and plastic bottles marking the crab pots.

Though I want all entrepreneurs including watermen to do well financially, I also like open waters. With so many users trying to catch the same crab, I looked into other fisheries that were still profitable, but not filled with too many workboats. For a couple of years, I ran a profitable eeling business. I maintained a live well on board to keep the larger eels fresh for air shipment to Germany, France, and Japan. I harvested and salted down the smaller eels and sold them to Eastern Shore trotliners. Eeling was good for me for a while, but it still didn't allow me the flexibility I needed to get my work done at MWA.

So I converted *Dawn* so she could dig soft clams using a hydraulic clam rig. With clamming, I could work hard on the days the weather was fit and then I could devote the rest of my time working at MWA. Locally, Marylanders absolutely loved to eat steamed clams drenched in butter. We also sold a small portion of our clams to recreational and charter fishermen who would grind up raw clams and use them for chum (bait) to lure in rockfish and blues.

One morning, I was digging for clams on my favorite clam bar, which was ten miles north of Annapolis not far from Sandy Point State Park. To the south of me, I could clearly see both spans of the Chesapeake Bay Bridge. This area was considered prime fishing grounds for crabs, oysters, fish, eels, and clams; this was a superb clamming bar. All morning long, the clams were coming up heavy and thick on my conveyer belt.

Because I was without another crewmember on board to help me pick clams, I was having trouble culling them fast enough. Even when I slowed down the conveyer belt, I knew a lot of them fell back overboard before I could get them into a bushel basket. The adult clams (keepers over two inches) had a distinctive brown ridge on both sides which told me the clams were growing fast in the warm waters because they had plenty of food. I was on track to hit my fifteen bushel limit before noon and be back in Rock Hall before 2 p.m. With no other workboats around me to slow me down, I kept my head down picking clams and enjoying the warm summer day.

As I eased forward to work a new section of water, I noticed something odd out of the corner of my eye. The view wasn't right, so I shut down the conveyor belt to look around. Sure enough, amongst all of the greenish-brown water normal for the time of year, I observed a large patch of blue water all around *Dawn*. It was a crystal blue color and the water was clear several feet down. It looked like pool water though it didn't smell like pool water. Though I had heard other watermen talk about this discoloration, I had never seen this color blue on the Chesapeake Bay in the summer. I passed through the section of blue water and returned to clam in what I considered normal waters. I harvested my limit and headed for home.

When I got home that afternoon, I called a few of my research and regulatory contacts in Annapolis to report what I saw. I wanted them to inspect the clam bar that evening but they were unable to get there on short notice. They shared that this was not their first encounter with a chlorine release in Maryland waters and assured me it would not be their last. To their credit, they did not speculate as to whether it was a spill or simply an over-release. I appreciated their candor and maturity about my sighting of blue water but I still didn't like the idea that chlorine in large doses was passing over our prime fishing grounds.

When I returned the next day to the same bar, the waters were once again a greenish-brown color. I set my clam rig down in the water and began to dig for clams. The clams were coming up thick again. But as I picked the clams, I noticed a number of the clams were slightly lighter in color. They weren't white like the dead ones often found on the beach, they were just faded some. I didn't like seeing these random whiter clams amidst all the brown ones. I managed to harvest fifteen bushels of clams again and went back home.

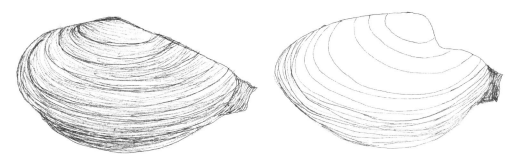

Brown and faded clams. *Courtesy of Ann Crane Harlan*.

When I returned the next day to clam on my favorite bar, I was uncomfortable with the number of clams that were fading to white. I was no longer comfortable that I could discern the difference between a dead white clam and a dying whitish clam. Disgusted with the idea that a careless chlorine release probably was causing this "white out," I left my favorite bar to go work another good spot. I was fortunate to be based in the central part of the Chesapeake Bay where many fertile, healthy clam bars were readily accessible.

This experience with the crystal blue water really forced me to think about how our nation had been using the Chesapeake Bay as a liquid landfill. I'll never really know how much chlorine, human sewage, ship ballast, military wastes, animal wastes, chemicals, and fresh water have been released (or dumped) into the Chesapeake Bay since I was born in 1937 but I bet it's a bunch. Today, in 2012, this issue troubles me even more. It's embarrassing to think that our country (including me) still uses fresh drinking water to flush toilets and wash cars when millions of people around the globe would go to war for access to fresh water.

Chapter Fifty-Eight
Divisive Ice

There were only four of us working the bar off Tolly Point that afternoon. The winds were blowing about thirty knots and the air temperature was only 20 degrees F. Working the clam bar as a group, we found enough ice free water that we could clam effectively and still have enough space to move around. A strong ebb tide was flowing which meant the water, ice, and wind were all flowing southwards towards the Atlantic Ocean. Not far from where we were working, we could see large sheets of ice moving down the Bay.

I was working without a crewmember that day. I had my clam rig lowered into about twelve feet of water and the clams were coming up nice and steady. I kept my eyes focused on the conveyor belt and only looked up now and then to make sure I wasn't getting too close to another waterman or some shifting ice. For just a moment, I kind of tuned the world out and got lost in my thoughts while I was picking clams. When I looked up to check my position, I saw that a large chunk of ice had come between me and the other clammers. The ice eased alongside *Dawn* but I wasn't too worried since my buddies were only a couple hundred yards away.

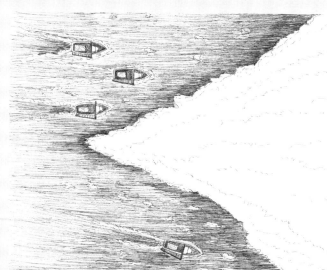

Clammers split by an ice wedge. *Courtesy of Ann Crane Harlan.*

In that brief moment while I was "in the zone," I missed an important window of time to play it safe. Instead of lifting up my clam rig and easing back around the ice floe, I decided to stay in that good spot and pick just a few more before moving to safety. Unfortunately, I had miscalculated the size and speed of the ice floe. Instead of easing around it as I had planned, this giant slab of ice had started pushing against my workboat and began pushing me south towards the Thomas Point shoal bar and away from my comrades.

Unable to use my steering or power systems to break free of this moving ice, I raised my clam rig fully out of the water and prepared to react to the situation based on the way the ice was pushing me. Moving at a slow but steady speed of two knots, *Dawn* struck the shoal bar hard. In an instant, I was hard aground on a sand bar in less than three feet of water.

Now hard aground, the slab of ice kept grinding against the hull right below the waterline. Had she been aground flat in the water, the ice would have slowly cut *Dawn* in half at the waterline. Had she been leaning to port, the ice would have climbed over and sunk her. I was lucky this time around, because the weight of the clam rig forced *Dawn* to lean to starboard, which forced some of the ice to go underneath the hull. As the ice kept grinding its way underneath my boat, I heard a loud popping noise which made me cringe. In less than two seconds, *Dawn* was lifted completely out of the water and was now adrift on an ice floe. I was now riding over top of Thomas Point shoal bar on a large slab of ice. I was safe, for the moment, but it was a creepy feeling to know I was utterly helpless against this flowing ice. It was absolutely quiet out on the Chesapeake Bay except for the blowing wind and an occasional sound made from the shifting ice. I stayed in the warm cabin so I could think of what would be my next smart move.

Nothing happened for over an hour. Periodically, the ice floe would collide with other slabs of ice but nothing changed my situation. The wind was blowing steady which helped weaken the structure of the ice. But still, there was nothing I could do to change my situation which made me both unsettled and edgy. Finally, the combined weight of *Dawn*, the clams, and the clam rig crushed through the slab of ice I was stuck on, which released me into deep water.

By now, I had drifted to the mouth of the Rhodes River but I didn't think I could find enough open water to get to a marina. So, I throttled *Dawn* up a little bit and headed for the South River which I thought would have enough open ice tracks for me to push through.

The ice in the tracks was no thicker than a pane of glass so I knew I could get through if I kept up my speed. But as I made a turn past one of the channel markers, I discovered that my steering felt "kind of spongy."

The steering became even more problematic as I eased along at less than a quarter speed. *Dawn* was getting "dumber and dumber," which meant she was getting heavy in the water. Finally, my boat was so heavy in the water that I took her out of gear and went aft to check some of the floorboards. As soon as I looked into the bilge, I knew I was in big trouble because it was full of water. Somewhere below the waterline, *Dawn* was taking on water fast and I was sinking in deep, cold water with no other workboats in sight.

Now powered by pure adrenaline, I revved up the engine and turned her directly for the shoreline. I steered *Dawn* out of the ice tracks and drove her right into ice way too thick for my forty-six-foot workboat to break apart. I knew the bow of *Dawn* was going to get crushed but I had already made the decision to sacrifice *Dawn* to save me. My only hope was to get into shallow water before *Dawn* broke apart or sunk. As I pushed her hard against the ice, I could hear her floorboards popping but I just kept the power on full. In one last surge of power, the engine sucked in a gulp of water and cut out.

There was nothing pretty about the way I beached *Dawn* in shallow water, but she did her job and got me close to shore. I managed to get her bow up into shallow water though the rest of her sank at the drop off. Now up to my armpits in freezing cold water, I managed to pull myself up to the bow where I was out of the water but very cold and wet.

The ice around *Dawn* was thick enough to hold my weight but the ice around the bow was already broken apart and was too unstable to walk on. I was in a bad situation and needed some help to get to shore. Though I had been too consumed with beaching *Dawn* to notice, an alert older man had seen my struggle while I was still out on the river and had already taken steps to help me out. Recognizing that I was trying to get to shallow water, he had already pulled his aluminum skiff onto the ice and was on his way to get me. He somehow knew that *Dawn* was not going to get all the way to shore. Walking carefully alongside his boat to protect himself from breaking through the ice, he helped me off *Dawn* and got me to shore. At that moment, I felt I was so lucky to have this man watching out for me from the shoreline. As an old timer myself, I now understand that he was not there by chance.

Chapter Fifty-Nine
Lunch in Tilghman

Right after I got home from a hot day of clamming on the Chesapeake Bay, I walked into my office to check my answering machine for messages. My office manager, Betty Duty, informed me that an associate from The Office of The President of The United States of America had called me at the MWA office earlier in the day. She said I was invited to attend a luncheon in Tilghman where I could meet Ronald Reagan in person and then hear him speak.

My first thought was one of disbelief. I assumed, wrongly, that one of my watermen buddies was pulling another prank on me. But when I called Betty in the morning to verify the integrity of the message, she assured me it was the real deal. Selfishly, I told her that I wish it was not a luncheon because I didn't like to miss a day of clamming. She reminded me I was only giving up one day of clamming for the once-in-a-lifetime chance to meet the most relevant man in America.

When I called The Office of the President the following morning, I assured them how pleased and proud I was to attend the luncheon as the lead representative from the Maryland Watermen's Association. I was looking forward to seeing members of the Talbot County Watermen's Association who were progressive fishermen and active supporters of MWA. In particular, I looked forward to spending time with MWA board member Captain Russell Dize. Russell was an experienced skipjack captain who had a working knowledge of every fishery in Maryland. Russell has been a standout member of MWA for many, many years and is what I consider "the best of the best."

I enjoyed meeting President Ronald Reagan and listening to his message. I was surprised to see how tall and rawboned he was. What really impressed me, however, was the way he listened to the watermen. He worked hard to understand our pain, fears, and our dreams by listening to our stories. He figured out, quickly, that harvesting seafood from the Chesapeake Bay was no easy task.

During his talk, I could see how easily and quickly he related to the watermen present. He seemed to enjoy being in the company of others. He exuded confidence, leadership, and hope in a humble way. He had this ability to look forward and help us all believe that good times are ahead. I found real integrity and a trust in his words and never once felt like he was expecting anything in return. He refrained from making political promises that would make his audience feel good over lunch but be impossible to implement in the future.

What a blessing it was for me and the other watermen present to be invited to meet and share a meal with such a special man.

Chapter Sixty
The Rockfish Moratorium

By the early eighties, scientists and regulators confirmed the striped bass fishery was in grave trouble. The watermen's number-one fishery and the recreational fishermen's number-one trophy fish was failing to repopulate itself in the wild. Every user group and stakeholder associated with the Chesapeake Bay was now deeply involved with the debate. By 1983, the commercial fishermen and the recreational fishermen were at complete odds with one another. I still recall how ugly and bitter the infighting was between us.

As watermen using a variety of different nets and netting systems, we simply didn't see the numbers of rockfish declining as sharply as the scientists were reporting. Our seasonal harvests had remained good and our net income remained solid as well. In hindsight, we probably just fished harder so we achieved the same results. Unfortunately, we probably didn't listen very well either because our fear of losing our jobs was jamming our capacity to listen fully.

Meanwhile, the numbers and influence of the recreational fishermen had really increased throughout the seventies and early eighties. Armed with fast boats, lots of hooks, and endless supplies of cheap clams for chum bait, these sportsmen could harvest a lot of rockfish without nets. Whether the fishery managers and the public knew it or not, the sheer numbers of these fishermen place a heavy load on the rockfish populations. It may surprise some readers to know that recreational fishermen were not required to purchase a fishing license nor did they have to report their daily catch to DNR. It irked me to see my watermen take so much heat from the media for fishing with nets while the recreational fishermen raced around the Chesapeake Bay unchecked. It also irked me when I observed a recreational fisherman casting a lure into a watermen's pound net to steal some easy rockfish for dinner.

Because the rockfish crisis was so acute, many of the long term solutions that would have generated sustainable results for the fishery were all put on the shelf. There wasn't time for leaders in Annapolis to restore the submerged aquatic vegetation. There wasn't enough money to address water quality problems caused by construction site runoff, aging sewage treatment plants or chronic polluters. The only strategies that received attention and media coverage were the ones that pertain to cutting the harvest. The experts had determined that only a reduction in harvest at this stage of the crisis could have any real effect in saving the fishery. The chronic polluters (like sewage treatment plants) didn't even get a slap on the wrist.

As MWA president, I couldn't see a good outcome for the watermen. I was disheartened by how much influence the recreational fishermen had gathered in this debate. I was also disappointed that the regulators and fishery managers had not been more forceful and assertive with their fishery stock assessment and their prognosis. Beat down pretty badly by many user groups and stakeholders, I believe MWA made a number of unintentional errors as we tried to protect our way of life.

First, I think we got emotionally fired up when the experts assigned the blame to overfishing by watermen. Second, in our anger, we stopped listening fully and missed the messages from the scientists. Third, we were too consumed with the harvesting results of the recreational fishermen when we should have been working on our harvesting performance. Because we failed to meet in the middle with our counterparts in Annapolis, they slammed the door on all watermen and took the best path for them which was to issue an indefinite harvesting moratorium. We unknowingly drew a line in the sand and then they used it against us. In hindsight, I believe we pushed too hard as an organization when the fishery was too far in decline.

As president, I should have recognized the fishery managers were backed into a corner and helped them find a better solution. Had we not pushed so hard for so long, we could have implemented our original recommendation which was to run a tightly controlled harvest which I believe could have achieved the same rebound effect without having to go to the more drastic measure of an indefinite harvesting moratorium.

The tipping point of the rockfish debate for me came when the leaders in Annapolis seriously started to reconsider that age old ploy of reclassifying the striped bass as a game fish in Maryland waters. With that seemingly innocent shifting of words, that would make it illegal for watermen to harvest and sell rockfish for a profit. By definition, consumers would then not be able to buy wild Maryland rockfish at the seafood counter or in a restaurant. With the rockfish classified as a game fish, only recreational fishermen would be allowed to catch rockfish for their pleasure in Maryland waters. As a 4th-generation watermen, I was aghast that this topic even reached the table for discussion.

A trophy rockfish. *Courtesy of Ann Crane Harlan.*

Knowing the moratorium was imminent, the board members at MWA focused our remaining strengths to insure the moratorium achieved something of long-term value. The last thing we wanted was to lose our fishery in the short term and not regain it in later years. We requested to have a better understanding of how the fishery assessment model worked. We wanted to better understand the assumptions being used to power the model. We also wanted to understand how each class of fish (1985, 1986, etc.) was counted and factored into the plan. We didn't want to change the model; we wanted to be able to understand the scientists as they shared their findings.

In addition, we insisted that all recreational fishermen be banned from harvesting rockfish right alongside us. We didn't want to leave them behind on this issue. Importantly, we wanted this restriction to include the catch and release part of the recreational fishery. We have learned that catch and release fishing, particularly when fish are approaching the time of year when they spawn, leaves the fish weakened and sometimes dead from the "play action."

Finally, we insisted that other states close down their commercial and recreational harvest to protect this migratory species. I will never forget testifying alongside Governor Harry Hughes and Delegate Clayton Mitchell (then Speaker of the House) in Washington, D.C. to make sure Congress fully understood that this fishery was important to America as well as Maryland. Our collective recommendation was that every state represented in ASMFC (Atlantic States Marine Fisheries Commission) would participate in a full and indefinite moratorium with Maryland. In time, the Atlantic Striped Bass Conservation Act was established which insured the best outcome for the rockfish. The Rockfish Moratorium went into effect on January 1, 1985.

The primary purpose of the moratorium was to stop all harvesting pressures so the "King of the Chesapeake" could rebound and reproduce abundantly again in the wild. Based on the science and the politics at the time, it was considered the only way to stop the downward spiral of the rockfish. With the stroke of a pen, a fishery that had served Maryland and America for centuries was put on ice. It was the lowest point of my professional life.

The stroke of a pen.
Courtesy of Ann Crane Harlan.

Chapter Sixty-One
A Night to Remember

In my role at MWA, I have met many special people who have helped the fisheries and the fishermen survive on the Chesapeake Bay. As a result, I am regularly invited to speak to different groups about watermen and our unique way of life. But the invitation I most remember and treasure was when I was asked to speak at a retirement gala for Senator Mathias at the Baltimore Convention Center in 1986.

I was invited to express our appreciation for the senator on behalf of all the watermen of Maryland. It was an honor for me to be asked to speak about this special man. Naturally, I said "yes" to this opportunity. Having testified in dozens of hearings and spoken to hundreds of different audiences before, I was sure I would be able to deliver a quality, positive message about the senator that would strengthen the watermen as well.

As I worked alone on *Dawn*, I started to think about the importance of this night for Senator Mathias and for me. I knew, intuitively, this speaking assignment was different and was going to be far more challenging. This time, I would not be talking about the life cycles of an oyster or what I thought caused the recent outbreak of pfiesteria on the Pocomoke River. Instead, I was attending a high-end, black-tie affair filled with people who respected and valued Senator Mathias. My only purpose for attending that night was to share how Senator Mathias had been so helpful to the Maryland watermen.

The more I thought about this evening, however, the more I got anxious about it. In fact, I was swept up with feelings of pure dread and became overwhelmed with the importance of my task. I worried that my broken English and thick Rock Hall drawl might distract or offend people in the audience. I worried over what to wear. I worried about getting lost in downtown Baltimore and whether I could find a parking spot. I got so wound up in the details, I didn't spend any time thinking about what I was going to say.

The night of The Gala, I did get lost in Baltimore and then had a devil of a time finding a parking space. Now, I was stuck in a long line of couples waiting to go through security and the line was not moving. At that moment, I felt all alone and I wished I had stayed home in Rock Hall where I belonged. I started to panic when I realized I should have been in the line at the speaker's entrance. I was overwhelmed again and filled with dread.

From the crowd, a friendly voice called out to me and said, "Larry, are you having problems getting inside?" I looked over to see the smiling face of The Speaker of the House, Clayton Mitchell. I said, "Clayton, I need to get inside right now." He smiled again, and said, "Come with me and I'll get you there." What a blessing to have him call out my name in that moment.

When I sat down at one of the head tables in front of over 1,000 people, another feeling of dread washed over me like a flood tide. The room was filled with perfectly dressed politicians, lobbyists, regulators, and business leaders. There was not a waterman in sight to calm me down or make me feel at home. Though I was dressed right and looked my best, I didn't feel like there was another soul in the building that looked, acted, or talked like me. I was miserable and lonely.

At my table, I was surrounded by lifelong supporters of Senator Mathias. As we took turns introducing ourselves, I was in awe with how each person there had developed a special relationship with the senator. When I told them I was a waterman, several of them smiled as if to say, "That's nice." When I told them I was there to speak at the podium, they smiled with a look of disbelief and again said, "That's nice." Finally, one guest looked right in my eyes and said, "Really, what are you going to talk about?"

I quipped back quickly with, "Sir, I have no idea yet." Everyone there roared with laughter as they considered how unlikely that was to be true. Unfortunately, I wasn't joking. I had spent so much time stewing over the details of the evening, I had not prepared any notes or memorized any talking points. As in the past, I was planning to talk from my heart when I got up to the podium (others might call that *winging it*).

The moment I was asked that question, I got panicky because I knew I wasn't really prepared to do my best. Another feeling of dread washed over me, so I tried to numb my nerves by drinking two glasses of wine. The wine settled me down some, but not enough to make a difference. For the next ten minutes, I sat in my chair lost in my thoughts as the other guests talked among themselves. I feared that I was clearly over my head this time and I was fast approaching a time when I would make a fool of myself.

The speaker before me was excellent and he received strong applause from the audience. This gave me ample time to walk up to microphone and get myself right. At first, I felt fine – until my eyes adjusted to the light. Once I saw all those people looking at me, my body turned to stone and I couldn't even tell if my head was still attached to my body. For a few dreadful seconds, I just stared at the crowd in silence. I knew I had no notes in my pocket and no compassionate staff member from MWA was there to save me, either. I couldn't find the first two or three words to get started and I know I was just oozing with discomfort.

My skin felt like it was on fire and then it started to tingle. I'm not certain if I was even breathing. Finally, the first few words rolled out of my mouth. I'm sure they were rough words, but they gave me enough time to remember why I was standing at the podium. I could hear my voice over the loudspeakers but I couldn't follow the words. Suddenly, a calming feeling came over me reassuring me that I would be all right and to press on. In that moment, I found my voice and my message just as if I were home in Rock Hall.

From then on, I no longer saw the crowd in front. I focused my eyes and my heart on Senator Charles "Mac" Mathias and all he had accomplished for Maryland and the watermen. Using my simple words, I told the audience why I loved the Chesapeake Bay and her working watermen. I told them what the waters were like when they teemed with fish, oysters, clams, crabs, and eels. I told them how declining water quality and infighting among user groups was unproductive and a terrible example for our young people to see. I told them about the time when Senator Mathias came to visit me on my workboat. I closed by sharing with the audience how much courage and strength it must have taken for him to promise and secure funding for the seven-year Bay Study. I thanked the audience for listening to me and then stepped away from the podium.

As I walked back away from the podium, the crowd rose up to give Senator Mathias a standing ovation for his service to the watermen. I was caught off guard by the roar and feared that maybe I had said something wrong or unintended. But when my new friends at the table received me back with affirming words, another wave of calm washed over me. I had successfully honored Senator Mathias and The Maryland Watermen's Association without a hitch.

With the pressure to perform now behind me, I enjoyed the rest of the evening tremendously as speaker after speaker paid tribute to

Senator Mathias. One by one, they each affirmed that "Mac" had run a great race for the Chesapeake Bay, Maryland, and The United States of America. From where I was sitting, I could see that he was pleased that so many people came to honor his role as a public servant. What an honor it was for me to be there, too.

As I drove home that night, I reflected back on all the good things that had happened to me that day. The way Clayton Mitchell managed to get me inside The Baltimore Convention Center on time. The way my table mates chose to encourage and welcome me to their table as a simple waterman. The way those first words finally flowed off my lips. The way I was provided with a calming peace at that podium that night. I was certain that this was one of the best nights of my life, if not the best.

By the time I had crossed over the Chesapeake Bay Bridge, I had made two important decisions about my future. First, I realized that it was The Holy Spirit, not me, that surrounded me with calmness so I could deliver my message with honor. Second, I realized that two glasses of wine was a poor substitute for properly preparing for a speech. This special night in Baltimore inspired me to change on the inside so I could grow into a better man on the outside. For me, that meant re-connecting with The God I had left behind.

Chapter Sixty-Two

Dawn II

My first workboat was an old rowboat given to me by Captain Willie in 1945. From that humble start, I owned a couple of other wooden rowboats and skiffs. As a teenager, I purchased *Sea Mite* – twenty-eight feet. And then I progressed to *Mary C* – thirty-eight feet, *Comet* – *forty-two feet,* and then *Dawn* – forty-six feet. All of my boats, in their time, were perfect for each particular stage in my career.

Dawn, in particular, had been an exceptional boat for me. I couldn't possibly count the number of crabs, eels, fish, oysters, and clams I harvested on her. For so long, this workboat was the one sure tool I could count on to make good money and also protect me from danger. She was a workhorse with beautiful lines and handled heavy seas well. She gave me good service when she was powered with gasoline, and gave me even better service and efficiency when I converted her over to diesel.

In the late eighties, I had made the decision to design and build my "lifetime workboat." It was my time to build the boat of my dreams which for me meant fiberglass, dual diesel engines and enough room in the cabin to keep my customers comfortable and enough room in the back to work every fishery on the Chesapeake Bay. I knew I wanted her to be forty-six feet long and that she, too, would be named after my daughter, Dawn.

Thinking back over that time in my life, I took quite a chance when I invested my hard-earned money into an expensive workboat when the waters and the fisheries around me were in such trouble. In some respects, it seemed almost dumb of me to intentionally build a new workboat when so many good used workboats were available for sale. The shad fishery had been closed for almost ten years. The oyster fishery was still open, but was clearly not healthy. Even the rockfish fishery was closed during this period of time. On the surface, it looked like a bad time to reinvest in the seafood industry of Maryland.

But I turned fifty in 1987, which proved to be an important turning point in my life. Socially, I was starting to wear out from too many late nights spent with shallow friends. Spiritually, I was questioning in earnest whether I really wanted to spend the rest of my life without God guiding my feet. Professionally, I loved working with the board and staff members at MWA and I was making very good money clamming on *Dawn*. Even though the fisheries were down and the water quality was getting worse, I was still making a good living as a waterman and I had zero interest in doing anything else with my life except being a waterman. My thinking was if I was doing well as a waterman without the shad, oyster, and rockfish fishery, then I should do fine when things turned around.

Culturally, watermen like me stayed in the game because we were fundamentally optimistic people by nature. We wouldn't venture out every morning in the cold if we didn't think the day was going to be profitable – or at least special. Deep in our core, most watermen believe in the raw power of nature; at some level we believe that all finfish and the shellfish will survive if humans just stop fouling the waters. Some watermen will say it is the laws of nature, while others might call it "luck." Many watermen are God fearing which means at some level they believe there is a God that is capable of saving and repopulating every species in Maryland. As long as there is one male and one female alive to breed in the wild, most watermen will not give up on the species or on their way of life.

Armed with the belief that man is good and God is great, I shared my dream of my lifetime workboat with master boat builder Phil Jones from Hooper Island (Dorchester County). Phil agreed to work on a time and materials basis with some cash paid up front to buy materials. I told him I didn't need a written contract or an estimate nor did I expect him to make a blueprint. A handshake from Phil was good enough for me, and he started to build *Dawn II* on the lawn beside his home. *Dawn II* was Phil's first effort to build a workboat out of fiberglass instead of wood.

When I had time, I would drive east to Hooper Island to see my dream come to life. I enjoyed visiting with Pam, Robert, and Paul as each played an important role in building my boat. Besides, visiting Hooper Island was a pleasure for me because the area was still wide open, wild, and undeveloped by comparison to Ocean City, Kent Island, or Annapolis.

It was quite a thrill for me when Phil called and said, "Come get her; she is ready." I couldn't wait to see her finished, so I gathered up my family for a trip down to Hooper Island. When I saw her resting in her cradle as a finished workboat, it was a very emotional moment for me. Her lines were beautiful and her stainless steel propulsion and steering systems were bright, shiny, and solid. I could see that Phil had managed to capture every part of my dream and then some. I felt that *Dawn II* was my masterpiece and was the greatest "thing" I had ever created.

While I stared in awe at my new boat, Phil and his team were working hard to lift her off the cradle and onto his transport system. The distance to the commissioning spot was only about two miles away but some of the equipment Phil used to transport *Dawn II* made me nervous. When he loaded her onto a rusty old trailer, I didn't think it was strong enough to hold the weight. And I surely didn't think Phil's old truck was going to make it all the way to the water. Phil knew I was nervous about his old rig hauling my precious workboat down the road, and he assured me that everything would be fine. His calming words helped some, but when I saw *Dawn II* going over the "bridge to nowhere" backwards, I cringed.

As promised, Phil delivered *Dawn II* to the water's edge without a scratch. I calmed down and started to enjoy the moment once the wheels on the truck stopped moving. To celebrate this big moment in my life, I had planned two additional activities. First, I invited a local pastor from Hooper Island to come bless her before she was launched. Second, I invited my entire family to share in my moment. To have my daughter, Dawn, with me that day to christen *Dawn II* was a high point of my life.

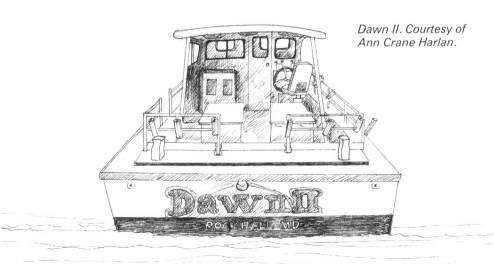

Dawn II. Courtesy of Ann Crane Harlan.

Chapter Sixty-Three
Icing the Clams

Though not a huge fishery, the soft clam market was an important part of the Maryland Seafood Industry. Roughly 300 watermen had invested thousands of dollars to purchase the equipment needed to safely and efficiently dig for clams in deep water. In return, these watermen made good profits clamming year round. Seafood buyers bought every clam we could harvest and rarely did we ever experience a weak market. In Maryland, our clams were sold to restaurants and seafood retailers, so any consumer who wanted some "steamers" could get them fresh. A significant portion of our clams were sold as fish bait for hook and line fishermen. Charter boat captains bought them by the bushel basket to attract rockfish and bluefish. A surprisingly large number of recreational fishermen bought bushel baskets of clams to use as chum, too.

The vast majority of our soft clams bought by seafood buyers were shipped north to fill massive orders for clams in New England. The demand for these clams was strong and steady and Maryland watermen received a premium price for fresh clams shipped north. Truckload after truckload of Maryland clams left Rock Hall six days per week to fill the strong demand for them. This export market was all but assured, as long as we could keep up with the demand. It was a great time to be a clammer and clearly was part of my best of times.

For years, the seafood buyers had developed very good shucking, handling, and shipping processes to insure our clams would remain fresh all the way to Massachusetts and the rest of New England. Most buying points in Maryland had advanced refrigeration systems and tons of ice on hand to keep clams cool all the way to the consumers. Locally, the seafood handlers employed dozens of expert clam shuckers who were paid by the pound to separate the clam from the shell. Back then, as now, the relationship between the local watermen and the seafood buyers was important and very strong.

Though the seafood handlers had developed excellent clam handling systems back in the sixties to handle this robust clam fishery, the individual watermen were not required to have advanced cooling systems on their workboats. Their primary role was to dig clams off the bottom of the Chesapeake Bay and deliver them directly to the seafood buying points (dock, truck, etc.).

For decades, Maryland clams were harvested and shipped to New England without a problem or concern whatsoever. Maryland had an excellent reputation for delivering high quality, fresh clams all over the East Coast. But that all changed one day when a concern (almost a rumor) was voiced from New England that maybe our Maryland clams might not be fresh enough to meet the refined standards of the "consumer." There was no formal allegation or complaint by a seafood buyer or a consumer, just a questionable concern voiced from an unknown source.

As dedicated clammers making a good living by exporting clams, we immediately were suspect about the nature and intent of this concern (which we treated as a charge). As president of the Maryland Watermen's Association, I dug deeply into the charge to ferret out the facts. Without a paper trail or a single spoiled clam to research the softly voiced concern, I was not able to definitively pinpoint the source of the freshness charge. In hindsight, maybe that was a blessing.

Like wildfire, word of this charge spread to every corner of the East Coast and the issue was impossible to ignore. The rumor persisted and a number of health officials from up north started to question the process that watermen were following to cool clams once they came on board. With all the emotions and fear removed, the charge being alleged was that our clams harvested in the summer months might not be getting cooled down fast to prevent a spike in bacterial counts.

In less than a week, our long-standing record of delivering high quality clams to New England was under siege. I was amazed how this cleverly placed concern had such a far-reaching impact. I was upset that our Maryland clams, an icon, were being called into question without any tangible proof of a problem. I remained frustrated that I could not find the person, or persons, who had started this crisis.

Immediately, the MWA board of directors convened to tackle this objection head on. We decided to stop efforts to track down the source of the charges because we didn't want to further confuse our consumers. We also didn't want to waste our limited resources on activities that would not directly increase the freshness of the clams.

Instead, we decided to use this window of opportunity created by our critics to fully study the actual freshness of our clams using good science and a broad team of experts. In principle, we knew our clam handling process was good but we also knew there were new technologies available that could make our clams better. Strategically, we resolved to protect our New England markets no matter what. We also resolved to clear this charge (presented as a concern) so our reputation would not be stained.

Because this freshness charge could potentially touch many different organizations in Maryland, we did not attempt to address this problem alone. Because there was a human health issue associated with this charge, we pulled in experts from all corners of Maryland to help us find the best outcome. Naturally, we asked our Annapolis-based resources to help out and immediately the Department of Health and the Department of Natural Resources (DNR) joined us. Since interstate shipping was directly associated with the charge, we asked for help from the Interstate Shellfish Sanitation Conference (ISSC). Locally, we invited our friends at United Shellfish Company, Inc. to lend their expertise in seafood handling and their significant knowledge of the New England clam markets.

With a great team in place, we now were ready to find practical and affordable ways to help our watermen cool down their clams on board their boats. Importantly, we didn't want to create any new problems for the watermen just to satisfy the concern. We also didn't want to wait until handling regulations were shoved down the throats of the clammers. Our ultimate goal was to create a new system that would cool our clams down fast and safely so we could deliver the freshest clams to our receiving points.

Before we developed something new, we decided to establish a baseline reading so we knew what our bacterial counts were using our existing clam handling processes. So our results would be viewed as credible, only trained scientists conducted the bacterial counts. We measured the bacterial counts at the conveyor, on the workboat, on the truck, on the cross dock, on the tractor trailer, and at the destination. We conducted the tests in several areas of Maryland and then replicated each test. The benchmark testing confirmed that our existing handling process was good and that clams were arriving fresh in New England.

Now, it was time to build a better way to cool down clams while on board our boats without shocking them with ice cold water or straight ice. Our biggest challenge in designing a new system was to find enough room on the workboat to hold the system. On my forty-six-foot *Dawn II,* I already had a forty-two-foot conveyer rig suspended over the starboard side with a heavy steel frame. Plus, I had twin engines to power her and a third diesel engine up front to power the clam rig. Finally, I had to leave enough room to hold fifteen bushel baskets for clams plus have room for one to three crewmembers to move around. Finding a good place to put a cooling system on *Dawn II* was not easy, and she is a large workboat compared to most.

Our early brainstorming inspired us to consider a few simple solutions. Our first thought was to only harvest at night when the air temperature was cooler. We scrapped this idea because Maryland nights can be plenty hot and we felt the additional risk to the watermen was not warranted. Another idea was to air cool the clams with large fans as they came up the conveyor belt. We considered placing large volumes of ice around each wooden bushel basket. We then considered building an icebox similar to the refrigerated boxes often used on pickup trucks. One by one, we dismissed each of these ideas as incomplete solutions.

Building on what we learned from the brainstorming discussion and early prototypes, we decided to substitute our wooden bushel baskets for the strong, light plastic baskets already in use by our seafood handlers. They were sturdy, easy to clean and more efficient to stack on board (saving space). We then developed an ice filled, cool water bath system where each full basket could be dipped under water for about ten minutes. This insured that all clams were cooled evenly and quickly. The clams were then iced down and placed in an insulated box. From our workboats, the seafood buyers loaded our clams directly onto reefer (refrigerator) trucks for immediate shipment.

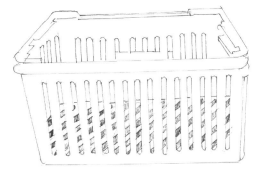

Wood and plastic bushel baskets. *Courtesy of Ann Crane Harlan*.

Through teamwork and a common purpose, we designed and built a much better system to cool and ship our clams to our primary market. But, our work was not done until our distribution channel had an opportunity to see our new system. We invited health and transportation experts from all over the East Coast to come to Maryland and follow our clam handling process from the water's edge clear to a shipping destination in Massachusetts. Using *Dawn II* as the demonstration vessel, we showed a number of people how we handled our clams from start to finish. It was disappointing, though not surprising, when individuals who initially challenged our freshness promise declined to attend our tour. In hindsight, I recognize now that our open invitation conveyed our confidence in our clams.

Chapter Sixty-Four

Rockfish Rebound

When the rockfish moratorium went into effect in 1985, life in Rock Hall and other fishing communities changed dramatically. Immediately, the focus on the crab fishery intensified. But just as quickly, the infrastructure that had been in place for decades to support the rockfish industry all but collapsed. Sales to watermen for supplies like ice, trucks, nets, fuel, and corks fell off dramatically. As a result, the watermen could no longer invest their money back into our town. The downstream effect of the moratorium was significant and long lasting. There was even a small number of young watermen who left the water altogether as a result of the moratorium. Who knows, maybe the next president of MWA will be in that generation of young people who saw no opportunity without a rockfish fishery.

For MWA, the years following the moratorium were hard. We continued to suffer from the stigma that commercial fishermen alone, not the recreational fishermen, had caused the fishery to collapse. The hurt persisted for a while and our level of trust in several state agencies was low. Watermen, in general, do not function at their best without a purpose or a mission. To survive this down period, most watermen poured all of their remaining strengths into blue crabs.

Fortunately for all involved, the rockfish returned to the waters of Maryland in abundance. By removing all the harvesting pressure from North Carolina to Maine for five consecutive years, the striped bass returned to historically high levels. I couldn't tell if the fish rebound was triggered by the lack of harvesting pressure or if it was a cyclical increase of nature (or some combination of both). I know the old timers, like Captain Willie, spoke of certain years when the rockfish just disappeared. The good news was the rockfish rebounded even though few improvements were made to Maryland's overall water quality.

The rockfish rebound was embraced by all watermen as a good sign for the future. I consider the reopening of the rockfish fishery (using nets of course) as one of the brightest moments in my professional life. A real bright spot that occurred during the moratorium was the formation of the Rockfish White Paper Committee. This group was formed to draft the laws and regulations that would guide the striped bass fishery once the moratorium was lifted. It was an interesting mixture of recreational fishermen, commercial fishermen, charter fishermen, DNR leaders, and a few moderate environmentalists. I liked serving on this committee because it helped me grow as a person and a professional. I also liked the fact that I was able to safely form relationships with folks who traditionally didn't like watermen. As part of this initiative, a small compensation fund was also established to reimburse watermen who carried scientists to measure and monitor stock levels.

On this committee, I was focused on three areas in particular. To begin with, I made sure that any proposed laws and regulations on the discussion table were practical for my watermen to implement. A regulation will not achieve its purpose if it is impossible to implement at the water's edge. Then, I made sure the guidelines imposed on the commercial fishermen were clear and firm. Though this sounds counterintuitive, I needed to take this hard line because the watermen took such a hard and unfair rap for causing the rockfish decline. I needed to keep my watermen protected from future allegations of overfishing when the rockfish fishery declined in the future. Finally, I insisted that recreational fishermen were required to account for their harvesting efforts too.

Once the moratorium was lifted, these new laws and regulations were put into effect. Commercial fishermen were loaded down with regulations so DNR had better controls on the annual outtake of rockfish from Maryland waters. Though I did not want our watermen to have to bear the costs (fees, time, money, etc.) of these new regulations, I believed it was far better to suffer through a web of regulations than it was to lose our ability to use nets at all. I got earfuls of criticism from MWA members who did not want to be hassled or lose profits because of the regulations. But my only goal was to make sure the most fishermen could use nets to harvest rockfish for as long as possible. For the right to fish with nets, I would sacrifice even more "ease and comfort" in the future.

I watched the recreational fishermen endure some growing pains along with the watermen. For the first time, they were required to purchase a salt-water fishing license and were required to follow daily creel limits. They, like watermen, could now be stopped by a marine law enforcement officer and receive citations for possessing the improper size or quantity of fish. This was an important positive outcome of the rockfish collapse because I don't believe the state agencies or the general public know how effective these recreational fishermen are at catching fish. Particularly with today's modern equipment and gear, a recreational fisherman can afford to catch the last rockfish in the Chesapeake Bay if they want to. Today, I'm certain all of the recreational fishermen (in aggregate) harvest more rockfish annually than all of the watermen harvest (in aggregate).

In the years since the rockfish moratorium was lifted in 1989, the rockfish have continued to flourish in spite of continued problems with water quality. Unfortunately, a tension continues to exist and persist between the recreational and commercial fishermen as we compete for the same natural resource – the rockfish. Even today, special interest groups try to convince lawmakers, regulators, and moderate environmentalists that the rockfish should be reclassified to become a game fish.

At MWA, we have no intention of allowing that reclassification to occur, as we believe it would destroy our way of life as watermen. To give credit where credit is due, I want to thank two leaders from the Baltimore County Watermen's Association for their lifelong contributions to fighting to make sure all watermen can fish with nets in Maryland waters. I firmly believe that if Captain Danny Beck and Captain Russell Spangler had not consistently voiced the MWA message against this initiative to leaders in Baltimore, Washington, D.C., and Annapolis for decades, we might have lost this battle over the reclassification. Had the use of nets been banned from the watermen, I'm not certain MWA would exist either. If Captain Frank Beck of Baltimore County was alive today, I'm sure he would be well pleased with the service these men delivered on behalf of all watermen.

Maryland State Flag.
Courtesy of Ann Crane Harlan.

Chapter Sixty-Five

The Podium

When I received an invitation to introduce President William Jefferson Clinton at The Living Classroom Foundation in Baltimore on February 19, 1998, I said yes immediately. I always say yes to opportunities that will enhance the awareness about the Chesapeake Bay and her working watermen. I was honored to be selected to introduce the president.

I wasn't anxious at all about giving my speech until I started getting hounded by several professional staffers from The Office of The President. Every caller wanted to see a copy of my speech but I repeatedly said, "No, I am not writing a speech out for a simple introduction." As the staffers got more persistent, I also got more firm and told them I was not going to miss the prime part of the season to write a speech that I wasn't going to use. Negotiating with me now, they said they would accept an outline or at least some talking points. To get them off my back, I told them I would get them a few talking points when I could.

But the calls kept coming and I finally had to put an end to it. When the sharp young professional called me back, I finally said, "Listen, I don't use written notes when I give a speech. If you insist on having a written speech in your hands before the event, then you have my blessing to find someone else to do the task. I am not going to write a speech." I went on to explain that my handwriting was poor and I often had trouble reading my own handwriting. I really scared her when I said, "I don't use notes at all because I just speak from my heart." In a panic, she offered to drive to Rock Hall to help me write my thoughts down.

She was only doing her job, I realized, and she was appropriately afraid that I would arrive unprepared and embarrass President Clinton. I knew full well that I was going to think through my talking points carefully because I didn't want to risk another close call like I did at Senator Mathias's retirement gala. Just to see her reaction, I accepted her offer to come to Rock Hall to help me write out my thoughts. But when I told her my boat leaves at 5 a.m in the morning, she wisely rescinded her offer to help me. Reluctantly, she gave in to my way after I promised to arrive on time, not to disparage the Democratic Party, and say only honorable things about the president. This effectively stopped the calls and the demands for a script so I could keep fishing.

To get there on time, I left early so I could find a parking spot close to the Living Classroom. Unfortunately, the directions my staff prepared for me were useless because of all of the security checkpoints and detours. As usual, I got overwhelmed by the fast-moving traffic and a jungle of road signs. In spite of my best efforts, I did get lost in Baltimore. Finally, I managed to get into the line that was leading to my destination. I also got through the first two security stops without too much problem.

But as I rolled down my window to talk to the professional policewoman guarding the speaker's entrance, things went bad real quick. As she eyed my Ford pickup and then heard my Rock Hall drawl, she was sure I was in the wrong place. When I told her I was here to introduce the President of The United States of America in about an hour, she said bluntly ,"You are not coming in here with that pickup truck," and she signaled me to drive away. But I couldn't drive away so I stayed right there and repeated who I was and why I was there. She said, "Sir, I don't believe you. This parking spot is reserved for special people only."

I said, "All right, just give me your name and badge number so I can tell the President why I couldn't get inside The Living Classroom." She shook her head in disgust and again pointed to the exit she wanted me to drive through. I didn't budge one inch and waited for her to make the next move. Though she was irritated with me, I could also see she was amused by me, my truck, and my request. After a few more words between us, she looked at me and said, "I don't want to believe you, but I kind of believe you, so I'm going to allow you to park in that corner spot right over there. But keep this in mind, sir, that if you don't introduce The President of the United States of America inside that building tonight, I will personally make sure that your truck is towed away and you will never, ever see it again."

I parked exactly where I was supposed to and immediately rushed to the door. I panicked when I turned the corner to see a massive mob of Clinton followers lined up waiting to get inside. I had no idea how to get past these lines and get inside. Just then, I spotted a woman walking against the flow walking on her tippy-toes looking for someone. I asked her who she was looking for, and she said, "Larry Simns." Both of us were deeply relieved and she rushed me past everyone and took me directly to meet with Vice President Albert Gore.

In a little hallway, I was introduced to Mr. Gore and we shared a short visit. All he wanted to know was enough information about me so he could introduce me. I gave him my credentials in about ten seconds and he informed me that was all he needed. In a nice way, he asked me how I was doing. With a nervous smile, I confessed that I was over my head being here. To his credit, he said, "Me too," and we both shared a calming laugh. It was an easy exchange and I enjoyed meeting him.

My calmness didn't last long, however, and my anxiety spiked through the roof when I walked inside the building and saw the crowd. This place was packed with dignitaries, politicians, environmentalists, and thousands of Americans who absolutely revered President Clinton. There was not one empty seat in the building. I could barely hear myself talk, let alone find a quiet place to calm myself.

Awkwardly, a familiar surge of uncertainty and doubt crept over me as I waited. This time though, I wasn't experiencing a feeling of dread, but just a healthy case of the butterflies. My thoughts were clear and I knew my sole focus was to represent the watermen by introducing The President of The United States of America to the audience that had gathered to see him. Even so, I privately hoped that I would get another lift from The Holy Spirit as I did when I was speaking in Baltimore in 1987.

As always, there was a long list of introductions leading up to my introduction. I knew it was my turn when Mr. Gore introduced me over the loudspeakers. Fortunately, one of the speakers before me was United States Senator Barbara Mikulski, which pleased me for two reasons. First, no political leader has ever been more supportive of the working man and woman of Maryland than Senator Mikulski. She had been a steadfast believer in MWA for as long as I could remember. Second, on a more humorous note, I was glad she was there speaking because she brought her speaking stool with her to the podium. I knew I was going to need that stool to reach a microphone after seeing how tall Mr. Gore and Mr. Clinton were.

I walked right up to the podium and before saying a word, I bent down to grab the speaking stool Senator Mikulski had left under the podium. I slid it under my feet and then stepped on it to gain some height but also to give me a starting point as the next speaker. Jolted by a rush of pure adrenaline, I opened up my comments by saying that, "I may not be as important as these fellows but right now I can be as tall as them when I'm standing on this stool." My self-effacing dry humor helped the crowd lighten up a bit. More importantly, my little joke helped me relax too and enabled me to find a pulse for an audience that was itching to hear The President.

After the crowd and I settled down from my "stool move," I revealed that I was not a speech maker. I explained that I could see people in the audience right now who were more qualified than I was to introduce The President. I acknowledged that I was honored and humbled to introduce The President of The United States of America. I told the crowd that only in America could a lowly fisherman be asked to introduce The President to such an important audience.

With my opening comments complete, I simply spoke from my heart about how and why the Chesapeake Bay had changed for the worst in my lifetime. I shared why I valued the watermen and why I felt they should always be a part of Maryland's future. I closed by sharing how impressed I was that a sitting president was willing to carve out some of his globally significant time to show his concern about the Chesapeake Bay. I then welcomed President William Jefferson Clinton to the podium.

As President Clinton approached the microphone, his first words to the audience and me were, "I've been in public life long enough to know when a guy throws a sucker punch, when he gets up there and says, 'Oh, I'm just this lowly president of'…" Before he could even finish his comment, the crowd and I erupted into laughter and we all sat back to listen to an amazing speech by The President.

Instantly, I watched this man capture the entire audience with his poise, charisma, and his words. He had an amazing ability to relate to others. He could speak with clarity, passion, and purpose and seemed to make contact with every person there. Watching him speak, I realized that he was ten times more impactful in person than he was on TV. He gave an amazing talk, and when he closed, he smiled back at me with a "thumbs up sign" to affirm his belief in the Chesapeake Bay and the Maryland Watermen's Association.

The Great Seal of Maryland. *Courtesy of Ann Crane Harlan.*

Epilogue

Bob and I first met for breakfast on October 30, 2008. We have worked steadily on this project while I led MWA and he learned to farm. Since then, the world around us has changed dramatically. Americans remain deeply embroiled in struggles with debt, war, oil, and divisive partisanship. An uncontrollable gushing of crude oil trashed prime fishing grounds in the Gulf of Mexico. The free world mourned the 10th anniversary of 911. And America elected a black man to live in The White House.

Closer to home, I have endured some important losses as well. A fourth bout of lung cancer finally overtook my dear friend Buster Elburn who served as an inspiration to so many searching for Jesus. The watermen community also lost a superb outdoor writer named Bill Burton and an equally significant environmentalist named Tom Wisener. Within my own family, we lost Donald "Ducky" Tolson who was a special stepfather to Dawn and Larry Jr. All of these men led significant, unique lives for America while they were here.

The arrival of Hurricane Irene and Tropical Storm Lee in the fall of 2011 bothered me greatly. I always cringe when I hear the floodgates at Conowingo Dam had to be opened; I just know millions of tons of excess fresh water, trash, sewage, toxins, and dirt will pour out of the Susquehanna River. For the first time in over fifty-five years, I fell overboard while we were moving *Dawn II* into safer waters in Shipyard Creek. The chemotherapy treatments weaken my strength but they also upset my sense of balance, and I missed a step while I was stepping down from *Dawn II*. Fortunately, my son, Larry, and my grandson, Brent, were there to lift me back onto the dock. Brent even dove into the muddy waters until he found my glasses.

Falling overboard at my age is a not-so-gentle reminder that my time is drawing near. There is a reason, beyond just the humor, that my family and friends around town call me "old time." I took this spill as a clear signal from God to get my house in order and to finish this book while I still had my strength. The summer of 2012 has been the hardest for me. I lost my beloved Golden Retriever "Cap," naturally. His full name was "Captain of the Chesapeake." A few weeks later, my close friend, Bob "Hoot" Gibson, passed away. On September 29, 2012, our dear friend, Lind Elburn (Buster's wife) passed on to see Buster in Him. For a small fishing community like Rock Hall, this has been too much loss to bear. Still, I am hopeful and thankful of my time on earth.

As President of the Maryland Watermen's Association, I am sometimes asked how I remain so optimistic about the Chesapeake Bay and her working watermen with all the gloomy reports about water quality and fishery declines. As a result of writing this book and reflecting back over my entire life, I can now answer that question with ease.

In my heart, I believe in young people and I am convinced they will learn from my generation and do better. I also believe the surviving watermen of Maryland will continue to persevere and adapt to this rapidly changing world and will one day be respected for the role they serve in Maryland. I believe technologies now in development will solve our water quality issues. I believe the infighting between the user groups and stakeholders will stop and we'll all work together to stop doing harm to the waters of Maryland. Most importantly, I believe the laws of nature are already in place to not only save but restore the Chesapeake Bay and the fisheries to her prime.

After all, with God, all things are possible!

Matthew 19:26 NIV

A Message for Future Commercial Fishermen

When I first cast my dream of becoming a waterman at age 6, I had no idea what it would take to build and sustain a career as a commercial fisherman. All I knew at the time was that being a waterman was my dream. In the years that passed since I made that primal decision, I have been blessed with many experiences, people, books, and places that helped me achieve my first goal of becoming a waterman. Ultimately, I was led to my true life's calling which was to lead the watermen of Maryland to the best of my abilities. In my wildest dreams, I could never have imagined that serving as a leader in the commercial fishing industry in Maryland could trump my first goal of becoming a waterman.

The Best of Times on the Chesapeake Bay has been written in part to inspire the handful of young men and women who will choose a career as a commercial fisherman. It doesn't really matter if you have chosen to be an Alaskan king crabber, a Gulf of Mexico shrimper, or a pound netter on the Chesapeake Bay, we are all connected by our love of water and nature. Therefore, we are all brothers in kind. As a parting gift to all young people, I share my "life lessons" with you so that it might help you find your "spot" in this world.

About Your Boat

Always keep your boat, dock, and gear in good shape. Your workboat, including the engine and propulsion systems, is your life blood and great care must be taken to keep your boat safe, seaworthy, and fully operational. A properly maintained boat will make you money and it will also save your life when the weather and your mistakes turn against you.

Remember that problems accumulate on board a workboat. Most watermen can handle one or maybe two problems that flare up while on the Bay. But when three or more problems stack up against you at the same time, it can mean big trouble fast. We have lost experienced watermen to problems that stack up quickly.

Always respect the raw power of the Bay. Wind, fog, ice, and waves are the primary natural forces that can kill you outright. But man-made problems like submerged objects, collisions, fire, and equipment failures can also trigger a disaster. Never believe that you are so experienced or so skilled as a captain that you can either out-muscle or out-hustle the forces in nature.

Since the 1950s, I have witnessed the quality of communication, navigational, vessel and life saving devices improve exponentially. Today, boats are safer, stronger, and more able to handle rough seas. I credit the United States Coast Guard and a few specialized companies for inventing affordable, comfortable, and effective equipment and processes that have protected fishermen all over the world. But remember, these amazing devices and systems can't save your life if they are not accessible or maintained.

There is no place for alcohol or illegal drugs on board a commercial fishing vessel. These substances subtly alter the critical thinking and reaction skills of fishermen, which can be deadly. If you have a problem with alcohol, get professional help and stay off the water until you are right. Remember, the commercial fishing community of America is a tight knit group, so a waterman with a drinking problem on Smith Island will not be able to find work in Valdez, Alaska without being discovered. Don't mess with alcohol on the water.

About Your Work

All watermen experience both good and bad times. The bad times far outnumber the good times, so it is important to invest your profits back into your equipment and your family. If you can adjust your style of living to sustain yourself during the hard times then you will be fine. If you choose to live "high on the hog" as if every year is going to be your best, the hard times will ultimately destroy your momentum and your career. Be sure to build in enough margin to weather hurricanes, injuries, and sharp drops in consumer demand.

Love working on the water with all your heart and soul or get off the water. If the thrill of the chase is not in you and if you don't feel a burning competitive urge to catch a lot and also more than your best friend – get out. There is no easy or big money as a waterman (anymore). The best of times that I have written about are not likely to return until the waters of Maryland are cleaned up. It will take decades, not years, to restore the Chesapeake Bay. Be content to work in nature, make deep friendships, and have a great year once in a while. Always remember that a bad day on the water is better than a great day on land.

Learn to turn off your body senses. A waterman must be able to work safely without sleep, food, and warmth and must be able to work with pain, mosquitoes, jellyfish, howling winds, and wicked currents. Whatever the burden, it must be suffered through until the work is done, whether it takes hours, days, or weeks. Be particularly careful about the hidden dangers that can creep up when you are working without enough sleep.

Pick the right partner to fish with. Life is too short to work with someone you don't like, trust, or have confidence in. Pick wisely before the season begins so that your weaknesses can be covered by another crewmember's strengths. If you happen to pick poorly, which we all have done, suffer gracefully and honor the commitment through the season so that other crew members are not harmed by your mistake.

About Your Career

When I was a young man, watermen pushed the outer edge of the fishing regulations pretty hard. In the fifties and sixties, it never dawned on me that the Chesapeake Bay could be fished too hard. In 2012, we know that each fishery has a biological threshold that can't be ignored. For fishermen, this means we must adapt our purpose. If a waterman can't make a good living following the rules inked in Annapolis, then he must leave the water. Today, isolated acts of poaching and abuse of the regulations is destroying a beautiful way of life for the watermen who play by the rules. These cowardly acts destroy our relationships with the public and force fishery managers to create more regulations instead of better ones.

Quality science is good for the commercial fishing industry. In the old days, we could not measure changes in water quality or fishery health. Typically, our primary measurement of success was fishery profitability which failed to fully account for fishery cycles or other variables like pollution, hurricanes, and diseases. It is hard for watermen when the findings of researchers result in a loss of income or increased costs. But, I believe the future of the commercial fishing industry in Maryland is forever linked to quality research and good natural resource strategy.

When I was in my prime fishing years, only watermen and commercial vessels used the Chesapeake Bay in the fall, winter, and spring. Back then, only watermen applied any real harvesting pressure on the natural resources. Today, there are many user groups coexisting on the same Chesapeake Bay. Now there are hundreds of thousands of well-equipped, experienced sportsmen competing for the same finite resource. Though it has been a painful adjustment for me personally, I now understand that each Maryland license holder is entitled to his or her share of the natural resources. In today's world, all user groups and stakeholders have an equal opportunity to enjoy but also steward the waters of Maryland.

Over my lifetime, Maryland has always been blessed with a strong fleet of capable, enduring watermen. There have always been great fishermen to harvest the seafood for consumers. Where we have fallen short is in our ability to identify and groom willing and able young fishermen who would serve as future leaders. In fact, as the number of working watermen continues to shrink, our leadership gap is getting larger. It takes a huge sacrifice of time, energy, and money to lead commercial fishermen but without new blood, the commercial fishing industry will fall apart. If you feel a calling towards leadership, raise your hand and get involved. You don't have to be articulate or perfectly dressed – just do your best.

Stay together and stay focused. I believe it will always be important for local watermen to have a place to voice concerns and ideas at the county level. I believe strongly in the county associations because they serve as our "boots on the ground." I also believe special fisheries and waters need a focused working group to handle unique issues (like the blue catfish invasion). But at the state level, watermen must always speak with one voice in Annapolis so natural resources managers and political leaders can make the best choices for the fisheries and the watermen. The primary reason the Maryland Watermen Association was created in 1973 was to send one clear, solid message to Annapolis.

Unless water quality and fishery problems are solved at the source, most issues can't be solved sustainably. Our water quality problems in Maryland are compound problems which means a "silver bullet" is unlikely to exist to fix the problem. Until our water quality problems are addressed at their origins, Maryland will continue to treat the symptoms and not the problem. Likewise, if all user groups and stakeholders continue to avoid mature dialogues, sustainable strategies will never be developed. Without good strategy, many well intended tactical efforts will result in wasted human effort and financial resources. If you are nudged to lead, be the waterman that will listen to all sides of an issue before judging others and their best efforts.

About Your Soul

When I started out as a fisherman, I was certain that hard work alone would create my success. By the time I was thirty, I was sure that my hard work and some good luck, which I call pluck, was all I needed to find success. In my forties, my physical strength started to betray me. At the same time, the water quality of Maryland also started to fail. As I was turning fifty, I stopped living a wild life and settled down. Around age fifty-five, I found the God I had left behind in my early twenties. I asked Him for forgiveness and a new plan for my life and asked him to guide my feet from that day forward. Don't make my mistake and try to have a good life all on your own. And finally, do not become a workboat captain responsible for the lives of others until you know who, for sure, is guiding your life and for what purpose. It is great to be a "Captain," but it is also a huge responsibility.

A Message for Seekers

The original purpose of this book was to share stories about the Chesapeake Bay and her watermen. But, as I recalled the stories and shared them with Bob, I found it was impossible to talk about my "Best of Times" without seeing the hand of God running through my whole life.

So, this message is for that emerging waterman or that one lost soul (like me) who needs to hear a simple testimony of faith right now. I hope you find what you are looking for in these pages!

I was totally prepared by my mother to follow God all the days of my life. For the first ten years of my life, I never missed a day of church and all the good things that came with that choice. In my early teenage years, I got swept up in the world of hunting and commercial fishing which served me well and left plenty of room for God to guide my feet. In my late teenage years, however, I allowed myself to be exposed to a few bad influences that altered the way I looked at the world. I was still a Christian and living a good life, but I saw the dark side of mankind and learned that earthly desires could wreck even strong men.

By the time I was twenty-one, I had allowed a gap to form between God and I. I was busy fishing and making money; I didn't think about how God might feel about me drifting from His strong hands. After I nearly lost my son Larry Jr. to a blood disorder and encountered a few close calls on the water, I kind of went wild. Instead of buckling down and protecting my family, I started working way too hard and living a full social life as well. I was always in motion and always surrounded by friends. But I was lonely.

For the next thirty years, I burned the candle at both ends all the time. I fished until I was exhausted, and then I would work like a dog to fulfill my duties as president of MWA. With the remaining hours available to me for sleep and to be with my family, I went out with my friends instead because I craved the social contact and the camaraderie that naturally appears wherever watermen are gathered.

In these years, I had lots of fun and my share of successes, failures, and heartaches. Even as an adult, I was still lonely and unsettled in my heart. Saddest of all, I distanced myself from Mom and Dad with my wild living.

Deep inside me, I knew I needed to change on the inside if I was ever going to be a good man on the outside. I wanted to live up to my God given potential that I was given at birth even though the first steps would be hard. So, around age fifty, I started to make some changes in my life so I could find peace and happiness while still enjoying some success as a waterman. As an extrovert, I knew I needed to continue my active social life. But I didn't think consuming alcohol was helping me anymore, so I started drinking non-alcoholic drinks while I was out with my friends.

Sensing a change was occurring, a few of friend's mocked me for trying to clean up my act, which hurt me initially. When I realized that they were unsupportive of my goal to become a better man, I severed my ties with them because gaining their approval had nothing to do with my purpose. I also started to apply the teachings I received from my Masonic mentor Pek Downey. I started using my gifts and strengths to help others, instead of just myself, and I made sure I had folks around me who could protect me from my weaknesses. I also reached back in my memory to consider how mentors like Ame, Uncle Josh, and Captain Lon might approach my struggles which helped me a lot.

I was encouraged by the results I achieved by making these small, yet awkward, steps towards becoming a better me. Even with the progress, I knew that something and someone was still missing from my daily life. I determined that the missing piece in my life was in the quality and quantity of close, real relationships with others and with God. I was missing that special person in my life who would love me – warts and all. To address this part of my life, I married my love, Carolyn, on November 27, 1992. I had known all along that there was a significant difference between dating and marriage and it was time for me to "man up" and be accountable for this relationship in front of my family, friends, and God. Almost immediately, my life turned more positive and fulfilling.

In addition to my wife, I still needed a true buddy to talk over issues "man to man." I needed an accountability partner to keep me honest and to keep me looking forward. Mostly, I needed a man in my life who would challenge me to become better and to prevent me from believing my own lies. Now aware of what I needed, I found that strength in Buster Elburn, Bob Gibson, and Pastor Hyman (among others). Buster, in particular, served as a superb accountability partner and we spent many days talking about our lives in the duck blind helping each other grow.

While all of these changes were occurring in my life, Bob Gibson continued to encourage me to attend his church in Centreville. His enthusiasm about The Word was hard to avoid. I was receptive to His message, but I was particularly moved by Bob's desire to help me. Bob helped me understand what was still possible in my life if I could muster up the courage to leave my troubles at The Cross. As I listened to his testimony over and over, I realized that it was possible that there was room in God's heart for one more sinner. Even me.

With Bob and his wife, Irene, as our guides, Carolyn and I started to attend church regularly. Since Buster and his bride, Linda, came too, I was not afraid or embarrassed to walk into church. Surrounded by true friends, I stopped worrying about the folks who might be judging me or my intentions for trying to become a better man. As I listened to the messages from Pastor J. D. Hyman, I saw a need to resume my walk with God. With friends around me to affirm my best efforts, I joined the Rock Hall Church of God (Pentecostal) on June 25, 2000.

I fully understood that when I joined the church I was also agreeing to tithe. Tithing, which is giving the first ten percent of your gross income to God, was a high hurdle for me to get over as waterman. Never sure what tomorrow might bring on the Chesapeake Bay, it was hard not to sock some of my earnings into a rainy day fund. But, Carolyn and I tithed because we said we would.

It didn't take long for my tithing commitment to be tested for real. Soon after joining the church, my body was hammered by prostate cancer which was likely curable with surgery but the recovery period was long. I actually had nightmares about the thought of going bankrupt because of the lost fishing days due to a lengthy recovery. However, through my friendship with Captain Greg Jetton, I was able to get lined up with Captain Charles Jacquette who stepped into my role as captain. And Larry Jr. stepped up his role as crewmember to help Charles and me out. My recovery period went faster than I expected and my year-end net profits were as good as ever. Carolyn and I were convinced that our decision to join the church, including our commitment to tithe, was the reason we survived my first bout with cancer financially.

As my knowledge about God deepened, I slowly came to the realization that God never left me alone on our walk. It was me, not Him, who walked away and all I needed to do to resume my walk with Him was to confess my sins with my mouth. With Bob Gibson's help, I learned the Sinner's Prayer. This simple prayer helped me leave my rough past behind me including all of its crippling guilt, regret, and shame. With God guiding my feet and accountability partners like Buster and Bob by my side, how could I really fail in the future?

A few years later, I received a second baptism in the Chesapeake Bay at Tolchester Beach. This was a full immersion baptism where my entire body was placed under water by Pastor James. In this way, a struggling Christian like me can receive a complete covering from The Holy Spirit which was liberating. By receiving initial and ongoing pastoring by Reverend Powell, Hyman, James and now Dan McCready, I slowly inch closer to becoming the man I want to be. I know I am still a work in progress and I'm okay with that. With God's help, I can be a better man today than I was yesterday and still be optimistic about tomorrow.

If God is willing to restore a man like me, why can't He restore the Chesapeake Bay, the American Shad fishery, and you, too?

The Cross. *Courtesy of Ann Crane Harlan*.

Author Thanks

My parents, Leila Ramsdell Rich and Robert L. Rich, Sr. for teaching Becky, Homer, and me to love the earth and its creatures.

Cynthia Voigt, author of *Homecoming*, for insuring that each of her English students could think, read, and write.

Pastor David Woolverton, for helping me find my strengths.

Debra Himelwright Rich, my bride, for supporting this project from day one to the finish line.

Dr. William Turner, author of *East of the Chesapeake*, for inspiring me to try something new, and for his encouragement.

Rene Nedelkoff, for guiding me through all the choices.

Judith A. Reveal of Just Creative Writing and Indexing, for her exceptional first edit services in 2010. She was the first to read our manuscript and affirm Larry's account.

Alex Hoyt for honoring a last request from John M. Bannan.

Robert L. Rich, III, for exceptional second edit services in 2011 which inspired me to rewrite the entire manuscript.

Ann Crane Harlan, our pencil and ink artist, who patiently worked with Larry and me so readers could see a piece of Larry's life in her drawings.

Chris White, author of *Skipjack*, for guiding Larry and me with our first few steps.

Brad Bortner for helping Larry and me to see a complex science issue more clearly.

Mr. Jones of United Shellfish for sharing the wisdom he learned in the seafood industry.

Paul Greenburg, author of *Four Fish*, for telling me to keep writing until it was good.

Joan Rich, for exceptional feedback whenever requested.

Peter Schiffer, for taking a chance on a fisherman and a farmer.

Charles G. Eser, for truthfully assessing my manuscript and encouraging our project all the way.

Vince O'Shea, for investing his time and expertise so Larry's account would be helpful to the next generations.

Jerry Fraser, for writing our Foreword and validating our purpose.

Heather R. Davidson, our professional photojournalist, for generously sharing her photographs.

Tom Horton, author of *Turning the Tide*, for reaching over to help a fellow man, in this case a waterman, deliver an important historical message about the Chesapeake Bay.

Pastor Dan McCready, for insuring that God was respectfully referenced and credited.

George F. Martin, Jr. of GMCO Maps & Charts for providing the cover map.

Tara Petrilli of Eye-Volt Design, for creating the cover design concept for this book.

Ann Crane Harlan on the Chester River.
Courtesy of James Herron.

Bibliography

Blackistone, Mick. *Dancing with the Tide.* (Tidewater Publishers, Centreville, MD, 2001)

Blandpied,Dave & Eloise. *Before the Refuge.* (Kent Printing Corporation, Chestertown, MD, 2005)

Buckley, Michael. *Voices of the Chesapeake Bay.* (Geared Up, LLC., Edgewater, MD, 2008)

Davidson, Heather R. *Maryland's Chesapeake Bay Watermen.* (Waterside Publishing, Manchester, Maine 2009)

Footner, Hulbert. *Rivers of the Eastern Shore.* (Farrar & Reinhart, New York, New York, 1944)

Greenberg, Paul. *Four Fish.* (Penguin Press, New York, New York, 2010)

Greenlaw, Linda. *Seaworthy.* (Penguin Group, New York, New York, 2010)

Harp, David W. & Tom Horton. *Water's Way.* (Elliott & Clark Publishing, Singapore, 1992)

Horton, Tom. *Turning the Tide.* (Island Press, Washington, D.C., 2003)

Ordeman, John T. *Frank W. Benson, Master of the Sporting Print.* (Schneidereith & Sons, Inc., Baltimore, MD, 1983)

Parker, James. *Kissed by a Minnow, Pinched by a Crab.* (James Parker Photography Group, Severna Park, MD)

Peffer, Randall S. *Watermen* (The Johns Hopkins University Press, Baltimore, MD, 1979)

Rudow, Lenny. *Fishing the Chesapeake.* (Tidewater Publishers, Centreville, MD, 2005)

Tada, Joni Eareckson. *Joni.* (Zondervan, Grand Rapids, Michigan, 2001)

Turner, William H. *East of the Chesapeake.* (Turner Press, Onley, VA, 2010)

Warner, William W. *Beautiful Swimmers.* (First Back Bay, Boston, MA, 1994)

Warren, Marion. *Bringing Back the Bay.* (The Johns Hopkins University Press, Baltimore, MD, 1994)

White, Christopher. *Skipjack.* (St. Martin's Press, New York, New York, 2009)

Reading References

(URL as of 8/1/12)

Alliance For The Chesapeake Bay – www.allianceforthebay.org

Atlantic States Marine Fisheries Commission – www.asmfc.org

Blue Crab Industry Design Team – www.bluecrab.info

Calvert Marine Museum – www.calvertmarinemuseum.com

Cecil College – www.cecil.edu

Citizens for a Better Eastern Shore – www.cbes.org

Chesapeake College – www.chesapeake.edu

Chesapeake Bay Commission – www.chesbay.us

Chesapeake Bay Foundation – www.cbf.org

Chesapeake Bay Journal – www.bayjournal.com

Chesapeake Bay Maritime Museum – www.cbmm.org

Chesapeake Bay Program – www.chesapeakebay.net

Chesapeake Bay Seafood Industries Association – www.cbsia.org

Commercial Fishermen of America – www.cfafish.org

Environmental Defense Fund – www.edf.org

Havre de Grace Decoy Museum – www.decoymuseum.com

Interstate Shellfish Sanitation Conference – www.issc.org

Living Classroom – www.livingclassrooms.org

Maryland Department of Natural Resources – www.dnr.state.md.us

Maryland Historical Society – www.mdhs.org

Maryland Watermen's Association – www.marylandwatermen.com

National Fisherman – www.nationalfisherman.com

Oyster Recovery Partnership – www.oysterrecovery.org

Phillips Wharf Environmental Center – www.pwec.org

Potomac River Fisheries Commission – www.prfc.state.va.us

Rock Hall Church of God – www.rockhallcog.org

Salisbury University – www.salisbury.edu

The Ward Museum – www.wardmuseum.org

Turner Sculpture – www.turnerscuplture.com

University of Delaware – www.udel.edu

Virginia Institute of Marine Sciences – www.vims.edu

Virginia Waterman's Association – www.virginiawaterman.com

Washington College – www.washcoll.edu

Larry's Glossary

Annapolis

A once-thriving seafood hub complete with a fish market and several raw bars. For decades, the downtown harbor was packed full of skipjacks, bugeyes, and all kinds of workboats. As the state capital, Annapolis, also served as the final authority concerning all commercial fishing laws and regulations which profoundly affected every waterman of Maryland. Annapolis was (and is) home to the United States Naval Academy, so it was a bright spot for America as well.

Atlantic Striped Bass

This migratory species was aggressively harvested by recreational and commercial fishermen throughout the eastern seaboard and currently remains a thriving part of the watermen's livelihood. Locally, this species of fish is called rockfish or stripers. The scientific name for the striped bass is *Morone saxatilis*.

Bay Bridge

The official name of this dual span bridge is The William Preston Lane Jr. Memorial Chesapeake Bay Bridge. The first span was opened in 1952 and the second was opened in 1973. Marylanders either call this structure the Bay Bridge or just "the bridge." This roadway changed the quality of life on the Eastern Shore in both good and bad ways.

Bilge

An enclosed area on a workboat between the frames at each side of the floor where seepage collects. Wood, fiberglass, aluminum, and steel hulls all require a bilge system to collect and purge seepage water.

Chesapeake Bay Watershed

This is the geographical area that receives rainwater that ultimately drains into the Chesapeake Bay. Parts of New York, Pennsylvania, Maryland, Delaware, Virginia, and West Virginia all drain into the Chesapeake.

Commercial Fishermen

These are men and women who generate their income by harvesting seafood. Dating back to at least biblical times, this ancient profession was once held in high regard around the world as a way to make a living and to provide nutrition for many.

Fishery

The occupation or industry of catching fish or taking other products (seafood, natural resources) from bodies of water; the right to fish certain waters as defined in *The Random House College Dictionary Revised Edition* 1975.

Menhaden

An important migratory species that serves many roles in the Chesapeake Bay. The scientific name for menhaden is *Brevoortia tyrannus*. Locally, watermen call them bunkers, buggies, or alewives. Menhaden are a critical baitfish source for migrating rockfish, bluefish, and shad. They are used by watermen for crab and catfish bait. Once rendered in a processing plant, menhaden are used as a human health supplement and fishmeal for aquaculture. Like oysters and clams, menhaden are filter feeders, capable of processing large volumes of excess algae caused by excess nutrients.

Natural Resources

The natural wealth of a country consisting of land, forests, mineral deposits, water, etc., again as defined in T*he Random House College Dictionary*. Among the watermen of Maryland, harvested species like crabs, oysters, clams, fish, eels, and horseshoe crabs are generally referenced as natural resources which might be confusing to some readers.

Overfishing

T*he Random House College Dictionary* defines overfishing as to fish an area excessively; to exhaust the supply of usable fish in certain waters; to fish so as to deplete the supply of fish in certain waters. The term overfishing (a.k.a. overharvesting) is used primarily by regulatory officials in relation to the overall population of a species. Local watermen are not able to measure fishery abundance on a macro basis so they do not use the term overfishing much. Watermen speak regularly in terms of compliance with established rules, regulations and laws.

Route 50

This is the east to west highway system that connects Baltimore, Washington, and Annapolis to Ocean City. Ocean City was (and remains) a thriving, beach resort that draws millions of people to Maryland's Eastern Shore every year. In the summer time, the bottleneck at the Bay Bridge is a burden for locals and often a serious obstacle for Maryland's emergency response systems. Officially, US Route 50 is called the John Hanson Highway. Back home, we just call it "50."

Watermen

A specific grouping of commercial fishermen that work the waters of Maryland, Virginia, Delaware, and North Carolina. Originally, these hardy fishermen migrated from Europe many generations ago. Maryland watermen harvest blue crabs, oysters, clams, fish, and eels using a variety of tools and methods.

Workboat

For centuries, all workboats were built out of wood and were powered by sail or oars. As diesel and gasoline engines were adapted for marine use, most sailing vessels were replaced by modern workboats of various lengths, widths, and designs. Depending on the fishing methods used and the types of water being fished, watermen would use small boats like garveys or skiffs and also large workboats to get the job done. The primary vessel type used in Larry's time was the classic, classy, and durable hull design called a deadrise.

A skipjack dredging for oysters. *Courtesy of Ann Crane Harlan*.

Chesapeake Bay Charts

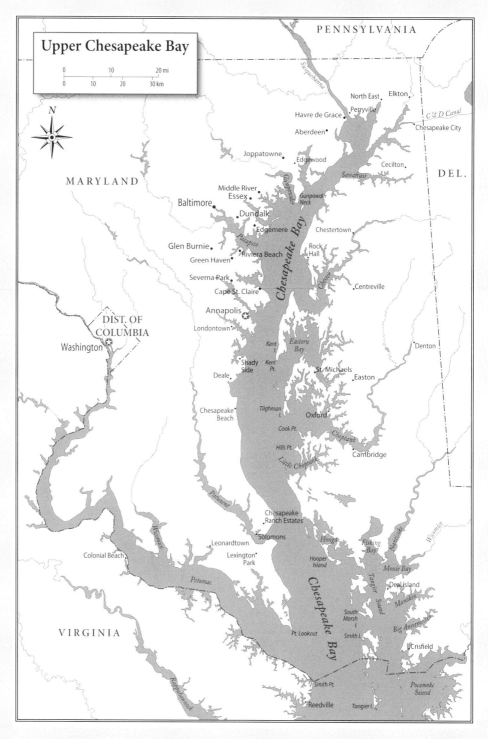

The Upper Chesapeake Bay. *Courtesy of Tara Petrilli of Eyevolt.*

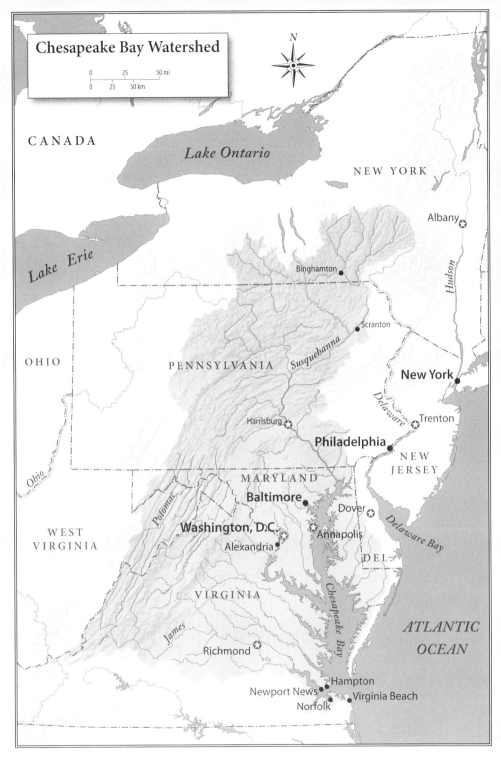

The Chesapeake Bay Watershed. *Courtesy of Tara Petrilli of Eyevolt.*

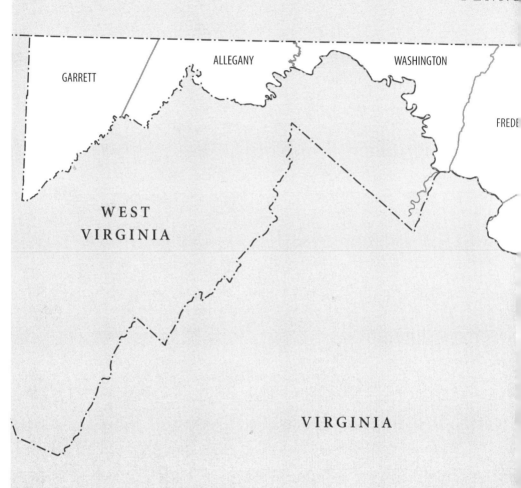

PENNS

ALLEGANY

GARRETT

WASHINGTON

FREDE

WEST
VIRGINIA

VIRGINIA

Maryland Counties

| 0 | | 25 mi |
| 0 | 25 km | |

N

Maryland County Lines. *Courtesy of Tara Petrilli of Eyevolt.*

Index